A Matter of Faith

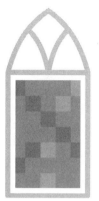

A Matter of
Faith
RELIGION IN THE 2004 PRESIDENTIAL ELECTION

David E. Campbell

Editor

BROOKINGS INSTITUTION PRESS
Washington, D.C.

ABOUT BROOKINGS
The Brookings Institution is a private nonprofit organization devoted to research,
education, and publication on important issues of domestic and foreign policy. Its
principal purpose is to bring the highest quality independent research and analysis to
bear on current and emerging policy problems. Interpretations or conclusions in
Brookings publications should be understood to be solely those of the authors.

Copyright © 2007

THE BROOKINGS INSTITUTION
1775 Massachusetts Avenue, N.W., Washington, D.C. 20036
www.brookings.edu

Library of Congress Cataloging-in-Publication data
A Matter of faith? : religion in the 2004 presidential election / David E. Campbell, editor.
     p.   cm.
   Chiefly papers presented at a conference sponsored by the University of Notre Dame's
Program in American Democracy in December 2005.
   Includes bibliographical references and index.
   ISBN-13: 978-0-8157-1328-9 (cloth : alk. paper)
   ISBN-10: 0-8157-1328-2 (cloth : alk. paper)
   ISBN-13: 978-0-8157-1327-2 (pbk. : alk. paper)
   ISBN-10: 0-8157-1327-4 (pbk. : alk. paper)
   1. Presidents—United States—Election—2004. 2. United States. Congress—Elections,
2004. 3. Christianity and politics—United States. 4. United States—Politics and
government—2001– I. Campbell, David E., 1971– II. Title.
   JK5262004 .M37 2007
   324.973'0931—dc22   2007007869

9 8 7 6 5 4 3 2 1

Printed on acid-free paper.

Typeset in Minion

Composition by Circle Graphics
Columbia, Maryland

Printed by R. R. Donnelley
Harrisonburg, Virginia

Contents

Acknowledgments

The chapters here, for the most part, were initially presented as papers at a conference sponsored by the University of Notre Dame's Program in American Democracy in December 2005 and generously supported by the Annenberg Foundation. I am indebted to Christina Wolbrecht, director of the Program in American Democracy, for her assistance in bringing this conference about. Both her organizational acumen and intellectual acuity have been extremely helpful.

The Program in American Democracy has benefited from the support of the university's College of Arts and Letters and, especially, Dean Mark Roche. I appreciate that Notre Dame provides an environment where rigorous scholarly inquiry into religion is valued.

All this logistical, financial, and institutional support would be for nothing, however, if not for the contributors to this volume. They represent a mixture of experience in the discipline—some are assistant professors, and some have reached emeritus status. Some have been working on religion and politics for a long time, while others are new to this area of research. Collectively, they have risen to the challenge of producing trenchant yet accessible research, and have managed to keep to a tight schedule. In particular, I would like to acknowledge John Green, who has generously provided guidance for this entire project.

Finally, I am thankful for the moral support provided by my wife, Kirsten, and my children, Soren and Katie. They constantly remind me of what matters most, and so this book is dedicated to them.

David E. Campbell
Notre Dame, Indiana

A Matter of Faith

The 2004 Election
A Matter of Faith?

David E. Campbell

Few observers of American politics deny that in recent years religion has come to play an increasingly important role in the nation's elections, especially the presidential election. To some, perhaps many, religion may appear to be a new factor in national politics. But today's focus on religion is really just a variation on what has been a common theme throughout U.S. history. In 1800, Thomas Jefferson had to deal with accusations that he was an atheist; in the late 1800s, William Jennings Bryan invoked biblical themes to support economic policy; in 1928, Al Smith faced anti-Catholic mobs on the campaign trail; in 1960, John F. Kennedy too had to forestall anti-Catholic sentiment that, while muted when compared with what Smith faced in 1928, lingered nonetheless.

Religion, then, has long been a feature in national elections. Yet that does not mean that the religious cleavages of the past correspond to those of the present. Rather, the last thirty years have seen a re-sorting of the parties' electoral coalitions along religious lines. No longer are Democrats and Republicans divided along the old lines, defined by whether they are Catholic or Protestant. Instead of religious *denomination,* the parties are divided by religious *devotional style*—that is, a way of being religious. People who are more devout—regardless of denomination—are more likely to favor the GOP. Obviously, such a statement is a generalization. There are exceptions; notably, as shown by Eric McDaniel in chapter 12 of this volume, religious devotion among African Americans does not lead them to favor the GOP. And as seen in chapter 13, by Lyman Kellstedt, Corwin Smidt, John Green, and James Guth, there are pockets of support for the Democrats among the devout. Nonetheless, these exceptions almost prove the rule, as Kellstedt and his coauthors also argue that there are few prospects for a religious left movement to rival that on the right.

How did the country reach the point that many voters cast their ballots along devotional rather than denominational lines? How did it get from the denominational fissures laid bare by John F. Kennedy's Catholicism to George W. Bush's "coalition of the religious," which brought together evangelicals and traditionalist Catholics? There are a number of milestones marking the way, with none as prominent as Jimmy Carter's 1976 presidential campaign. Carter's candidacy centered on his identity as a personally devout churchgoer who had been "born again." He did not emphasize the content of his beliefs or his denominational affiliation but simply reassured voters that his religious background meant that he was a moral and ethical person.

It is one of the great ironies of American politics that by injecting his personal religiosity into presidential politics, Jimmy Carter—a Democrat—was at the vanguard of the movement that has come to define the Republican Party. Beginning around 1980, pundits and scholars alike began to speak of the New Christian Right as a movement closely associated with the GOP. Religious conservatives' influence within Republican circles increased to the point that in 1992, delegates at the Republican national convention cheered Pat Buchanan's declaration of a culture war in America. While conventional wisdom holds that the Republicans pushed the rhetoric appealing to religious conservatives too far in 1992, Buchanan's once-prominent role in the GOP is nonetheless instructive. As a Catholic with a strong following among evangelical Protestants, Buchanan embodies the cross-denominational nature of the new face of religion in American politics. There is, perhaps, a parallel between Buchanan's failure to rally the nation in 1992 and Barry Goldwater's landslide loss in the 1964 election. Both showed party strategists the outer edge of support for themes that later came to fruition in more moderate form. Goldwater's harsh libertarianism set the stage for the ascendance of Reagan's sunny version of small-government conservatism in 1980. Likewise, Buchanan's incendiary rhetoric paved the way for George W. Bush's more subtle use of language and references to themes that resonated among the growing evangelical base of the GOP while also attracting social conservatives from other religious traditions.

And then came 2004, when religion took center stage. In the immediate wake of Bush's reelection, the pundits were abuzz with the discovery that exit polls showed that a plurality of voters had selected "moral values" as the most important issue affecting their vote. Of those who gave priority to moral values, a strong majority went for Bush. Similarly, many commentators suggested that Bush mobilized the Republicans' socially conservative base by stressing his opposition to gay marriage, which was the subject of referenda in eleven states on election day—including the critical battleground state of Ohio. The moral values interpretation of the election, however, was quickly contested. Op-ed pages were filled with columns debating whether the election of 2004 turned on moral values or whether it was really about the economy, the Iraq war, and terrorism.

The debate over moral values continues in the pages that follow. In chapter 4, Sunshine Hillygus argues that when the electorate is viewed as a whole, moral values hardly seemed to have been a priority for most voters in the 2004 election; instead, it was largely about other issues. Scott Keeter elaborates on that conclusion in chapter 5 by demonstrating that while moral issues like gay marriage and abortion did not matter to most voters, they were very much on the minds of a crucial constituency for the GOP—white evangelical Protestants.

The question of whether the 2004 election hung on moral values is important, if only because it figured so heavily in postelection commentary and for many observers has become the defining theme of the election. Nonetheless, the role of moral values is only a starting point for understanding how religion was woven into the 2004 presidential election. As a primer for the more extensive discussion in the chapters to follow, the remainder of this introductory chapter briefly examines three other ways in which religion left an imprint on the 2004 campaign. Each provides a window into both the present and the likely future role of religion in shaping the American electoral landscape. The first is George W. Bush's *evangelicalism,* the second is John Kerry's *Catholicism,* and the third is Howard Dean's *secularism.*

Bush's Evangelicalism

Viewed from a distance, George W. Bush's religious background broadly resembles that of most American presidents, including his father's. Bush grew up attending establishment Protestant churches within both the Episcopalian and Presbyterian traditions; on marrying his wife, Laura, he formally affiliated with the United Methodist Church. A closer look, however, makes clear that when it comes to religion, Bush is more like Jimmy Carter than his own father. Bush's faith is better understood through his devotional style than his denomination, for he is an evangelical Christian. Evangelicalism is not a denominational affiliation per se, such as Catholicism or Lutheranism. Rather, evangelicals are defined by their strong emphasis on Bible study and a personal embrace of Jesus Christ, often following a turning point in their life. If there is any doubt about Bush's faith, one need only consult the small library of books and DVDs[1] on the subject that are widely disseminated within the growing evangelical subculture.[2] As detailed in chapter 10, by Geoffrey Layman and Laura Hussey, Bush is widely thought to have a bond with the evangelical community (or at least among highly committed evangelicals); he is seen as "one of their own." No single moment better captures the connection Bush has made with the evangelical community than a well-known comment he made during a debate in the early stage of the 2000 Republican primaries. When asked to name his favorite political philosopher, Bush paused and then said plainly, "Christ, because he changed my heart." I have no idea whether Bush's response was a cleverly orchestrated effort to establish his bona fides among evangelical voters or simply a spontaneous remark. Whatever the motivation, his comment was pitch-perfect to the evangelical ear.

Because Bush's religion has received a lot of attention, one might assume that his public remarks are replete with religious comments. In fact, statements like his reference to Christ in the 2000 primary season are rare. While Bush does use language with a religious theme in many of his speeches, so have other presidents. Indeed, Bush's religious language is often subtle, consisting of allusions to hymns or phrases used in religious discourse that still have meaning when unmoored from their religious context. Most famously, Bush has often used the term "a culture of life," which he borrowed from Pope John Paul II.

In other words, when speaking to the electorate, Bush's use of religious language is not substantially different from that of other recent presidents. Where Bush differs from his predecessors is in the way that the evangelical community has embraced him; as either a cause or a consequence of that embrace, Bush has directed a lot of attention and resources to mobilizing the

1. Consider the following examples: David Aikman, *A Man of Faith: The Spiritual Journey of George W. Bush* (Nashville: W Publishing Group, 2004); Paul Kengor, *God and George W. Bush: A Spiritual Life* (New York: Regan Books, 2004); Stephen Mansfield, *The Faith of George W. Bush* (New York: Tarcher, 2003); and *George W. Bush: Faith in the White House* (New York: DVD distributed by Good Times DVD).

2. Smith (1998).

evangelical vote. In the wake of Bush's popular vote loss to Al Gore in 2000, his chief campaign strategist, Karl Rove, even went so far as to suggest publicly that Bush had failed to capitalize on his evangelicalism by not energizing enough evangelicals to get to the polls. Since Rove's words, spoken during a forum sponsored by the American Enterprise Institute in December 2001, are referenced in multiple chapters, they are quoted here:

> We probably failed to martial [sic] support among the base as well as we should have. If you look at the model of the electorate, and you look at the model of who voted, the big discrepancy is among self-identified, white, evangelical Protestants, Pentecostals, and fundamentalists. If they were a part of the voters of what they should have been if you had looked at the electoral model, here should have been 19 million of them and instead there were 15 million of them. Just over 4 million of them failed to turn out and vote. And yet they are obviously part of our base. They voted for us, depending on who they were and where they were, by huge margins, 70 and 80 percent margins. And yet 4 million of them didn't turn out to vote that you would have anticipated voting in a normal presidential election year. I think we may have failed to mobilize them.[3]

This is a remarkable statement given that, as shown by John Green, Lyman Kellstedt, Corwin Smidt, and Jim Guth in chapter 2, traditionalist evangelicals constituted 25 percent of Bush's voting coalition (having given Bush 87 percent of their votes and turned out to vote at a rate exceeded by only Jews and atheists/agnostics, groups that are mere slivers of the population).

However, while evangelicals' identification with Bush is an important aspect of his coalition, its significance at the polls should not be overstated. Just as Catholics had been voting Democratic before John F. Kennedy ran for president, evangelicals had been voting Republican before Bush appeared on the scene. Bush's bond with evangelicals is, then, perhaps analogous to the connection between Kennedy and his fellow Catholics. Such ties are based on a common identity. Because he was universally identified as a Catholic, Kennedy did not need to speak publicly about his Catholicism; because he is widely identified as an evangelical, Bush does not need to say much about his faith.

That Bush himself may not say much about his religion hardly means that religious themes have been absent from the appeals made by the Bush campaign, particularly in 2004. Because religion can be an explosive topic with the potential for alienating voters uncomfortable with overt religious rhetoric, the Republicans narrowly targeted only those voters most likely to respond

---

3. American Enterprise Institute (2001, p. 5).

positively to such appeals. As Quin Monson and Baxter Oliphant demonstrate in chapter 6, in 2004 the parties employed new technology to accomplish a timeless political strategy—delivering the right message to the most receptive voters. In years past, precinct captains knew their party's supporters in the neighborhood and made personalized appeals to ensure that they turned out on election day. In a telling sign of the times, technology has replaced the neighborhood precinct captain. The parties draw on extensive databases to learn everything they can about voters: their party registration, marital status, magazine subscriptions, and even church membership. That wealth of information means that direct mail can be designed—the term of art is "microtargeted"—to match voters' interests. Voters profiled as likely social conservatives because of, say, the church that they attended or the magazines to which they subscribed were targeted to receive campaign mail that highlighted "morality issues," such as abortion and gay marriage. Even on those potentially inflammatory topics, however, the ad copy is much like the speeches in which Bush invokes religious language: subdued and inclusive. In chapter 7, Quin Monson and I describe how Bush's ads never described him as opposing marriage for homosexuals; rather, they emphasized his support for traditional marriage. Never was anything derogatory said about homosexuals per se.

The reason for the subtlety is no secret. While Bush received strong support from social conservatives, that single constituency was not enough to win a presidential election. He also needed support from voters for whom social issues take a backseat to economic or, especially in 2004, national security issues. These other Bush voters are likely to be social moderates. Even within the social conservative camp, the GOP needs to cast as wide a net as possible, which is why Bush typically avoids specifics on the subject of religion. He can attract the widest possible coalition by finding common cause with those who think of themselves as "religious" rather than adherents of a particular religious tradition. Indeed, the creation of a new coalition that transcends denominational boundaries is what James Davison Hunter originally meant by the term "culture war."[4] Hunter was speaking of alliances that link people of orthodox beliefs across denominational lines—whether Protestants, Catholics, Mormons, or followers of other traditions. Take the example of evangelicals and Mormons, which is particularly revealing. These two groups seem to compete for the distinction of being the religious group with the highest level of support for the GOP, even though they have deep theological differences

---

4. Hunter (1991).

and a history of mutual antagonism. The Republicans have also managed to win considerable support from traditionalist Catholics, who are more important numerically. To think that groups with such long-standing disagreements could unite politically represents a historically remarkable development that is not fully appreciated by many political observers.

Owing to its coalition of the religious, the Republican Party faces a difficult balancing act. On one hand it has at its base a core of evangelical supporters who have been fully incorporated into the internal party apparatus of the GOP and play a role not unlike the role once played by labor unions in the Democratic Party. It is thus extremely unlikely that anyone could ever win the Republican nomination for the presidency without receiving, as it were, the blessing of key evangelical leaders. On the other hand, evangelicals alone do not make for election victories. Successful Republican candidates must also appeal to voters who, while perhaps socially conservative, are not evangelicals themselves. As of this writing, each of the leading contenders for the 2008 Republican nomination has his (to date, they are all men) own particular challenge in achieving a balance between shoring up the evangelical base and reaching beyond it to other voters. John McCain, for example, must convince evangelicals that he did not really mean it when, during the 2000 campaign, he said that certain leaders of the religious right were "agents of intolerance."[5] Similarly, Rudy Giuliani must play up his heroic post-9/11 image and play down his social liberalism and marital history. Perhaps the contender with the rockiest religious road to travel is Massachusetts governor Mitt Romney. Such a statement may seem puzzling, as Romney would appear to have a lot going for him. After all, he has held firm on gay marriage by convincing the Massachusetts Supreme Judicial Court that same-sex nuptials should be limited to residents of Massachusetts only; he opposes stem cell research; and, over time, he has become increasingly pro-life on abortion. When his positions on those issues are combined with his business background, his turnaround of the once corruption-ridden Salt Lake City Olympics, and his squeaky-clean private life, it would seem that he deserves a place on the top tier of Republican presidential hopefuls. But whether his bid for the presidency has legs rests on whether evangelicals in the GOP primaries are willing to vote for someone of Romney's faith. He is a member of the Church of Jesus Christ of Latter-day Saints, more commonly known as the Mormons. Even though evangelicals and Mormons share a lot of political ground, in religious terms they are miles apart. To see

---

5. "Excerpt from McCain's Speech on Religious Conservatives," *New York Times,* February 29, 2000, A16.

the gulf that Romney needs to bridge, walk into almost any Christian bookstore, where you will find a shelf of books disparaging his faith as a "cult." Many of the devout Christians who shop in such bookstores also vote in Republican primaries. Romney's candidacy therefore will be an interesting test of how far the Republican coalition of the religious extends. Only time will tell whether he will become the Mormons' Al Smith (who suffered an ignominious defeat, thereby reinforcing the perception that Catholics were viewed with suspicion by the Protestant establishment) or John F. Kennedy (whose victory marked the official acceptance of Catholics into the American mainstream).

Kerry's Catholicism

Bush's evangelicalism demonstrates the significance of evangelicals, a relatively new group, to the GOP coalition. The candidacy of John Kerry, on the other hand, demonstrates the exodus from the Democratic coalition of Catholics, a group that was once squarely at its center. There is no better way to analyze the changing Catholic voter than by comparing Kerry in 2004 to Kennedy in 1960, as Matthew Wilson does in chapter 9. As has been widely noted, there are enough uncanny surface parallels between Kennedy and Kerry (not to mention their shared initials) to rival the supposed parallels between Kennedy and Lincoln. Both Kennedy and Kerry were highly decorated military veterans serving as Democratic senators in Massachusetts. Even more important, both were Catholic. It is almost as though the Democratic Party decided to run a controlled experiment to compare the electoral fortunes of a Catholic candidate in 1960 and 2004. As described by Wilson in his chapter, since 1960 the Catholic electorate has undergone a dramatic shift. While Kennedy—hardly a model of Catholic piety—took a stratospheric 82 percent of the Catholic vote, Kerry took less than 50 percent. In other words, Kerry did no better among Catholics than among the population as a whole. That probably says more about contemporary American Catholics than about Kerry, since that was about the same share of the Catholic vote won by Al Gore in 2000. Catholics have so fully assimilated into the larger American culture that they are no longer a distinctive political group. Even more significant is that Bush actually beat Kerry—by a long shot—among churchgoing Catholics, taking 74 percent of their votes. Here again is evidence that the salient religious divide in America is no longer defined by denomination but by devotion. If Al Smith or John F. Kennedy had been told that one day an evangelical Protestant would attract a majority of votes from churchgoing Catholics, they undoubtedly would have laughed the prediction away.

As Wilson compellingly argues, Catholic voters have changed because they no longer see their attachment to the Democratic Party as a matter of group loyalty. Today's Catholics are far more likely to vote on the basis of issues rather than the legacy of an institutional connection to the party that historically had been their political home, at least in part because Catholics often were of low socioeconomic status. While some of the Catholic shift is owed to the rising socioeconomic status of American Catholics, the fact that churchgoing Catholics vote Republican to a greater extent than nominal Catholics suggests that the devotional divide applies to Catholics as well as Protestants.

Will the Democrats ever be able to win back the Catholic vote? Barring a political earthquake, it appears that the same devotional divide found within the general electorate will continue to be replicated among Catholics, at least in the short to medium term and at least among Anglo whites. Latinos, however, are a fascinating and important exception. Latino Catholics, who because of immigration and high birth rates are an increasing share of the overall American Catholic population, lean heavily Democratic—just like earlier waves of immigrant Irish, Italians, and Poles. At the same time, Latino evangelicals look more like Anglo evangelicals than other Latinos. As David Leal explains in chapter 11, which discusses religious influences on the Latino vote, Latino Catholics supported Kerry while Latino evangelicals favored Bush. The Latino example is a reminder that today, neither religion nor ethnicity is political destiny.

Dean's Secularism

The final religious theme from the 2004 election comes not from the general election but from Howard Dean's failed campaign for the Democratic nomination. What makes Dean interesting is not the religion that he professes but the perception that he is not very religious at all. Next to Bush's evangelicalism and Kerry's Catholicism, Dean's perceived secularism—and the reaction to it— is equally revealing about the role of religion in the American electoral process.

The arc of Dean's rise and fall should be familiar to students of presidential primaries: a fresh face appears on the national stage, only to stumble in the early stage of the primaries, never to recover. Dean had a meteoric rise to the top of the Democratic charts, followed by a fall of Shakespearean proportions. While many people remember the infamous Dean scream as the ostensible reason for his implosion, the reality is that underlying the reaction to the scream was a lot of uneasiness about Dean among leading Democrats. Long before his holler made him the butt of late-night comedians' jokes, many prominent Democrats had expressed concern that he was unelectable because he was too liberal. Tied up in the indictment of Dean's liberalism were related accusations that he was too secular to win in the heartland. In January 2004, the *New Republic* put Dean on its cover and said that he had a "religion problem." More accurately, Dean could be said to have an *irreligion* problem: Franklin Foer labeled him as "one of the most secular candidates to run for president in modern history."[6]

My point is not to delve into Dean's religious background or the question of whether his religious beliefs had any bearing on whether he would make a good president. What matters is the belief among some prominent Democrats that a winning presidential candidate must not be perceived as too secular. To quote Foer again: "One day, a truly secular candidate might be able to run for president without suffering at the polls. But that day won't be soon."

Dean's popularity with the Democratic base, coupled with uneasiness about his perceived secularism, underscores the dilemma facing Democrats. Just as the Republicans need to be careful that their core evangelical supporters do not push the GOP too far in an overtly religious direction, so the Democrats need to be careful that their secular base does not alienate religious moderates who, as shown by Kellstedt and his coauthors, constitute a sizable share of Democratic supporters. Some in the Democratic Party see a hopeful model for reconciling these two countervailing forces in the recent campaign of Virginia governor Tim Kaine. Kaine, a Mass-attending Catholic Democrat, won convincingly in the red state of Virginia, at least in part by highlighting his background as a missionary overseas. Perhaps even more important, he couched some of his more controversial, liberal-leaning policy positions in religious terms. When criticized by his Republican opponent for opposing capital punishment, he ran television ads in which he said, "My faith teaches life is sacred. That's why I personally oppose the death penalty."[7]

As in any election, there are many reasons why this particular candidate won that particular race, including the fact that he ran in the wake of a popular Democratic predecessor. It is therefore difficult to know the extent to which his religious background was a factor in the election. Perhaps the most judicious conclusion is that it certainly did him no harm and likely did him some good.

Inevitably, two consecutive losing presidential bids have led the Democratic Party to search for a winning strategy in 2008. Should the "Kaine model"

6. Foer (2003–04).
7. Dao (2005, p. A23).

come to be seen as the way forward by the Democratic rank and file, the attention paid to religion in 2008 will dwarf the attention it received in 2004. If so, perhaps the devotional divide will cease to be the salient cleavage that it has been in recent presidential contests.

Perhaps. The Democrats, however, are a long way from endorsing the Kaine model, and any such prediction is extremely premature. As shown by John Green and John Jackson in their chapter on delegates to the 2004 party conventions, the Democrats have a strongly secular base, many of whom will presumably object to using religious language for *any* purpose—including the advocacy of traditionally liberal positions. Even among the many devout Americans who vote Democratic, there is an almost palpable reluctance to employ religion in the service of electoral politics. The more likely scenario for 2008 therefore is the continuation of the trend observed in 2004—and in 2000, 1996, 1992, and before. The Republican Party will be the one to use overt displays of religiosity, phrased to include all Judeo-Christian faiths but nonetheless having evangelical undertones. In that case, the devotional divide will continue and likely deepen.

A Guide to the Book

The three themes highlighted here hardly exhaust the ways in which religion worked its way into the 2004 presidential election. But I hope that they have whetted the reader's appetite for a deeper discussion of whether the 2004 contest was "a matter of faith," which is the central question of the chapters to follow. The remainder of the book begins with a section entitled "The Big Picture," which includes two chapters that scan the horizon of the 2004 electoral landscape. First is "How the Faithful Voted," by John Green, Lyman Kellstedt, Corwin Smidt, and James Guth. These four scholars draw on the Fourth National Survey of Religion and Politics, the single best source of data on how religion relates to the political choices of the mass public, to lay out the facts of who voted for whom. John Green and John Jackson then provide a complementary chapter on religion and the 2004 party activists, namely the delegates to the Republican and Democratic national conventions. Next is a section entitled "The Moral Values Election?" which centers on the debate over the degree to which moral values determined the outcome of the 2004 contest. First, Sunshine Hillygus reminds readers that moral values were hardly the only thing on voters' minds in 2004, while Scott Keeter demonstrates that, of those who were thinking of moral values, many were evangelicals. These two chapters offer a thorough discussion of the debate over moral values in 2004. As the specifics of that debate fade in years to come, these two chapters will remind readers of how moral values did or did not matter in 2004.

The third section, "Mobilizing the Faithful," delves into the specifics of how religious conservatives were mobilized in 2004. As noted, one tactic that came to the fore during 2004 was the use of highly targeted direct mail appeals. Using an innovative new survey, J. Quin Monson and Baxter Oliphant detail how and how often those appeals used moral and religious themes. The following chapter, by J. Quin Monson and me, is a case study of how the appeals actually affected the 2004 vote. It shows that contrary to the opinions expressed by a number of political scientists in the immediate wake of the election, gay marriage was a key issue in the vote for Bush. Barbara Norrander and Jan Norrander then explore public opinion on stem cell research, which, because it parallels the abortion debate, has the potential to be a divisive issue with staying power.

In the fourth section, "Religious Constituencies," the book narrows the focus to specific religious groups, with chapters on the voting behavior of different segments of the population. Matthew Wilson uses the contrast between the sharply divergent experiences of John F. Kennedy in 1960 and John Kerry in 2004 as a lens through which to view the changing political allegiances of American Catholics. Geoffrey Layman and Laura Hussey present another story of change over time as they highlight the growing allegiance of evangelicals to both the Republican Party and George W. Bush. David Leal and Eric McDaniel then add ethnicity and race as further dimensions to the story of religion in American politics. Leal explains how religion affected the Latino vote in 2004, while McDaniel discusses the politics of the black church. In the final chapter in this section, Kellstedt, Smidt, Green, and Guth examine one of the more intriguing topics in the volume: the prospects for a religious left movement to counterbalance the religious right.

The book concludes with a chapter by David Leege, who interprets the preceding chapters through a variety of theoretical lenses and offers recommendations for a future research agenda to explore the intersection of voting behavior, religion, and politics.

What, then, can the reader expect to learn from this book? For the most part, the authors concur that the 2004 election *was* a matter of faith, although there are some healthy differences of opinion on the degree to which faith mattered. Religion thus endures as a theme in the politics of the present, as it has been in the past. And by all indications, religion's influence seems likely to persist into the future. As we look forward to 2008 and beyond, any attempt to understand the direction of American presidential politics without accounting for the religious factor will be incomplete at best—and futile at worst.

The Big Picture

How the Faithful Voted

Religious Communities
and the Presidential Vote

John C. Green, Lyman A. Kellstedt, Corwin E. Smidt,
and James L. Guth

I t is widely recognized that religion played a major role in the 2004 presidential election and that recognition has enlivened the debate over the meaning of the election results, including the importance of "moral values," the effect of religious mobilization, and the contribution of particular religious communities to the outcome.[1] It is on the latter point that there is perhaps the most confusion. How did the faithful vote? What role did they play in party coalitions? Did the patterns of electoral participation by religious groups in 2004 differ from the patterns of electoral participation by religious groups in previous elections?

This chapter addresses these basic questions by describing how the most important religious communities voted in 2004, examining the role that they played in party coalitions, and then comparing the 2004 results to those in the three previous presidential elections. Drawing on a set of surveys that include extensive measures of religion, these descriptions and comparisons add a new dimension to recent scholarship on the subject.

In 2004, President George W. Bush received strong support from a coalition of evangelical Protestants and Christian traditionalists, improved his standing among Catholics, and secured some additional votes from religious

1. Muirhead and others (2005).

minorities. Senator John Kerry presided over a more complex coalition of religious minorities, less traditional Christians, and the unaffiliated, to which he added gains among mainline Protestants. These 2004 voting patterns developed slowly over the last twelve years, and to appreciate them fully, a brief overview of the American religious landscape and its relevance to national politics is in order.

The American Religious Landscape and National Politics

Using survey research to describe the American religious landscape, let alone identify its relevance to national politics, is a daunting task. However, a quarter-century of research has produced two powerful conceptual tools for these purposes: *religious tradition* and *religious traditionalism*.[2]

A religious tradition is a group of religious denominations, movements, and congregations with similar beliefs, behaviors, and origins. This concept taps the "belonging" aspect of religion: the affiliation of individuals to particular religious communities. By definition, religious traditions are characterized by foundational doctrines and normative practices—in short, a particular kind of "traditional" belief and behavior.[3]

However, individual members of a religious tradition are unlikely to have equal commitment to its foundational doctrines and religious practices, so there may be diverse communities within a religious tradition based on degree of traditionalism. Members who strongly affirm traditional beliefs and practices can be called "traditionalists," an especially appropriate term for individuals who consciously seek to preserve their tradition against the encroachments of the modern world. Still other members hold to the doctrines and practices central to their tradition, but with less consistency and fervor than the traditionalists; these can be dubbed "centrists," for lack of a better term.

In some ways, the opposites of the traditionalists are the "modernists," members of a religious tradition who have adapted traditional beliefs and behaviors to accommodate the modern world; this term is especially appropriate for individuals who consciously seek to advance such adaptations. Finally, others are simply nominal "members" of their tradition, belonging but neither accepting its doctrines nor engaging in its normative practices. Of course, members who reject the basic tenets of their tradition can switch to another, more congenial one—or choose to be unaffiliated with any tradition.

2. Leege and Kellstedt (1993); Green and others (1996); Kohut and others (2000); Layman (2001).
3. Kellstedt and others (1996); Kellstedt and Green (1993); Green (2000b).

In analogous fashion, there may be considerable diversity among the unaffiliated, reflecting, for example, noninstitutional religiosity, indifference to religion, and the adoption of secular beliefs.

Thus defined, religious traditions and traditionalism can connect religious people to politics, jointly and separately.[4] Throughout most of U.S. history, religious traditions were the primary means by which the political connection occurred. In most cases, the distinctive religious perspectives of the religious traditions were regularly translated into characteristic voting patterns. In fact, American party coalitions were in large part alliances of "ethno-religious" groups, with some traditions identifying with the Democrats and others with the Whigs and later the Republicans.[5]

That pattern changed in the late twentieth century, when traditionalism began to display strong independent effects on politics. In fact, the effects were so strong that some scholars spoke of a "restructuring" of American religion: in most (if not all) religious traditions, traditionalists increasingly differed from modernists, and the growing ranks of the unaffiliated population were seen by some observers as allies of the modernists in this new structure.[6] These factions' differences in belief and behavior had important political implications. For example, traditionalists of all sorts have slowly turned toward the Republican Party, while the modernists and the unaffiliated have shifted gradually toward the Democratic Party.[7] These shifts have reduced the political distinctiveness of religious traditions as a whole. Religious tradition and traditionalism both were relevant to the presidential vote in 2004.

The U.S. Religious Landscape in 2004

Table 2-1 maps the U.S. religious landscape in 2004, illustrating both membership in religious traditions and, where possible, the degree of traditionalism within them. It is based on data from the Fourth National Survey of Religion and Politics, and the categories are calculated to be comparable with those in the previous surveys in this series, dating back to 1992. (See the appendix for survey details.) Within the major traditions, four categories are shown, constructed from measures of beliefs and behaviors. As the labels suggest, the "traditionalists" scored highest on the traditionalism scale, followed by the "centrists," "modernists," and "nominals," who scored the lowest. Three

4. Layman and Green (2006).
5. Jensen (1971); Kleppner (1979); McCormick (1974); Noll (1990).
6. Wuthnow (1988 and 1989); Hunter (1991 and 1994).
7. Layman (2001).

Table 2-1. American Religious Landscape in 2004

Percent

Religious community	Proportion of adult population	Belief in a personal God	All great religions equally true	Weekly worship attendance	Highest religious salience
Protestants					
Evangelical Protestant	25.1	69.9	19.5	62.7	57.7
Traditionalist	10.7	93.0	9.1	95.8	80.2
Centrist	9.7	69.3	19.8	50.3	51.4
Modernist	3.3	27.3	37.2	19.1	26.7
Nominal	1.5	0.0	54.4	1.7	6.7
Mainline Protestant	16.4	34.7	44.3	33.3	31.3
Traditionalist	4.5	73.2	14.6	75.8	60.3
Centrist	5.5	32.4	47.9	28.1	36.4
Modernist	4.4	13.1	58.0	11.4	8.0
Nominal	2.0	1.3	70.0	1.2	3.7
Latino Protestant	2.6	61.0	28.6	65.7	67.0
Black Protestant	9.3	54.0	23.5	59.0	67.2
Catholics					
Non-Latino Catholic	17.5	31.8	49.9	49.2	33.9
Traditionalist	4.2	64.5	32.9	92.3	72.8
Centrist	7.4	31.3	47.1	53.2	32.2
Modernist	3.8	13.6	59.5	20.9	12.3
Nominal	2.1	1.2	75.0	0.0	0.0
Latino Catholic	4.5	34.4	49.4	46.9	51.1
Other traditions					
Latter-day Saints	1.4	64.3	24.1	71.4	69.1
Other Faiths	2.5	29.1	36.6	46.5	42.7
Jews	1.9	10.5	52.8	23.7	25.7
Other Non-Christians	1.4	10.7	64.3	42.9	42.1
Unaffiliated	17.3	6.1	47.6	3.6	11.2
Unaffiliated believers	4.8	18.8	33.7	8.9	28.1
Seculars	9.0	1.7	54.0	1.9	6.1
Atheists/agnostics	3.5	0.0	50.0	1.4	1.4
Entire sample	100.0	40.0	37.4	43.1	41.0

Source: Fourth National Survey of Religion and Politics, Bliss Institute of Applied Politics, University of Akron, March–May 2004 ($N = 4,000$).

roughly analogous categories were developed for the unaffiliated population. (See the appendix for details on how all the categories were calculated.)

Religious Communities

When smaller religious groups were included, this process generated twenty-two distinctive religious communities in the United States, many of which are quite small and have relatively few cases even in this large sample. Many of the table entries, therefore, must be viewed with caution. Indeed, the full range of groups is presented to assess broad patterns, not to offer a definitive description of any given religious community.

The first column in table 2-1 lists the size of each category as a percentage of the U.S. adult population. The remaining four columns report measures of religious belief and behavior: the percentage of respondents who believe that God is a person (as opposed to an impersonal force); the percentage of respondents who agree with the statement that "all the world's great religions are equally true and good" (as opposed to only one religion being true); the percentage who attend worship services weekly (or more often); and the percentage for whom the salience of religion is at the highest level (religion is important to the respondent and offers a great deal of guidance).

Belief in a personal God is part of all the major religious traditions in the United States, while the view that all religions are equally true marks a departure from such traditions. Nevertheless, that view has become common enough to receive a name, "lay liberalism."[8] Regular worship attendance is a normative practice in all the major traditions, while salience captures the subjective importance of faith to the individual. Three of these measures were used to define the twenty-two categories in table 2-1; lay liberalism was not part of the definition, but it is included here for illustrative purposes (see appendix for details). Taken together, these patterns fit well with the existing scholarship on religion and politics.[9]

Evangelical Protestants. In the 2004 survey, nonminority evangelical Protestants were the largest religious tradition, including one-quarter of the adult population, and the traditionalists were the single largest subgroup (and the largest category in the entire table). But note that the centrist evangelicals were nearly as numerous, and about one-fifth of all evangelicals were modernists or nominals. Overall, evangelical Protestants were the most traditional in religious belief and practice: more than two-thirds believed in a personal God, less than one-fifth were "lay liberals," three-fifths reported attending worship weekly or more often, and nearly three-fifths claimed that religion was highly salient in their lives.

However, there also were striking differences among the evangelical subgroups on all those measures. For instance, note the dramatic decline in belief in a personal God and an almost parallel increase in lay liberalism as one

8. Hoge, Johnson, and Luidens (1994).
9. See Kohut and others (2000); Smidt and others (2003); Leege and Kellstedt (1993).

moves down the table from the traditionalists to the nominals. Likewise, nearly 96 percent of the traditionalists reported weekly worship attendance, while just under 2 percent of the nominals did, and 80 percent of the traditionalists reported high religious salience, compared with only about 7 percent of the nominals.

Mainline Protestants. Nonminority mainline Protestants made up a little more than 16 percent of the adult population in 2004, but unlike evangelicals, they were more evenly divided internally, with about equal numbers of traditionalists, modernists, and centrists (who were the largest single group). Each of these groups was roughly one-half the size of the centrists among evangelicals; the nominal group was about the same size as its evangelical counterpart. Overall, mainline Protestants were markedly less traditional than evangelicals, exhibiting roughly one-half the level of adherence to the items in table 2-1. But here, too, note the internal differences: traditionalist mainliners approached their counterparts among evangelicals in belief and behavior, while the centrists and modernists scored below their counterparts. Of special note is the dramatic increase in lay liberalism, rising to 70 percent among nominal mainline Protestants.

Minority Protestants. The remaining Protestant categories represent ethnic and racial minorities. Latino Protestants, drawn for the most part from evangelical denominations, are best thought of as a subtradition, comparable to ethnic European Protestants in the nineteenth century. Although a small group (a bit larger than nominal mainliners), they are rapidly growing and of considerable interest politically. Black Protestants are best thought of as a separate religious tradition, with special institutions, beliefs, and behaviors based on the history of slavery and segregation in the United States. One of the largest categories, black Protestants, was about as numerous as centrist evangelicals. Both Latino and black Protestants reported relatively high levels of traditional belief and practice, roughly comparable to those of centrist evangelicals. (Table 2-1 does not report differences based on traditionalism within these groups, partly because of their small size and partly because the political effects are modest. Although the traditionalists in these groups tended to be more conservative than their co-religionists, ethnic and racial identities were more important factors.)

Roman Catholics. Non-Latino Catholics were the second-largest tradition in table 2-1, making up a little more than 17 percent of the adult population, about the size of mainline Protestants, and having about the same proportion of traditionalists, centrists, modernists, and nominals. Overall, non-Latino Catholics also showed relatively low levels of traditionalism, but there were strong differences between the traditionalists and the nominals in terms of religious belief and behavior. Like their Protestant counterparts, Latino Catholics are separated out in the table. They were about as numerous as traditionalist Catholics and resembled centrist Catholics in belief and behavior.

Other Religious Traditions. Four categories cover smaller religious traditions. One group is the Latter-day Saints, a small but distinctive religious tradition. "Other Faiths" is a composite category, including traditions as diverse as the Eastern Orthodox, Christian Scientists, and Unitarian-Universalists. The Jewish community is another group, followed by "Other Non-Christians," a composite category of Muslims, Buddhists, and Hindus, among others.[10] All four categories are small, with each roughly comparable in size to the nominals within each of the three large Christian traditions. The degree of traditional belief and behavior declines from the Latter-day Saints to Other Non-Christians, although this pattern may reflect an "Abrahamic faith" bias in the religious measures used, if not a Christian one. Nonetheless, the pattern for lay liberalism is revealing: only about 25 percent of the Latter-day Saints agreed that all religions are equally true, while the figure rose to almost 66 percent for those in the Other Non-Christians group.

Unaffiliated. The final three categories represent unaffiliated individuals. Taken together, the unaffiliated accounted for just over 17 percent of the adult population, rivaling the size of mainline Protestants. As the name implies, unaffiliated believers reported some religious beliefs, although only rarely traditional ones, and they were about as numerous as modernist mainline Protestants. Seculars, defined by a general lack of religious affiliation, belief, or behavior, were one of the largest categories in the table, about the size of centrist evangelicals. Self-identified atheists and agnostics, who largely lack traditional beliefs as such, were about as numerous as modernist Catholics. Lay liberalism does not show as strong a pattern across these groups, perhaps because the question implies the general efficacy of religion, which many non-religious people do not accept.

Religious Communities and the 2004 Election

Table 2-2 reports the two-party presidential vote and estimated turnout in the 2004 election across the religious landscape, with religious communities ordered according to percentage of votes for Bush. Religious communities

10. It is worth noting that the denominations combined in the two polyglot groups exhibited similar voting behavior in 2004.

Table 2-2. Religious Communities and the 2004 Presidential Election

Percent (arranged by Bush vote percentage)

Constituencies	Adult population	Bush voters	Kerry voters	Voters
Republican constituencies				
Latter-day Saints	1.4	97.0	3.0	69.2
Traditionalist evangelicals	10.7	87.9	12.1	70.8
All evangelicals	25.1	77.5	22.5	63.2
Traditionalist Catholics	4.2	73.9	26.1	77.6
Centrist evangelicals	9.7	70.4	29.6	56.3
Traditionalist mainliners	4.5	65.6	34.4	77.8
Latino Protestants	2.6	62.9	37.1	49.3
Swing constituencies				
Modernist evangelicals	3.3	57.1	42.9	55.5
Nominal evangelicals	1.5	56.6	43.4	62.2
Centrist Catholics	7.4	52.3	47.7	68.4
All non-Latino Catholics	17.5	52.7	47.3	66.9
Entire sample	100.0	51.2	48.8	60.8
All mainliners	16.4	50.0	50.0	69.2
Centrist mainliners	5.5	49.1	50.9	70.6
Modernist mainliners	4.4	43.1	56.9	55.6
Democratic constituencies				
Modernist Catholics	3.8	38.1	61.9	54.8
Unaffiliated believers	4.8	37.0	63.0	42.7
Latino Catholics	4.5	31.4	68.6	43.1
Nominal mainliners	2.0	31.0	69.0	76.4
Other Faiths	2.5	29.7	70.5	61.9
Seculars	9.0	29.5	70.5	52.6
Nominal Catholics	2.1	28.9	71.1	63.9
All unaffiliated	17.3	28.1	71.9	52.3
Jews	1.9	26.7	73.3	86.5
Atheists/agnostics	3.5	20.0	80.0	60.9
Other Non-Christians	1.4	17.6	82.4	44.7
Black Protestants	9.3	17.2	82.8	50.4

Source: Fourth National Survey of Religion and Politics, Post-Election Sample, Bliss Institute of Applied Politics, University of Akron, November–December 2004 ($N = 2,730$).

that favored Bush are at the top and those that backed Kerry are at the bottom, with the closely divided groups at the middle of the table. As a point of reference, the overall two-party vote and turnout is located in the middle of the table. In addition, the overall figures for evangelicals, mainliners, Catholics, and the unaffiliated are included as well.

Before we turn to a more detailed discussion of these patterns, a few basic features are worth noting. First, there are important differences among the major religious traditions. Compare, for instance, the Bush vote among all evangelical, mainline, and black Protestants; also note the difference between the Kerry vote among all non-Latino Catholics and among all the unaffiliated. Even these broad definitions of religious tradition help explain the presidential vote, revealing the continuing importance of religious belonging.

Second, there were systematic political differences within all the major religious traditions based on traditionalism: traditionalists always voted more heavily for Bush, while modernists and nominals were always less supportive. That pattern holds to some extent even among the unaffiliated, with atheists/agnostics markedly more Democratic than unaffiliated believers. Finally, note the enormous variation in voter turnout within and among religious traditions. In 2004, traditionalists outpolled the modernists—and so did the nominals. Turnout among the unaffiliated was relatively low. Low turnout also characterized some religious minorities, but others, such as Jews, voted at very high rates.

By itself, table 2-2 presents something of a challenge to the conventional wisdom on religion and politics: it shows that both the Republicans and the Democrats had strong religious constituencies in 2004. More important, this arrangement facilitates a discussion of the complex connections between religious communities and the presidential vote.

Republican Constituencies

The first three groups in table 2-2 voted nearly three-quarters or more for Bush. The president's strongest constituency was the Latter-day Saints. Past research has often found this group to be the most Republican of religious traditions, reflecting both its religious traditionalism and its geographic concentration in the GOP strongholds of the Mountain West.[11] However, the 97 percent backing for Bush in this survey is likely an exaggeration produced by the small number of cases.

However, Bush's most important religious constituency was traditionalist evangelicals: 70 percent turned out to vote and 88 percent voted for Bush. Traditionalist Catholics were the next most supportive; they turned out at a rate of about 78 percent and gave Bush almost 75 percent of their ballots. These top Bush groups accounted for 16.3 percent of the adult population in 2004 (as measured in the first column of table 2-2).

The next three groups—centrist evangelicals, traditionalist mainliners, and Latino Protestants—supported the president with more than 60 percent of

11. Campbell and Monson (2007); Kellstedt and others (1995).

their ballots. Turnout varied substantially among these groups. More than 75 percent of traditionalist mainliners voted (much like traditionalist Catholics), but the other two groups, especially Latino Protestants, lagged behind the national figures. These three groups made up another 16.8 percent of the adult population in 2004.

Swing Constituencies

The next five categories were, in political parlance, "swing groups," in which the candidates won by small margins. Three went for Bush: modernist and nominal evangelicals and centrist Catholics. Here the level of turnout varied, with modernist and nominal evangelicals turning out below or at the national figure, while centrist Catholic turnout was above it. Centrist Catholics were strongly pursued by both campaigns, and Bush's slight edge here was emblematic of the 2004 election's close outcome.

Kerry won the remaining two swing groups: centrist and modernist mainline Protestants. Here, too, the level of turnout varied, with modernist mainliners voting less than the nation as a whole, and centrist mainliners turning out at a higher rate (much like traditionalist evangelicals). Kerry's narrow margin among centrist mainliners was also emblematic of the election results. All told, these five swing groups made up 22 percent of the adult population in 2004.

Democratic Constituencies

The remaining religious communities strongly backed Kerry. The next seven groups in the table gave him solid support, beginning with modernist Catholics and the unaffiliated believers, better than 60 percent of whom voted Democratic. However, both groups turned out less than the nation as a whole. The next seven groups voted Democratic by 60 percent or more, including modernist Catholics, unaffiliated believers, Latino Catholics, nominal mainline Protestants, Other Faiths, seculars, and nominal Catholics. Here turnout varied as well: Latino Catholics and seculars voted at a relatively low level while nominal mainline Protestants voted at a very high rate, about 76 percent. Taken together, these seven groups accounted for 28.7 percent of the adult population in 2004 (about 12 percentage points larger than the Bush counterpart groups).

The final four religious communities in the table were Kerry's strongest supporters, voting Democratic at a rate of more than 73 percent. These categories included Jews, atheists/agnostics, Other Non-Christians, and black

Protestants. Jews reported the highest turnout rate overall (which may be a bit exaggerated by the small number of cases); the other groups turned out at the national level, except for black Protestants, who voted at a significantly lower rate. Taken together, these groups made up 16.1 percent of the adult population in 2004 (about the size of Bush's top religious constituencies).

The patterns in table 2-2 are quite powerful: religion in the United States was strongly linked to the 2004 presidential vote in a systematic fashion. However, these patterns raise the question of the impact of other sociodemographic factors that are known to influence voting behavior. While it is beyond the scope of this chapter to offer a full model of the 2004 vote, we have tested the impact of these data elsewhere,[12] and the results were consistent with other recent work.[13] The conclusion of this body of research is that religious tradition and traditionalism have an independent effect on the presidential vote when analysts control for other sociodemographic variables, including income, gender, education, age, and region. Only race and ethnicity are as powerful—but they are closely linked to religion and thus are included in these religious categories.

Religious Communities and Party Coalitions in 2004

Table 2-3 reports the two-party vote in another way: the relative importance of the religious communities to the total Bush and Kerry vote, thus bringing together the groups' vote, turnout, and size in the adult population. This table describes the religious components of the party coalitions in 2004, adding to 100 percent of the Bush and Kerry vote (by column).

The Bush Coalition

The single largest religious community in the Bush coalition was traditionalist evangelicals, accounting for just under 25 percent of all his ballots. The second-largest group was centrist evangelicals, at about 12 percent. Taken together, the two largest evangelical groups made up 35 percent of the Bush vote. If modernist and nominal evangelicals are added in, then evangelical Protestants as a whole provided the president with 40 percent of his support at the polls.

12. Guth and others (2006); also see Olson and Green (2006).
13. See Petrocik (2006); Layman and Green (2006); Leege and others (2002); Layman (2001); and Kohut and others (2000).

Table 2-3. Religious Communities and Presidential Voter Coalitions in 2004

Percent (by column)

Constituencies	Bush voters	Kerry voters	All voters
Republican constituencies			
Latter-day Saints	3.7	.1	1.9
Traditionalist evangelicals	23.4	3.4	13.6
Traditionalist Catholics	7.7	2.9	5.3
Centrist evangelicals	11.9	5.2	8.6
Traditionalist mainliners	7.0	3.9	5.5
Latino Protestants	2.6	1.6	2.1
Swing constituencies			
Modernist evangelicals	2.9	2.2	2.6
Nominal evangelicals	1.5	1.2	1.4
Centrist Catholics	8.0	7.6	7.8
Centrist mainliners	6.5	7.1	6.8
Modernist mainliners	3.3	4.6	4.0
Democratic constituencies			
Modernist Catholics	2.9	4.9	3.8
Unaffiliated believers	2.0	3.6	2.8
Latino Catholics	1.9	4.4	3.1
Nominal mainliners	1.5	3.6	2.6
Other Faiths	1.4	3.2	2.2
Seculars	4.6	11.6	8.0
Nominal Catholics	1.3	3.4	2.3
Jews	1.4	4.1	2.7
Atheists/agnostics	1.5	6.5	4.0
Other Non-Christians	.4	1.7	1.0
Black Protestants	2.6	13.2	7.8
Entire sample	100.0	100.0	100.0

Source: Fourth National Survey of Religion and Politics, Post-Election Sample, Bliss Institute of Applied Politics, University of Akron, November-December 2004 (*N* = 2,730).

Bush received another 18.4 percent of his vote from other traditionalists among Catholics and mainline Protestants, plus the Latter-day Saints. Thus, the combined traditionalist categories accounted for more than 40 percent of all Bush ballots. Other centrist groups provided Bush with another 14.5 percent of his vote, while the sum of all centrists accounted for 26 percent. High turnout among the traditionalist groups and centrist Catholics helped Bush, but the slim majorities from less traditional evangelicals benefited the Democrats.

So, Bush was reelected with strong support from nonminority Christian traditions, especially evangelicals and religious traditionalists, but with significant backing from Catholics and centrists. However, all these groups accounted for only about 75 percent of the total Bush vote; Bush's slim margin of victory therefore required a broader coalition. One source of extra votes was ethnic and racial minorities. Led by Latino Protestants, these groups provided 7.1 percent of the Republican vote. Another source of support was mainline Protestant and Catholic modernists and nominals, at 9.0 percent. Meanwhile, the three unaffiliated groups and the non-Christian categories provided another 9.9 percent. In sum, Bush received more than 25 percent of his ballots from religious communities that largely backed Kerry.

The Kerry Coalition

Kerry's single most important group was black Protestants, at 13.2 percent of his total vote. Adding Latinos brings the total from ethnic and racial groups to just under 20 percent of all Kerry ballots. The non-Christian categories added another 5.8 percent, bringing the total from religious minorities to more than 25 percent of the Kerry vote. However, the second most important source of Democratic votes was the seculars, at 11.6 percent. All the unaffiliated groups combined accounted for just over 20 percent of all of Kerry's support. Finally, adding up all the modernist and nominal groups (including the evangelicals) produced another 20 percent of Kerry's ballots. The high turnout among nominal mainline Protestants and Jews clearly helped Kerry, but he would have done better with higher turnout from black Protestants, Latino Catholics, seculars, and unaffiliated believers.

Kerry's coalition was more diverse than Bush's in religious terms, drawing heavily from religious minorities, the unaffiliated population, and less traditional Christians. But like Bush, Kerry needed broader support to render the election a toss-up. One source of extra votes was the centrist categories, which provided Kerry with 20 percent of his ballots. In addition, Kerry received more than 10 percent of his ballots from traditionalists of various kinds. All told, Kerry obtained more than 25 percent of his ballots from religious communities that largely backed Bush—about the percentage that Bush received from groups that otherwise strongly supported Kerry.

The 2004 Vote in Temporal Perspective

Were the 2004 results substantially different from those of other recent presidential elections? Table 2-4 presents the presidential vote of the major religious communities from 2004 back to 1992. For ease of presentation, the categories are kept in the 2004 order and the 2004–1992 percent change is listed in the final column. This table reports the Republican portion of the

Table 2-4. Religious Communities and Presidential Vote, 2004–1992

Percent of two-party vote (arranged by 2004 Bush vote percentage)

Constituencies	Bush 2004	Bush 2000	Dole 1996	Bush 1992	Change 2004–1992
Republican constituencies					
Latter-day Saints	97.0	94.4	78.6	66.7	30.3
Traditionalist evangelicals	87.9	87.3	81.7	83.5	4.4
Traditionalist Catholics	73.9	60.7	54.0	53.3	20.6
Centrist evangelicals	70.4	63.2	57.9	68.1	2.3
Traditionalist mainliners	65.6	75.9	65.6	63.8	1.8
Latino Protestants	62.9	28.6	24.2	38.1	24.8
Swing constituencies					
Modernist evangelicals	58.2	42.4	35.3	45.3	12.9
Nominal evangelicals	55.2	44.0	47.8	28.6	26.6
Centrist Catholics	52.3	49.6	48.8	46.6	5.7
Entire sample	51.2	49.5	46.8	47.3	3.9
Centrist mainliners	49.1	51.5	52.9	58.7	−9.6
Modernist mainliners	43.1	55.7	46.3	53.8	−10.7
Democratic constituencies					
Modernist Catholics	38.1	40.0	34.0	33.9	4.2
Unaffiliated believers	37.0	28.0	35.0	60.0	−23.0
Latino Catholics	31.4	28.6	26.3	25.0	6.4
Nominal mainliners	31.0	51.2	45.5	40.0	−9.0
Other Faiths	29.1	25.6	17.6	14.3	14.8
Seculars	29.5	42.2	46.5	25.9	3.6
Nominal Catholics	28.9	37.5	44.4	61.5	−32.6
Jews	26.7	23.3	18.4	17.9	8.8
Atheists/agnostics	20.0	30.6	40.6	32.1	−12.1
Other Non-Christians	17.6	37.0	18.2	18.8	−1.2
Black Protestants	17.2	3.5	11.2	9.5	7.7

Source: National Surveys of Religion and Politics, Bliss Institute of Applied Politics, University of Akron. 1992 ($N = 2,265$); 1996 ($N = 2,350$); 2000 ($N = 3,000$); 2004 ($N = 2,730$).

two-party vote, but since the Democratic portion is its reciprocal, the patterns can be used to discuss both parties. Table 2-5 presents the turnout in the same fashion; both tables are discussed together. The proportion of the U.S. adult population represented by the various religious communities remained about the same over this period.

Traditionalist evangelicals were a strong Republican constituency throughout the period, with more than 80 percent voting for Republican candidates. The GOP did, however, improve its support by some 4 percentage points and increased turnout by almost 5 percentage points between 1992 and 2004 (see tables 2-4 and 2-5). The GOP made bigger gains among other of its constituencies. For instance, the Republican vote among Latter-day Saints

Table 2-5. Religious Communities and Turnout, 2004–1992

Percent

Constituencies	Voted 2004	Voted 2000	Voted 1996	Voted 1992	Change 2004–1992
Republican constituencies					
Latter-day Saints	69.2	63.3	36.3	66.7	2.5
Traditionalist evangelicals	70.8	64.7	63.7	65.9	4.9
Traditionalist Catholics	77.6	63.8	62.3	75.0	2.6
Centrist evangelicals	56.3	47.6	45.3	46.8	9.5
Traditionalist mainliners	77.8	62.8	67.0	75.6	2.2
Latino Protestants	49.3	38.5	50.0	36.8	12.5
Swing constituencies					
Modernist evangelicals	61.8	42.7	40.0	56.7	5.1
Nominal evangelicals	69.0	44.3	39.7	40.0	29.0
Centrist Catholics	68.4	59.1	57.1	72.4	−4.0
Entire sample	60.8	54.3	51.9	54.6	6.2
Centrist mainliners	70.6	50.8	58.5	62.2	8.4
Modernist mainliners	55.6	54.3	54.0	60.5	−4.9
Democratic constituencies					
Modernist Catholics	54.8	56.3	57.1	55.5	−0.7
Unaffiliated believers	42.7	42.3	32.9	32.1	10.6
Latino Catholics	43.1	36.3	47.6	36.6	6.5
Nominal mainliners	76.4	63.8	61.5	60.5	15.9
Other Faiths	60.6	69.7	61.5	63.8	−3.2
Seculars	52.6	46.3	40.2	37.0	15.6
Nominal Catholics	63.9	39.4	56.9	55.8	8.1
Jews	86.5	72.6	47.6	69.8	16.7
Atheists/agnostics	60.9	70.3	40.2	65.5	−4.6
Other Non-Christians	44.7	64.4	32.5	63.0	−18.3
Black Protestants	50.4	53.9	56.9	40.9	9.5

Source: National Survey of Religion and Politics, Bliss Institute of Applied Politics, University of Akron. 1992 ($N = 2,265$); 1996 ($N = 2,350$); 2000 ($N = 3,000$); 2004 ($N = 2,730$).

increased by some 30 percentage points and their overall turnout inched up as well. (These patterns, plus the sharp decline in turnout in 1996, may be exaggerated by the small number of cases in this group.) Another Republican success story was Latino Protestants, who exhibited a dramatic increase in both turnout and the GOP vote over the period, with the biggest gains on both counts occurring between 2000 and 2004.

A more important change occurred among traditionalist Catholics, who became 20 percentage points more Republican over the period. Although their overall turnout was up marginally since 1992, it jumped substantially between 2000 and 2004. Centrist Catholics also moved in a Republican direction, but in a slow, steady fashion. This group's turnout also expanded sharply between 2000 and 2004, although it declined modestly over the entire period.

The net result was that Bush obtained a majority of both groups in 2004. Indeed, John Kerry's Catholicism appears not to have helped much with these Catholic communities and his less traditional Catholicism may even have been a hindrance.

A more complex pattern appears among other evangelical and mainline Protestant categories. The GOP vote among centrist evangelicals increased slightly over the period, although their turnout expanded considerably, mostly between 2000 and 2004. There was an increase on both counts among modernist and nominal evangelicals, especially the latter, with big gains also occurring between 2000 and 2004. In fact, modernist and nominal evangelicals gave majority support to a Republican presidential candidate in 2004 for the first time since 1992. These changes may reflect the nature of the various campaigns: in the 1990s the Democratic presidential ticket contained Southern candidates with evangelical backgrounds of a less traditional sort (Clinton and Gore), who may have had some appeal among less traditional evangelicals. The 2004 Democratic ticket had no such appeal, and Bush campaign strategist Karl Rove deployed a full-court press to obtain evangelical votes. Indeed, these results suggest that he was successful in his stated objective of mobilizing more evangelicals in 2004 than 2000.[14]

Something of an opposite pattern occurred among mainline Protestants. The GOP vote among traditionalist mainliners increased over the period, but the high-water mark was in 2000, with the Republican vote declining by 10 percentage points between 2000 and 2004. Indeed, Republican support decreased sharply among centrist, modernist, and nominal mainliners over the entire period (by about 8, 11, and 9 percentage points, respectively), but those trends were temporarily arrested in 2000. Perhaps George W. Bush's family background and membership in the United Methodist Church had special appeal to mainliners of all sorts in 2000. However, that connection certainly did not work in 2004, when all the mainline groups voted sharply less Republican. At the same time, mainline turnout increased, often sharply. For example, turnout among nominal mainliners grew by more than 12 percentage points between 2000 and 2004.

These largely opposite trajectories for evangelical and mainline Protestants may well be related. The consolidation of evangelicals in the Republican coalition may have had the effect of pushing away mainline Protestants, once the religious mainstay of the GOP. While that pattern may have something to do with "moral values," such values would not explain the Republican drift of

14. American Enterprise Institute (2001); Green (2004c).

modernist and nominal evangelicals in 2000 or the Democratic shift of traditionalist mainliners in 2004. Instead, the cause may have been other issues associated with the Bush administration, such as the war in Iraq. In any event, these data show the continuing importance of religious tradition to the presidential vote.

Thus, the Democratic presidential candidates made gains among mainline Protestants over the period and especially in 2004. The net result was that the mainliners were evenly divided between the major parties in 2004. The Democrats also made gains among a collection of other groups in 2004, including modernist Catholics (the group where Kerry himself may belong), seculars, nominal Catholics, and atheists/agnostics. But interestingly, Kerry lost significant ground among unaffiliated believers. The trajectories of all these groups over time were complicated by Ross Perot's independent campaigns in 1992 and 1996. Perot had considerable appeal to less traditional believers, apparently drawing votes away from Bill Clinton as well as from his Republican opponents. Several of these groups (seculars, unaffiliated believers, nominal Catholics) showed sizable increases in turnout over the period, but modernist Catholics showed little change. Meanwhile, voting among atheists/agnostics declined, especially between 2000 and 2004.

Despite strong Democratic support among ethnic and religious minorities, the party steadily lost some ground among Latino Catholics, Jews, and black Protestants. All three groups showed increased turnout over the entire period as well, although fewer black Protestants voted in 2004 than in 2000. Republican gains among black Protestants in 2004 were relatively large, but mostly because the GOP's performance in 2000 was so abysmal. A similar pattern of Republican gain and increasing turnout held among the Other Non-Christians group in 2000, but dissipated in 2004, when both turnout and the GOP vote declined. It is possible that this pattern reflects the Bush administration's conduct of the war on terrorism—but the small number of cases here requires a cautious interpretation.

Tables 2-6 and 2-7 show the religious composition of presidential vote coalitions from 1992 to 2004 (based on the two-party vote). Despite the complex changes in turnout and votes reported in the previous tables, the relative shapes of these coalitions were remarkably stable over the period. Still, there were some shifts in the religious character of the major party coalitions worth noting.

The Republicans made relative gains among their top three groups in 2004, so that traditionalists made up 7.8 percentage points more of George W. Bush's 2004 coalition than his father's coalition in 1992. Over the period, the GOP

Table 2-6. Religious Communities and Republican Presidential Voter Coalitions, 2004–1992

Percent (two-party Republican vote by column)

Constituencies	Bush 2004	Bush 2000	Dole 1996	Bush 1992	Change 2004–1992
Republican constituencies					
Latter-day Saints	3.7	2.2	2.1	2.1	1.6
Traditionalist evangelicals	23.4	24.9	20.7	18.1	5.3
Traditionalist Catholics	7.7	8.4	6.6	6.8	0.9
Centrist evangelicals	11.9	9.5	10.7	13.5	−1.6
Traditionalist mainliners	7.0	8.5	8.1	7.8	−0.6
Latino Protestants	2.6	1.0	1.6	1.7	0.9
Swing constituencies					
Modernist evangelicals	2.9	1.8	1.2	5.1	−2.4
Nominal evangelicals	1.5	1.4	2.1	0.4	1.3
Centrist Catholics	8.0	7.6	7.9	10.1	−2.1
Centrist mainliners	6.5	6.5	10.5	7.8	−1.1
Modernist mainliners	3.3	4.4	3.7	5.9	−2.4
Democratic constituencies					
Modernist Catholics	2.9	3.6	3.5	4.2	−1.3
Unaffiliated believers	2.0	1.8	1.4	2.5	−0.5
Latino Catholics	1.9	1.8	1.9	1.5	0.4
Nominal mainliners	1.5	2.8	1.9	1.7	−0.2
Other Faiths	1.3	1.3	0.8	0.6	0.7
Seculars	4.6	5.5	6.4	3.2	1.4
Nominal Catholics	1.3	1.2	2.3	1.7	−0.4
Jews	1.4	1.3	1.7	1.1	0.3
Atheists/agnostic	1.5	2.5	2.5	1.9	−0.4
Other Non-Christians	0.4	1.3	0.4	0.6	−0.2
Black Protestants	2.6	0.6	1.9	1.7	0.9
Entire sample	100.0	100.0	100.0	100.0	

Source: National Survey of Religion and Politics, Bliss Institute of Applied Politics, University of Akron. 1992 (*N* = 2,265); 1996 (*N* = 2,350); 2000 (*N* = 3,000); 2004 (*N* = 2,730).

also made slight advances among ethnic minorities, mostly between 2000 and 2004, and some very modest long-term gains among seculars and Jews.

In contrast, the Democrats made relative gains among the unaffiliated groups, so that the Democratic coalition became 8.5 percentage points "less affiliated" over the period (see table 2-7). They also made a long-term gain among mainline Protestants, for a total of 3.7 percentage points, and posted a 2.5 percentage point gain among nominal Catholics. They also made very modest gains among Latino Catholics, nominal evangelicals—and interestingly, traditionalist evangelicals.

Table 2-7. Religious Communities and Democratic Presidential Voter Coalitions, 2004–1992

Percent (arranged by 2004 Bush percentage)

Constituencies	Kerry 2004	Gore 2000	Clinton 1996	Clinton 1992	Change 2004–1992
Republican constituencies					
Latter-day Saints	0.1	0.1	.5	.9	−0.8
Traditionalist evangelicals	3.4	3.5	4.1	3.2	0.2
Traditionalist Catholics	2.9	5.3	4.9	5.3	−2.4
Centrist evangelicals	5.2	5.4	6.8	5.7	−0.5
Traditionalist mainliners	3.9	2.7	3.8	4.0	0.1
Latino Protestants	1.6	2.5	4.3	2.5	−0.9
Swing constituencies					
Modernist evangelicals	2.2	2.4	1.9	5.5	−2.9
Nominal evangelicals	1.2	1.8	2.0	0.9	0.4
Centrist Catholics	7.6	7.6	7.3	10.4	−2.8
Centrist mainliners	7.1	5.9	8.2	4.9	2.0
Modernist mainliners	4.6	3.4	3.8	4.5	0.3
Democratic constituencies					
Modernist Catholics	4.9	5.3	6.0	7.4	−2.5
Unaffiliated believers	3.6	4.6	2.2	1.5	2.1
Latino Catholics	4.4	4.4	4.8	4.0	0.4
Nominal mainliners	3.6	2.7	2.0	2.3	1.3
Other Faiths	3.2	3.7	3.2	3.4	−0.2
Seculars	11.6	7.5	6.5	8.1	3.5
Nominal Catholics	3.4	1.9	2.6	0.9	2.5
Jews	4.1	4.2	6.8	4.3	−0.2
Atheists/agnostics	6.5	5.4	3.2	3.6	2.9
Other Non-Christians	1.7	2.1	1.5	2.5	−0.8
Black Protestants	13.2	17.6	13.5	14.3	−1.2
Entire sample	100.0	100.0	100.0	100.0	

Source: National Survey of Religion and Politics, Bliss Institute of Applied Politics, University of Akron. 1992 (*N* = 2,265); 1996 (*N* = 2,350); 2000 (*N* = 3,000); 2004 (*N* = 2,730).

How the Faithful Voted

The questions posed at the outset of this chapter can now be answered. Both the Republican and Democratic parties had strong religious constituencies in 2004. For the GOP and President Bush, traditionalist evangelicals were the single most important constituency, serving as the backbone of a coalition dominated by other evangelicals and traditionalists. This pattern developed steadily throughout the 1990s and reached its fullest expression in 2004. However, a broader coalition was responsible for Bush's narrow victory, which rested on winning centrist Catholics and making modest gains among ethnic and religious minorities.

For the Democrats and Senator Kerry, the two most important constituencies were black Protestants and seculars. Indeed, Kerry assembled a complex coalition drawn in roughly equal parts from ethnic and religious minorities, the unaffiliated, and modernist and nominal Christians. This pattern also developed in the 1990s and was in full flower by 2004. The Democrats also made significant gains among mainline Protestants between 2000 and 2004. But like his rival, Kerry had a broader coalition that included crucial votes from centrists and traditionalists.

Taken together, these findings reveal the great diversity within the American religious landscape, with its many distinctive communities defined by religious tradition and traditionalism. Differences between religious traditions remained important despite the striking differences among traditionalists, centrists, modernists, and nominals within the major religious traditions. These patterns persist when one controls for other socioeconomic factors.

Given the development of the religious elements of the Republican and Democratic presidential coalitions over the last several elections, there is every reason to expect that these basic patterns will continue into the future and that they will be an important factor in the 2008 campaign. However, because the coalitions were so closely balanced in 2004, it is difficult to predict the outcome of the next several elections with any certainty. After all, even modest changes in the votes of a few religious communities could swing the results one way or another. In addition, each party's religious coalition encompasses contradictions that may be difficult to manage in the rough and tumble of politics. For the Republicans, the tensions among Christian traditionalists, centrists, and religious minorities could prove problematic. For the Democrats, tensions between its unaffiliated and less traditional followers on one hand, and its supporters among religious minorities and centrists on the other, could be every bit as daunting.

Appendix. Surveys and Religious Categories

This chapter is based on the Fourth National Survey of Religion and Politics, conducted by the Bliss Institute at the University of Akron in collaboration with the Pew Forum on Religion and Public Life, with additional support provided by the Paul B. Henry Institute for the Study of Christianity and Politics at Calvin College and the William R. Kenan Jr. Endowment at Furman University.[1] The survey, conducted in the spring of 2004, was based on interviews of a national random sample of 4,000 adult Americans (eighteen years of age or older). Members of the initial sample were then reinterviewed after the 2004 election; the later sample included 2,730 respondents.

This survey was the fourth in a series of surveys conducted at the University of Akron since 1992, using the same pre- and postelection design and roughly the same number of respondents in the samples.

Religious Tradition. The National Survey of Religion and Politics for each year contains an extensive series of questions to determine the specific religious affiliation of respondents as accurately as possible. Despite the precision of the measure, there were some ambiguous responses, which were coded with the aid of other religious variables, including "born again" status, religious identity, and attendance at worship services. These affiliations were then recoded into the eleven religious traditions in table 2-1. This standard classification is based on the formal beliefs, behaviors, and histories of the denominations or churches involved, with the most detail dedicated to sorting out the many kinds of Protestants in the United States.[2] Black Protestants and Latinos were separated on the basis of race and ethnicity.

Traditionalism. The survey contained extensive measures of religious belief and behavior. Five belief items were found in all four surveys (view of the Bible; belief in God; belief in an afterlife; view of the Devil and of evolution), as were five behavior items (frequency of worship attendance; frequency of prayer; frequency of Bible reading; frequency of participation in small groups; and level of financial contribution to a congregation). In most cases, these items were worded the same way across surveys. However, in a few cases improvements in question wording over time produced some differences between surveys. In order to maintain the same conceptual basis for the traditionalism scale, these items were adjusted by means of other religious

1. Green (2004a); Green and others (2005).

2. See Kellstedt and Green (1993); Green and others (1996); Layman (2001); Layman and Green (2006); Guth and others (2006).

measures not used in the overall analysis in order to have the same range and frequency as the items in the 2004 survey.

The final belief and behavior items were then subjected to separate factor analyses in each of the surveys. The factor loadings were quite similar on all the analyses. A belief and behavior factor score was then generated and the two scores were subjected to a second factor analysis to extract underlying traditionalism. This final factor analysis also generated a factor score, which was adjusted to the mean score for all four surveys for each religious tradition. This adjustment was very modest but corrected for the peculiarities of each survey.[3]

In the final step, the adjusted traditionalism scale was divided into four categories within the three largest religious traditions. The cut-points were the mean traditionalism scores of four levels of religious salience. These cut-points were chosen because they were specific to the religious traditions, unambiguous, and consistent across surveys. Also, traditional religiosity stresses the importance of religion over other aspects of life.[4] Unaffiliated believers were defined by scoring in the top two-thirds of the belief factor score in each survey.

Although this categorization process is complex, it was remarkably robust, with a wide range of alternative measures, methods, and cut-points producing essentially the same results.[5]

Turnout Estimate. As in other surveys, voting behavior was overreported in the National Surveys of Religion and Politics. A more accurate estimate of turnout was calculated using likely voter screens, reports of past voting behavior, interest in politics, and demographic factors. Reported turnout was adjusted to the actual national turnout. The unadjusted results produced very similar results.

3. See Layman and Green (2006) for a similar approach, but one in which the belief and behavior items were used independently.

4. Guth and Green (1993).

5. For other versions of these categories, see Guth and others (2006); Dionne (2006); and Green (2004a). For a version of these categories for a popular audience, see John C. Green and Steve Waldman, "Tribal Politics," *Atlantic,* January-February 2006, pp. 10–14.

Faithful Divides
Party Elites and Religion
John C. Green and John S. Jackson

The results of the 2004 presidential campaign provoked an unusually strident debate about the impact of "moral values" on the outcome of the election and added fuel to the ongoing argument over the "culture war."[1] Some scholars argue that the culture war is real and consequential, rooted in fundamental moral divisions that will soon dominate political discourse. In their view, the American public is deeply polarized, leaving little middle ground or room for compromise.[2] To these advocates, "moral values" had, as they expected, a great impact in 2004. However, other scholars argue that the culture war is much exaggerated. Cultural disputes involve only small minorities of the population and have modest effects on political discourse. Moreover, they say, the public is not especially polarized on such matters, with most people holding moderate views and open to compromise. In any event, the populace is focused on other concerns.[3] To these advocates, "moral values" had limited impact in 2004 and that impact was overstated.

Despite their disagreements, both sides agree on two things. First, political elites, including party elites, are critical to the values divide, whether they

1. See Ferguson (2005); White (2005); Pomper (2005); Muirhead and others (2005).
2. Hunter (1991); White (2003); Greenberg (2004).
3. Williams (1997); Wolfe (1998); Fiorina, Abrams, and Pope (2005).

reflect a culture war raging in the public or instigate such "wars" themselves in their bid for power. Second, the disputants agree that religious communities are important to the values divide, whether in terms of bitter sectarian rivalries focused on sexual morals or religious coalitions concerned with an expanded issue agenda. These points of agreement provide fertile ground for investigating party elites and religion in 2004.

This chapter undertakes such an investigation, using a survey of national convention delegates in 2004. Consistent with other recent studies, we find evidence of "faithful divides" among major party elites: differences in religious affiliation and observance were important characteristics of Democratic and Republican delegates. These differences were often systematically linked to political attitudes, most clearly on cultural issues such as abortion, but to a lesser extent on liberal or conservative ideology and the Iraq war, where partisanship seemed to play a greater role. Overall, the party elites represented their co-religionists within the party's base reasonably well, both in aggregate numbers and on attitudes toward issues. Furthermore, the views of both "religious liberals" and "religious conservatives" were deeply embedded in elite party politics. These faithful divides contributed to the marked polarization among party elites.

Party Elites, Religion, and Values

Delegations to the major party presidential nominating conventions are among the broadest and most accessible bodies of party elites, and as a consequence, they have been extensively studied.[4] Delegates constitute what Kirkpatrick called "the presidential elite"; they are strategically located to influence national politics and they wield their influence in both formal and informal terms.[5]

In formal terms, once every four years national convention delegates become the embodiment of the national parties, elected to serve as each party's highest plenary body. In addition to formally nominating presidential and vice presidential candidates, they adopt the party's platform, enact the rules under which the next presidential nominations will be conducted, and hold a giant "pep rally" for the party's candidates.[6] The success or failure of the national conven-

---

4. McClosky, Hoffman, and O'Hara (1960 and 1964); Jackson, Brown, and Bositis (1982); Miller and Jennings (1986); Maggiotto and Wekkin (2000); Abramowitz, McGlennon, and Rapoport (1986).
5. Kirkpatrick (1976).
6. David, Goldman, and Bain (1960).

tions reveals the extent to which the party is united and ready for the general election in the fall.

In addition to their formal duties, the delegates represent critical components of the major parties' resources and organizational personnel. Many are envoys from state and local party organizations, which are the constituent parts of the national committees and the convention itself. Others belong to key interest groups or social movements allied with the party. Still others are part of the presidential primary campaigns, particularly that of the winning candidate, while many are connected to their party's congressional, state, and local officeholders. Finally, the delegates are a slice of the "life of the party" at the grassroots, embodying the priorities, opinions, and ferment within each party's larger activist pool. And when the conventions are over, the delegates return home to conduct the fall campaign and other party business.

Thus, presidential nominating conventions are a good place to observe the most important features of national politics, including the role of religion. Past research has found religion to have mattered among convention delegates. For example, Herbert McClosky, Paul Hoffman, and Rosemary O'Hara's surveys of delegates in the 1950s found strong evidence of religious elements in New Deal party coalitions, with the Democratic coalition containing Catholics, Southern Protestants, and religious minorities while the Republicans were dominated by mainline Protestants.[7] Later delegate surveys by Jeane Kirkpatrick and by Warren Miller and Kent Jennings in the 1970s and 1980s found that these religious alliances were under stress as new political forces, including the "religious left" and the "religious right," remade national politics.[8] Still later, Geoffrey Layman showed the emergence of new religious alignments among convention delegates in the 1980s and 1990s, including partisan shifts by some of the major religious communities but also religious divisions within those communities.[9]

In one sense, religion has long contributed to the "values divide" in American politics. After all, the New Deal–era disputes between Catholics and mainline Protestants were about the values of social justice and economic opportunity. And in the latter half of the twentieth century, the "religious left"

---

7. McClosky, Hoffman, and O'Hara (1960).

8. Kirkpatrick (1976); Miller and Jennings (1986).

9. Layman (2001). Additional evidence of this "great divide" has been found among a wide variety of political elites and activists, including members of Congress (Guth and Kellstedt 2001), campaign contributors (Green, Guth, and Fraser 1991), state convention delegates (Green, Rozell, and Wilcox 2001), and interest group activists (Guth and others 1995).

aggressively advocated the values of equality and individual rights. Recent disputes over values relating to proper sexual behavior and traditional families arose alongside disagreements over the values of environmental protection, world peace, and social stability. Religious communities have been central to these disputes, producing a series of "faithful divides" in politics. However, different sets of religious values have divided the faithful in different ways.

As described in chapter 2, two aspects of religion are especially useful in describing these divides among the faithful: religious traditions and traditionalism. Historically, religious traditions were the primary means by which religion was connected to politics, with different traditions developing strong links to one or another of the major political parties.[10] Indeed, the party coalitions of the New Deal era were examples of such "ethno-religious" alliances.[11] During the last half of the twentieth century, however, traditionalism began to exercise an independent influence on politics, with more traditional members of religious traditions shifting in a conservative, Republican direction and less traditional members shifting in a liberal, Democratic direction.[12] The liberal social movements of the 1960s and 1970s and the conservative social movements of the 1980s were early examples of the consequences of this "restructuring." Thanks in large part to the efforts of the "religious left" and "religious right," traditionalism emerged as a powerful factor in party politics—as found by Layman in the "great divide" of the 1990s.[13]

The culture war debate is a product of this shift in the political impact of religion. It remains to be seen whether this new kind of faithful divide, based on traditionalism, will eventually displace the older divides based on religious tradition or if a new kind of division will emerge from the heat of current religious and political debates. Making such predictions is difficult because the process through which religious values influence party elites is complex. For example, two psychological processes are at work in forging these connections: opinion constraint and cognitive dissonance.[14] On one hand, religious values can produce highly constrained opinion among party elites, generating a distinctive religious perspective on issues. On the other hand, cognitive dissonance within party elites because their personal views differ from the

10. McCormick (1974).
11. McCloskey and others (1960).
12. Kohut and others (2000).
13. Kirkpatrick (1976); Miller and Jennings (1986); Layman (2001).
14. For opinion constraint, see Kirkpatrick (1976). For cognitive dissonance, see Layman and Carsey (2002).

dominant view of their co-partisans can reduce the distinctiveness of religious values. Thus, there may be degrees of religious influence on party elites, ranging from cases in which religious and partisan values reinforce each other to cases in which they are sharply at odds.

Data Sources

This exploration of religion and party elites is based on the 2004 Party Elite Study (PES).[15] In the late summer of 2004 we mailed questionnaires to a systematic random sample of approximately 1,000 Democratic and 1,000 Republican national convention delegates during the week immediately following each party's national convention. We received 458 usable returns from the Democrats, for a response rate of 45.0 percent, and we received 502 usable returns from the Republicans, for a response rate of 46.5 percent (both figures exclude undeliverable mail). In most respects, survey respondents were not systematically different from nonrespondents. One exception was race, and the data were weighted to correct for the discrepancy, for a final weighted total of 500 cases in each party. (A good if rough figure for the margin of error for each survey is plus or minus 5 percentage points.) The 2004 survey was similar in design to the previous PES surveys, dating back to the 1970s.[16]

As in past PES surveys, many of the attitudinal questions were adopted from the American National Elections Study (NES), a fact that allowed us to compare the delegates' attitudes with those of their co-partisans among the general public using the 2004 NES survey.[17] Both the PES surveys and the NES contained similar measures of denominational affiliation and frequency of worship attendance. We coded denomination affiliation to the major religious traditions using the same coding system employed in chapter 2 in this volume. This measure of religious tradition was then simplified and combined with weekly worship attendance, a measure of religious traditionalism, to create the eleven religion categories used for the analysis.

15. Green and Jackson (2007); Jackson, Bigelow, and Green (2006).

16. On previous PES surveys, see Jackson and Hitlin (1976); Jackson, Brown, and Bositis (1982); Buell and Jackson (1991); Jackson (1992); Jackson and Clayton (1996); Green, Jackson, and Clayton (1999); and Jackson, Bigelow, and Green (2003).

17. The measure of worship attendance in the 2004 NES was slightly different from that used in past NES surveys and in the PES. We corrected the measure to match the distribution for weekly attenders using measures of congregational activity. In one case, the Iraq war, the Fourth National Survey of Religion and Politics was used as the point of comparison (see chapter 2).

A Religious Profile of the 2004 Convention Delegates

A good place to begin is with a religious profile of the national convention delegates in 2004. Table 3-1 lists membership in religious traditions and frequency of worship attendance. By these standard measures, the rival party elites differed substantially from one another.

The Democratic delegates who met in Boston to nominate John Kerry were quite diverse in religious terms. The single largest group was Catholics, accounting for more than 25 percent of all the Democratic delegates. The two next-largest groups were mainline and black Protestants (about 20 percent and 15 percent, respectively). These three groups accounted for about 60 percent of all Democratic delegates. The religiously unaffiliated made up another 14 percent and evangelical Protestants about 8 percent of the Democratic convention. The remaining 17 percent was accounted for by minority faiths: Jews and Liberal Faiths (Unitarians, Humanists, Wiccans) each were about 6.5 percent; Other Non-Christians (Muslims, Hindus, Buddhists) were less than 2 percent; and Other Christians (Latter-Day Saints, Eastern Orthodox, Christian Scientists) were less than 1 percent.

Table 3-1. 2004 National Convention Delegates: Religious Affiliation and Worship Attendance

Percent

Religious affiliation/worship attendance	Democrats	Republicans
Affiliation		
Catholic	28.0	23.2
Mainline Protestant	19.4	31.3
Evangelical Protestant	8.4	29.3
Black Protestant	14.6	5.0
Unaffiliated	14.0	3.6
Jewish	6.4	2.2
Liberal Faith	6.6	0.4
Other Christian	0.8	4.6
Other Non-Christian	1.8	0.4
All	100.0	100.0
Attendance		
More than once a week	7.6	17.0
Once a week	19.4	36.8
Several times a month	14.0	15.8
Several times a year	23.0	15.8
Seldom	24.2	10.8
Never	12.0	3.8
All	100.0	100.0

Source: Authors' survey.

In contrast, the Republican delegates that met in New York to renominate George W. Bush were less diverse in religious terms. The single largest group was mainline Protestants, who made up 31 percent of all Republican delegates. However, evangelical Protestants, at 29 percent, were nearly as numerous. Thus, 60 percent of the GOP delegates were white Protestants. Catholics were the third-largest group, with a bit under 25 percent of the total. Black Protestants and those in the Other Christians group each accounted for about 5 percent of the Republican delegates. The remaining 6 percent included the unaffiliated (3.6 percent), Jews (2.2 percent), and those in the Liberal Faiths and Other Non-Christians groups (less than one-half of 1 percent each).

These affiliation profiles reveal both historical patterns and recent trends. On the first count, the strength of Catholic Democrats and mainline Protestant Republicans reflects the dominant roles these religious traditions played in party coalitions in the New Deal era. Likewise, the greater presence of black Protestants and other religious minorities has long been a hallmark of the Democratic coalition. But there is also strong evidence of recent departures from these historic patterns. For example, in 2004 the Democrats contained many mainline Protestants and the Republicans many Catholics; the Democrats had also acquired a significant number of unaffiliated delegates, while the GOP made gains among evangelical Protestants. From a religious perspective, the Republican delegates were more diverse than in the past. These religious patterns had developed slowly over several decades and consolidated in the 1990s.[18]

One reason for the changes was the increased importance of religious traditionalism in politics. During the 2004 campaign, journalists discovered a "religion gap" among voters based on worship attendance.[19] Table 3-1 shows just such a division among the delegates. For instance, only about one-quarter of the Democrats reported attending worship once a week or more (27 percent), compared with more than one-half of the Republicans (53.8 percent). Similarly, more than one-third of the Democratic delegates claimed to attend worship seldom or never (36.2 percent), compared with roughly one-sixth of the Republicans (14.6 percent). Although the GOP clearly had an advantage on this measure of religious traditionalism, the Democrats were hardly a nonreligious lot, with almost 66 percent attending a few times a year or more often.

18. Layman (2001). The distribution of these religious groups did vary somewhat from 1996 to 2004 in both parties, but typically within the margin of error of the surveys. The mean size of the religious categories over this period closely resembled the distribution in table 3-2.

19. Green and Silk (2004).

Table 3-2 combines religious tradition and worship attendance and organizes the results for ease of presentation. First, the four largest religious traditions were divided into "weekly worship attenders" (weekly or more often) and "less observant" (less than weekly worship attendance). Second, the four smallest groups were combined into a single category ("All Other Faiths") and were also divided by worship attendance. This composite category is questionable on conceptual grounds and must be viewed with some caution, but it makes some sense empirically when broken out by party. Finally, the categories were listed in order of mean ideology score, ranging from the most conservative religious group to the most liberal.

It is worth taking a moment to review this combined religion category. Among the Democrats, the less observant were a majority in all the religious traditions, except for black Protestants, where there was a close division. Taken together, the less observant accounted for 59 percent of all Democratic delegates. In contrast, weekly attenders made up a majority of the categories for the Republicans, with two exceptions: Catholics, who were evenly divided, and mainline Protestants. Overall, weekly attenders accounted for 53.4 percent of all the GOP delegates. So, in addition to some important differences by religious tradition, the rival party elites also showed some important differences by the worship attendance measure of traditionalism.

Table 3-2. 2004 National Convention Delegates: Affiliation and Attendance

Percent

Religious affiliation/worship attendance	Democrats	Republicans
Evangelical Protestant		
Weekly attender	3.2	23.6
Less than weekly attender	5.2	5.7
Mainline Protestant		
Weekly attender	4.4	11.3
Less than weekly attender	15.0	20.0
Catholic		
Weekly attender	9.6	11.6
Less than weekly attender	18.4	11.6
Black Protestant		
Weekly attender	7.6	2.8
Less than weekly attender	7.0	2.2
All Other Faiths		
Weekly attender	2.4	4.8
Less than weekly attender	13.2	2.8
Unaffiliated	14.0	3.6
All	100.0	100.0

Source: Authors' survey.

Religion and Delegate Attitudes

Do the religious differences among party elites matter politically? One way to answer that question is to look at the political attitudes of the Democratic and Republican delegates by religious category. Because convention delegates were highly polarized in 2004, we can focus on a few key attitudes to explore the impact of religion, including self-identified ideology, abortion, and the war in Iraq.[20] These topics not only cover the major issues in American politics, they also reveal a range of relationships to religion.[21]

Ideology. Table 3-3 looks at self-identified ideology, one of the most general of political attitudes. About 12.5 percent of the Democrats claimed to be "very liberal," and almost 40 percent claimed to be "liberal." However, almost 50 percent of the Democrats identified themselves as "moderate" or "conservative." This evidence goes against the common stereotype of the Democratic Party as a bastion of intense liberalism. In fact, the Republicans fit the common stereotype of a conservative party much better: about 20 percent claimed to be "very conservative," more than 50 percent claimed to be "conservative," and just 25 percent characterized themselves as "moderate" or "liberal."

Religion helps explain these differences in ideological self-identification. Note that the "very liberal" Democrats were concentrated among the Unaffiliated and All Other Faiths groups. The other religious groups contained far fewer delegates with a "very liberal" identification. Turning to the center of the spectrum, moderate Democrats were concentrated among weekly attendance Christians, especially Catholics and evangelical and black Protestants. However, level of attendance produced a mixed pattern by religious tradition. Catholics and black Protestants who attended services weekly included more moderates than their less observant co-religionists. But evangelical and mainline Protestants who attended services weekly were *less* moderate than those who were less observant. This difference may be a product of the relatively small number of cases in the weekly attendance categories. But it also could be that the Democratic delegates contain some hints of the religious left, discussed in chapter 13.

Among Republicans, the "very conservative" delegates were concentrated among weekly attenders, especially among evangelical and black Protestants. And in every religious tradition, the less observant were less intense in their conservatism. Turning to the center of the spectrum, the unaffiliated and

20. Jackson, Bigelow, and Green (2006).
21. Controls for other demographic variables had little effect on these patterns, reflecting the high social status of the delegates.

Table 3-3. 2004 National Convention Delegates and Ideology

Percent

Religious affiliation/ worship attendance	Democrats			Republicans		
	Very liberal	Liberal	Moderate/ conservative	Liberal/ moderate	Conservative	Very conservative
Evangelical Protestant						
Weekly attender	0.0	38.9	61.1	7.6	42.4	50.0
Less than weekly attender	12.0	16.0	72.0	13.8	58.6	27.6
Mainline Protestant						
Weekly attender	9.1	45.5	45.5	28.8	60.7	12.5
Less than weekly attender	9.3	36.0	54.7	41.0	52.0	6.0
Catholic						
Weekly attender	2.1	18.8	79.2	31.6	54.4	14.0
Less than weekly attender	12.9	48.4	38.7	32.8	58.6	8.6
Black Protestant						
Weekly attender	0.0	40.5	59.5	7.7	53.8	38.5
Less than weekly attender	0.0	58.3	41.7	27.3	72.7	0.0
All Other Faiths						
Weekly attender	25.0	58.3	16.7	12.5	62.5	25.0
Less than weekly attender	21.2	34.8	43.9	21.4	57.1	21.4
Unaffiliated	30.0	37.1	32.8	44.4	44.4	11.1
All	12.6	38.6	48.8	24.7	53.0	21.9

Source: Authors' survey.

mainline Protestants were the most moderate, followed by both groups of Catholics. In all the religious categories, the less observant were more moderate than their co-religionists, with a partial exception for Catholics, where the difference was very small. Put differently, the most observant Republicans also had the most conservative ideology.

In sum, among the most intensely ideological groups of delegates, distinctive religious values reinforced the dominant partisan perspective. For example, weekly attendance evangelicals among the Republicans and the unaffiliated among the Democrats exhibited the most constrained opinion and the least cognitive dissonance. For other groups, the impact of religion was not so consistent, producing less intensely ideological responses.

Abortion. Table 3-4 considers attitudes on abortion, the quintessential cultural issue in American politics. Overall, the Democratic delegates were strongly pro-choice, with 75 percent agreeing with abortion on demand and

Table 3-4. 2004 National Convention Delegates and Permissibility of Abortion

Percent

Religious affiliation/ worship attendance	Democrats			Republicans		
	Always	Sometimes	Never	Always	Sometimes	Never
Evangelical Protestant						
Weekly attender	77.0	25.0	0.0	1.7	57.6	40.7
Less than weekly attender	84.0	12.0	4.0	3.4	79.4	17.2
Mainline Protestant						
Weekly attender	59.1	40.9	0.0	10.9	27.3	16.4
Less than weekly attender	73.3	26.7	0.0	33.0	66.0	1.0
Catholic						
Weekly attender	38.8	51.0	12.2	5.2	77.6	17.2
Less than weekly attender	75.3	24.7	0.0	25.4	69.5	5.1
Black Protestant						
Weekly attender	73.0	27.0	0.0	0.0	61.5	38.5
Less than weekly attender	88.9	11.1	0.0	50.0	40.0	10.0
All Other Faiths						
Weekly attender	91.7	8.3	0.0	8.3	79.2	12.5
Less than weekly attender	87.9	12.1	0.0	7.1	85.8	7.1
Unaffiliated	90.0	10.0	0.0	42.1	57.9	0.0
All	76.0	22.6	1.4	15.2	67.6	17.2

Source: Authors' survey.

virtually none agreeing that abortion should be banned. In contrast, the Republicans were best described as diverse or "moderately pro-life," with 67.6 percent favoring some restrictions on abortion. Indeed, only a little more than 17 percent advocated banning all abortions—and almost the same number favored abortion on demand. This pattern goes against the conventional wisdom that the GOP is a bastion of intense pro-life sentiment. It is also somewhat surprising given that over several recent presidential campaigns the Republican platforms and presidential candidates have been clearly pro-life.[22]

Religion has a strong and consistent association with attitudes toward abortion. First, the effect of worship attendance was straightforward. In both parties, weekly attenders were always more pro-life than their less observant co-religionists. For the Democrats, the patterns by religious tradition were a bit more complex. Catholics were the least pro-choice, followed by mainliners and then by black and evangelical Protestants; hence the moderation of the latter two groups observed in table 3-3 does not extend to abortion. For

22. Craig and O'Brien (1993, p. 314).

the Republicans, a clearer pattern appears: evangelicals were the most pro-life, followed by black Protestants, Catholics, and mainline Protestants.

In sum, delegates who were part of religious communities characterized by liberal cultural values tended to hold pro-choice positions on abortion, while those belonging to religious communities characterized by "traditional morality" tended to hold pro-life positions. Here, too, a notable level of opinion constraint extends across the religious, partisan, and ideological dimensions. Religion and partisanship provide powerful values systems that help their adherents organize the confusing, dissonant world, and they can reinforce each other substantially.

Iraq war. Table 3-5 reports delegate opinion on the Iraq war, the most contentious foreign policy issue of the 2004 campaign. Overall, the rival party elites were deeply polarized, with more than 69 percent of the Democratic delegates claiming that the war was "fully unjustified," while 75 percent of the Republican delegates said that it was "fully justified." Given that level of polarization, there was relatively little room for religion to matter. However, there were some religious differences worth mentioning.

Table 3-5. 2004 National Convention Delegates and Justifiability of the Iraq War

Percent

Religious affiliation/ worship attendance	Democrats			Republicans		
	Fully unjustified	In between	Fully justified	Fully unjustified	In between	Fully justified
Evangelical Protestant						
Weekly attender	62.5	37.5	0.0	0.8	16.1	83.1
Less than weekly attender	68.0	28.0	4.0	0.0	24.1	75.9
Mainline Protestant						
Weekly attender	68.2	31.8	0.0	0.0	18.2	81.8
Less than weekly attender	66.7	33.3	0.0	1.0	28.0	71.0
Catholic						
Weekly attender	62.5	37.5	0.0	0.0	32.8	67.2
Less than weekly attender	65.6	34.4	0.0	1.7	23.7	74.6
Black Protestant						
Weekly attender	65.8	34.2	0.0	0.0	15.4	84.6
Less than weekly attender	65.7	34.3	0.0	0.0	36.4	63.6
All Other Faiths						
Weekly attender	83.3	16.7	0.0	4.0	32.0	64.0
Less than weekly attender	72.3	27.7	0.0	0.0	7.1	92.9
Unaffiliated	81.4	18.6	0.0	0.0	42.1	57.9
All	69.1	30.7	0.2	0.8	24.0	75.2

Source: Authors' survey.

Among the Democrats, those in the Unaffiliated and All Other Faiths groups were most likely to regard the war as "fully unjustified." Members of the major Christian traditions were a bit less decisive in their rejection of the war. Here the level of worship attendance mattered little, although weekly attendance Catholics and evangelicals were the least opposed to the war.

Among Republicans, the patterns were a bit clearer. Members of the Protestant traditions were the most supportive of the war, especially weekly worship attendees. In contrast, non-Protestants showed less support for the war, with weekly attenders most skeptical. (One exception was the less observant members of the All Other Faiths group, who backed the war nearly unanimously.) Unaffiliated Republicans, like unaffiliated Democrats, were the least supportive of the war. Taken as a whole, these patterns bear a modest resemblance to the evidence on ideology.

It is interesting that the war in Iraq did not more clearly divide the delegates along faith-based lines. Some on the left and the antiwar protesters have tried to make opposition to the war a clear moral imperative. In fact, these data may reveal a conflict over moral imperatives: opponents of the war may well have opposed it because it threatened the values of world peace and domestic security, while proponents may well have understood it as preserving the values of freedom and security. Thus, it appears that attitudes on the war were more influenced by partisanship than religion.

Overall, both religious tradition and traditionalism were associated with political attitudes among party elites in 2004. On some occasions, religious values and partisanship reinforced one another, producing intense and consistent opinion. This confluence tended to contribute to polarization of the major parties. However, in other cases religion and partisanship did not point in the same direction, reducing the intensity and coherence of opinion.

Party Elites and Partisan Publics

How well did the party elites represent their co-religionists among their party's followers in the general public? One crude way to answer that question is to compare the relative size of religious groups among each party's delegates with their size among partisans in the public. Table 3-6 offers such a comparison, using the 2004 National Election Study. Here a rough standard is useful: disparities within 5 percentage points between the delegates and public partisans can be regarded as unimportant (and the religious group is judged as "reasonably well represented" by the delegates), while disparities of

Table 3-6. Representation and Religion: 2004 Convention Delegates and Their Partisan Publics

Percent

Religious affiliation/ worship attendance	Democrats		Republicans	
	Delegates	Public	Delegates	Public
Evangelical Protestant				
Weekly attender	3.2	5.4	23.6	20.8
Less than weekly attender	5.2	8.4	5.8	15.8
Mainline Protestant				
Weekly attender	4.4	5.4	11.0	8.8
Less than weekly attender	15.0	5.7	20.0	10.7
Catholic				
Weekly attender	9.6	9.9	11.6	10.5
Less than weekly attender	18.6	14.7	11.6	12.6
Black Protestant				
Weekly attender	7.4	13.5	2.8	0.8
Less than weekly attender	7.0	9.6	2.2	1.4
All Other Faiths				
Weekly attender	2.4	3.2	4.8	2.1
Less than weekly attender	13.2	5.1	2.8	2.7
Unaffiliated	14.0	19.1	3.6	13.8
All	100.0	100.0	100.0	100.0

Source: Authors' survey; 2004 National Election Study.

more than 5 percentage points can be regarded as important (and the groups judged as under- or overrepresented by the delegates).

The 2004 Democratic delegates represented the evangelical Protestants among their party's supporters reasonably well if one takes the divisions by worship attendance separately. However, if the two categories are combined, evangelical Democrats were underrepresented at the national convention by 5.4 percentage points. The Democratic delegates also underrepresented black Protestants, especially the weekly attenders, by 6.1 percentage points. In contrast, the Democrats overrepresented less observant mainline Protestants by 9.3 percentage points and members of the All Other Faiths group by 8.1 percentage points. Interestingly, by these standards Catholics and the unaffiliated were reasonably well represented among the Democrats.

The 2004 Republicans present a simpler picture. Evangelicals who attended services weekly were reasonably well represented by the GOP delegates, but the less observant evangelicals were significantly underrepresented, as were the unaffiliated, by 10 and 10.2 percentage points, respectively. The opposite occurred for mainliners, among whom the less observant were significantly overrepresented, by 9.3 percentage points. Interestingly, Catholics, black Protestants, and those in the All Other Faiths group were reasonably well represented at the Republican convention (and probably overrepresented).

What was the source of these disparities? One possibility is religious mobilization. For example, the activities of the "religious left" over time may help account for the overrepresentation of less observant mainline Protestants among the Democratic delegates. Certainly there was something of a revival of religious left activities in 2004.[23] Similarly, the efforts of the "religious right" may help account for the fact that weekly attendance evangelicals were well represented among Republican delegates but less observant evangelicals were not. There is no doubt that the Republicans placed great stress on mobilizing the faithful in 2004, especially in key states such as Florida and Ohio.[24]

Another possibility is the impact of social status. Delegates in both parties are affluent, educated, and well-connected politically, and some of the underrepresented religious communities, such as black Protestants and evangelicals, are much less so. The fact that Catholics were well represented in each party may reflect both possibilities. Both liberal and conservative interest groups have been active in the Catholic community, and Catholics enjoy relatively high social status.[25]

Based on our analysis of political attitudes, we can draw a cautious assessment of the likely impact of these discrepancies. The Democratic delegates were probably a bit more liberal on ideology, abortion, and the Iraq war due to the overrepresentation of less observant mainliners and those in the All Other Faiths group as well as the underrepresentation of evangelical and black Protestants. In similar fashion, the Republican delegates might have been more moderate if they did not underrepresent less observant evangelicals and the unaffiliated. However, any such increase in moderation might well have been offset if less observant mainliners had been well represented.

Another crude answer to the question of representation can be provided by comparing the attitudes of delegates to those of their co-religionist co-partisans in the public. Figures 3-1 through 3-3 offer a simple version of such a comparison by plotting the attitudes of the eleven religious categories used in this analysis for two pairs of groups: Democratic delegates and public, and Republican delegates and public. The attitudinal measure is the percent of each

23. Waldman (1995).
24. Magleby, Monson, and Patterson (2007).
25. Kohut and others. (2000).

Figure 3-1. Delegates and Partisans: Ideology[a]

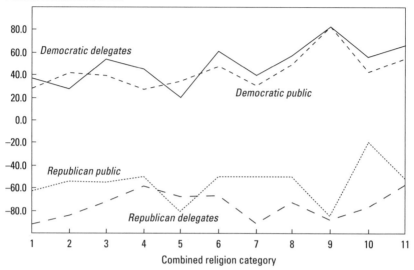

Percent conservative/liberal

a. Combined religion categories: 1 = weekly attender evangelicals; 2 = less observant evangelicals; 3 = weekly attender mainliners; 4 = less observant mainliners; 5 = weekly attender Catholics; 6 = less observant Catholics; 7 = weekly attender black Protestants; 8 = less observant black Protestants; 9 = weekly attender members of All Other Faiths group; 10 = less observant members of All Other Faiths group; 11 = unaffiliated.

group that holds the liberal or conservative position on the issue in question.[26] The eleven religious categories are listed in the same order as in tables 3-2 through 3-8, so the overall pattern of the graph is arbitrary. However, comparing the shape of the graph pairs reveals the extent to which delegate and citizen opinions are similar. Put another way, if the views of the delegates and their co-religionist co-partisans reflect the effects of religion, then the graphed lines should move together, even though the views of the delegates and the partisan public may differ substantially for other reasons—including the elite status of the delegates.

Figure 3-1 plots self-identified ideology for the two delegate-public pairs. The first thing to note is that the Democratic and Republican delegates (the darker lines) tend to hold more consistently liberal or conservative views than

26. For both the delegates and the general public, the attitudes are measured as the percent of the group that held liberal views (for the Democrats) or conservative views (for the Republicans). For ideology, all "liberal" and "conservative" responses were used, respectively. For the issues, the variables were coded as in table 3-8.

their partisan publics (the lighter lines), although subgroups of the Republican delegates deviate more often by being more moderate. As one might expect, the Democrats are on the liberal side of the scale (upper half) and the Republicans on the conservative side (lower half). These patterns are consistent with the literature, which has regularly found delegates to have more "extreme" opinions that their co-partisans in the public.[27]

The second thing to note in figure 3-1 is the similarity in the shapes of the graphs for each pair across the eleven religious groups, even though the elites and masses often differ in level of liberalism or conservatism.[28] For the Democrats, the shapes of the graphs match most closely from the weekly attender Catholics (group 5) to the unaffiliated (group 11). The shapes of the graphs do not match as well for white Protestants (groups 1 through 4), although the differences are not huge, and that fact may reflect in part the small number of white evangelicals among the Democratic delegates. The Republican graphs match much less well on ideology. For one thing, the Republican delegates are often more conservative than their co-religionists among rank-and-file Republicans. For white Protestants (groups 1 through 4), both lines move in a more moderate direction from weekly attending evangelicals to less observant mainliners, where the lines almost meet. Then the lines diverge for weekly attender Catholics (group 5), where the delegates were more moderate, and less observant Catholics (group 6). Both graphs are then roughly constant for black Protestants (groups 7 and 8) and move in a moderate direction for less observant members of the All Other Faiths group.

Figure 3-2 is a similar plot for abortion attitudes. Here the Republican graphs match more closely.[29] Among the Republicans, the most important differences were in the middle of the graph, with less observant Catholics (group 6) and weekly attender black Protestants (group 7). From the weekly attender black Protestants through group 10 (the less observant in the All Other Faiths group), the public was more pro-life than the Republican delegates. Here the Democratic graphs matched less well. For instance, there were notable differences between elite and public views among evangelical Protestants, both groups of black Protestants, and the unaffiliated. In all cases, the delegates were more purely pro-choice than the public (although among less observant mainline Protestants the differences are small).

27. McClosky, Hoffman, and O'Hara (1960); Miller and Jennings (1986); Maggiotto and Wekkin (2000).

28. For ideology and the Democrats, $r = .79$ for the two series; for the Republicans, $r = .17$.

29. For abortion and the Democrats, $r = .60$ for the two series; for the Republicans, $r = .67$.

Figure 3-2. Delegates and Partisans: Abortion[a]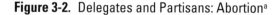

Percent pro-life/pro-choice

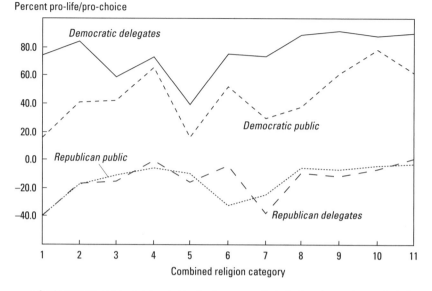

a. Combined religion categories: 1 = weekly attendance evangelicals; 2 = less observant evangelicals; 3 = weekly attendance mainliners; 4 = less observant mainliners; 5 = weekly attendance Catholics; 6 = less observant Catholics; 7 = weekly attendance black Protestants; 8 = less observant black Protestants; 9 = weekly attendance members of All Other Faiths group; 10 = less observant members of All Other Faiths group; 11 = unaffiliated.

Figure 3-3 plots opinion on the Iraq war. Here the rival party elites took much more extreme positions than their publics. However, note that the shapes of the graphs match each other well for each party. For the Democrats, the uniform antiwar sentiment of the delegates parallels that of the Democratic public, with opposition peaking for weekly attenders in the All Other Faiths and the Unaffiliated groups. Among the Republicans, support for the war among the delegates also paralleled support in the GOP public, reaching a maximum with members of the All Other Faiths group.[30]

Of course, all this evidence on representation must be viewed with considerable caution since there are many factors that cannot be taken into account in these simple comparisons. But taken together, the evidence suggests two tentative conclusions. First, in 2004 the rival party elites represented the religious constituencies within their partisan publics reasonably well in the aggregate, and furthermore, the disparities that existed might not

30. For the Iraq war and the Democrats, $r = .80$ for the two series; for the Republicans, $r = .41$.

Figure 3-3. Delegates and Partisans: Iraq War[a]

Percentage war fully justified/unjustified

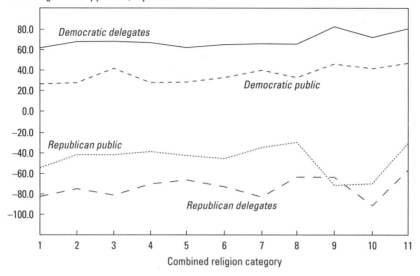

Combined religion category

a. Combined religion categories: 1 = weekly attendance evangelicals; 2 = less observant evangelicals; 3 = weekly attendance mainliners; 4 = less observant mainliners; 5 = weekly attendance Catholics; 6 = less observant Catholics; 7 = weekly attendance black Protestants; 8 = less observant black Protestants; 9 = weekly attendance members of All Other Faiths group; 10 = less observant members of All Other Faiths group; 11 = unaffiliated.

have changed the party's overall positions on the issues very much. Second, although party elites tended to hold more liberal or conservative views than their co-partisan publics, their attitudes tended to reflect the general political differences across religious communities. The best matches between delegates and the public tended to occur for religious constituencies long associated with each party. However, there were significant discontinuities in both parties as well. These patterns suggest that religion influences the views of delegates, even though it is not always the dominant factor in structuring their issue positions.

Party Elites and Religious Activists

This evidence on the representativeness of party elites leads to two questions: are party elites responding to the views of their co-religionists, or are partisan publics taking cues from party elites within their faith? Those questions are difficult to answer. However, the literature suggests that party elites are likely to be the most important factor in this relationship.[31] Certainly, in recent times both the "religious left" and "religious right" have directed extensive efforts at mobilizing religious communities during elections, and the 2004 campaign was no exception.

Throughout most of the twentieth century, religious mobilization was concentrated on the liberal side of the political spectrum.[32] Religious liberals led important social movements, such as the civil rights and peace movements, and they also participated prominently in largely secular movements, such as the feminist, environmentalist, and gay rights movements. Although most analysts believe that the "religious left" was attenuated in the 1990s, there was renewed activism in 2004.[33] Table 3-7 presents data on whether the delegates considered themselves supporters of religious liberals, sympathetic to their goals, neutral, skeptical of their goals, or opponents.[34]

Overall, about 25 percent of the Democratic delegates claimed that they supported religious liberals, and nearly 40 percent said that they were sympathetic to their goals. Hence, more than 60 percent of these delegates had a positive view of religious liberals. Roughly 20 percent were neutral, and only about 15 percent were skeptical or opposed. Supporters of religious liberals were concentrated among weekly worship attenders, with most found among mainline Protestants and those in the All Other Faiths group. The other religious categories contained markedly fewer supporters but a larger number of sympathizers. Weekly attendance Catholics included the fewest supporters of religious liberals and had the least positive view of them overall. There also was little strong support for religious liberals among weekly attendance black Protestants.

Republican delegates generally had a negative view of religious liberals. Overall, 40 percent identified themselves as opponents, and 39.5 percent were skeptical of their goals. Hence, about 80 percent of these delegates held negative views of religious liberals. Roughly 15 percent were neutral, and only

31. Layman (2001).
32. Olson (2007).
33. McMahon (2005).
34. The PES data have some evidence on attitudes toward religious liberals and conservatives over time. Interestingly, support for religious liberals increased dramatically between 1996 and 2004 for Democratic delegates, rising from about 1 percent claiming to be supporters to the 26 percent reported here. Opposition to religious liberals among Republican delegates declined over the period, but the low point was in 2000. Meanwhile, support for religious conservatives among Republican delegates was about the same in 1996 and 2000 but dropped substantially in 2004. However, opposition to religious conservatives among Democrats was essentially constant over the period.

Table 3-7. 2004 National Convention Delegates and Relationship with "Religious Liberals"

Percent

Religious affiliation/ worship attendance	Democrats					Republicans				
	Supporter	Sympathetic	Neutral	Skeptic	Opponent	Supporter	Sympathetic	Neutral	Skeptic	Opponent
Evangelical Protestant										
Weekly attender	25.0	43.8	6.3	12.5	12.5	0.0	1.2	5.8	22.1	70.9
Less than weekly attender	25.0	20.8	25.0	16.7	12.5	0.0	0.0	28.0	24.0	48.0
Mainline Protestant										
Weekly attender	59.1	9.1	18.2	4.5	9.1	2.1	6.4	21.3	38.3	31.9
Less than weekly attender	22.2	41.7	20.8	12.5	2.8	1.1	4.5	20.5	51.1	22.7
Catholic										
Weekly attender	6.4	38.3	34.0	19.1	2.1	4.2	2.1	14.6	41.7	37.5
Less than weekly attender	27.0	37.1	25.8	7.9	2.2	2.1	4.2	12.5	58.3	22.9
Black Protestant										
Weekly attender	22.9	28.6	28.6	14.3	5.7	0.0	0.0	0.0	42.9	57.1
Less than weekly attender	17.6	61.8	8.8	5.9	5.9	0.0	25.0	0.0	0.0	75.0
All Other Faiths										
Weekly attender	50.0	33.3	16.7	0.0	0.0	4.8	4.8	9.5	52.4	28.6
Less than weekly attender	39.1	43.8	7.8	1.6	7.8	0.0	0.0	16.7	33.3	50.0
Unaffiliated	22.6	35.5	24.2	6.5	11.3	5.9	5.9	17.6	29.4	41.2
All	26.2	37.7	21.0	9.2	5.9	1.7	3.5	14.9	39.5	40.4

Source: Authors' survey.

about 4 percent had positive views. Indeed, just a handful of Catholics, main-liners, and members of the All Other faiths group were supporters. Here, too, opposition was common among weekly worship attenders. Weekly atten-dance evangelicals and black Protestants were strongly opposed to religious liberals, but so were two small groups, less observant black Protestants and members of the All Other Faiths group, and one large group, less observant evangelicals. Most of the other groups were less opposed but quite skeptical of the religious liberals' goals.

Religious conservatives were not especially active in American politics until the late 1970s, but since then they have become major players. Nearly all analysts agree that "pro-life," "pro-family," and "pro-marriage" groups were quite active in the 2004 campaign. Table 3-8 reports the results of a question about the delegates' relationship to "religious conservatives."[35]

Overall, 50 percent of the Democratic delegates claimed to be opponents of religious conservatives—about twice the number that were supporters of religious liberals. Another 38 percent of these delegates said that they were skeptical of the goals of religious conservatives. Thus, nearly 90 percent of Democratic delegates had a negative view of religious conservatives. Roughly 10 percent were neutral, and only 3 percent had positive views. In fact, other than a handful of evangelicals, there were no supporters at all. The strongest opponents of religious conservatives were the unaffiliated, followed by members of the All Other Faiths group. Black Protestants included the fewest opponents but the largest number of skeptics.

The Republican delegates had a much more positive view of religious con-servatives. Overall, nearly 40 percent claimed to be supporters of religious conservatives—about the same number as were opponents of religious liberals. Another 30 percent were sympathetic to the goals of religious conservatives. Hence, about 70 percent of the Republican delegates had a positive view of this group. Roughly 17 percent were neutral and about 14 percent had negative views. The absence of GOP opposition is remarkable given the well-publicized disputes between the "religious right" and more moderate Republicans in the early 1990s. The supporters were concentrated among weekly attendance evangelicals and black Protestants and also included less observant evangeli-cals. One surprise was the lack of strong support from weekly attendance Catholics. Beyond evangelicals, the less observant groups contained the fewest supporters but a large number of sympathizers. The unaffiliated had the most negative views of religious conservatives.

35. Green, Rozell, and Wilcox (2003, 2006).

Table 3-8. National Convention Delegates and Relationship with "Religious Conservatives"

Percent

Religious affiliation/ worship attendance	Democrats					Republicans				
	Supporter	Sympathetic	Neutral	Skeptic	Opponent	Supporter	Sympathetic	Neutral	Skeptic	Opponent
Evangelical Protestant										
Weekly attender	7.7	7.7	7.7	46.2	30.8	76.1	18.8	3.4	1.7	0.0
Less than weekly attender	4.0	0.0	8.0	40.0	48.0	55.2	24.1	13.8	3.4	3.4
Mainline Protestant										
Weekly attender	0.0	9.5	4.8	33.3	52.4	35.2	35.2	14.8	11.1	3.7
Less than weekly attender	0.0	1.5	4.4	48.5	45.6	16.2	28.3	28.3	18.2	9.1
Catholic										
Weekly attender	0.0	7.0	11.6	44.2	37.2	26.3	36.8	19.3	14.0	3.5
Less than weekly attender	0.0	2.4	15.3	32.9	49.4	12.7	43.6	29.1	10.9	3.6
Black Protestant										
Weekly attender	0.0	0.0	25.0	50.0	25.0	61.5	7.7	23.1	7.7	0.0
Less than weekly attender	0.0	6.1	12.1	60.6	21.2	30.0	50.0	10.0	0.0	10.0
All Other Faiths										
Weekly attender	0.0	0.0	0.0	33.3	66.7	29.2	54.2	8.3	8.3	0.0
Less than weekly attender	0.0	3.2	8.1	25.8	62.9	15.4	46.2	23.1	7.7	7.7
Unaffiliated	0.0	0.0	0.0	22.4	77.6	17.6	29.4	29.4	11.8	11.8
All	0.4	2.9	9.2	37.9	49.6	37.9	30.9	17.4	9.6	4.1

Source: Authors' survey.

These assessments of religious liberals and conservatives reveal a high degree of polarization of the rival party elites. Indeed, the degree of polarization is greater than on abortion or ideology. In terms of opposition to religious liberals and conservatives, the polarization rivals that on the Iraq war.

Faithful Divides in 2004 and Beyond

In conclusion, we have found that in 2004 the major party elites were characterized by faithful divides based on religious tradition and traditionalism. These religious differences were systematically linked to political attitudes, most clearly on cultural issues such as abortion and to a lesser extent on ideology and the Iraq war, where partisanship seemed to play a larger role. Overall, the party elites represented their co-religionists within their party's public reasonably well, both in aggregate numbers and attitudes toward issues. Furthermore, views of "religious liberals" and "religious conservatives" were deeply embedded in elite party politics. These faithful divides contributed to the marked polarization among party elites.

These patterns reflect a profound change in the relationship between religion and politics in recent times. In the mid-twentieth century, the major religious traditions were a source of social identity that linked individual members to particular parties. Adherence to doctrine and practice played only a small role in such political links, so that many aspects of religious and political life were compartmentalized. In this sense, the major religious traditions were like "big tents" that enclosed adherents who were characterized by great variation in their level of traditionalism. This situation contributed to a web of cross-cutting cleavages on many issues, resulting in low levels of opinion constraint and high levels of cognitive dissonance within members of the major party coalition. Although party elites tended to have more coherent views than the public at large, they largely reflected these characteristics, contributing to a moderate and nonpolarized politics. Indeed, the "big tent" terminology was regularly applied to the nonideological parties of that era as well.

Today there is a degree of nostalgia for that style of politics, with its lower levels of religious mobilization, ideological coherence, and confrontation. But it is worth remembering that this kind of politics was strongly criticized at the time. For example, many political scientists disliked the nonideological political parties of the era and advocated "more responsible parties."[36] Such parties would be more coherent in policy terms, and among other things, they

---

36. Committee on Political Parties (1950).

would move beyond the often bitter divisions based on race, region, ethnicity, and religious identity that then plagued national politics. To a considerable degree, the advocates of "responsible" parties have gotten their wish.[37]

One part of these developments has been a profound change in the role of religion. Although religious traditions are still relevant to party politics, the degree of traditionalism has become important as well. In some respects, this reflects developments within American religion, as conscious preservers of traditional values confronted conscious promoters of modern values. Most of the "big tents" still exist formally, but the rival groups congregate in opposite corners of the tents, and some have moved outside of them. No doubt the political agenda has contributed to the divisions as well, by politicizing some long-standing religious differences.

The result has been a drive toward more consistent political cleavages, with higher levels of opinion constraint and lower levels of cognitive dissonance within members of party coalitions. Religious and political values increasingly overlap, aided and abetted by the political efforts of activists on the "religious left" and "religious right." Despite some exceptions, the rival party elites tend to exhibit these characteristics, contributing to polarized politics. Indeed, "polarization" has become the commonplace description of this state of affairs not only in party politics, but in the White House, Congress, and state governments as well.[38]

There is a powerful logic to a political alignment defined on one hand by people who are traditionalist in religion and conservative in politics and on the other by those who are modernist in religion and liberal in politics. One pole is compelled by the old-fashioned gospel of personal salvation, the rugged individualism of the marketplace, and American nationalism. The other pole is motivated by the modern gospel of social reform, government responsibility for economic outcomes, and the ceding of some national sovereignty to international organizations. However, these polar positions do not fit all issues equally well, nor do they affect all religious communities to the same degree or in the same fashion. Just as the "big tent" religious traditions and political parties of the past had a degree of coherence, today's intersection of religious traditionalism and partisan ideology also has a degree of incoherence.

It is in this regard that political leaders, including party elites, play a critical role, actively structuring political alignments out of the raw material of social characteristics and public opinion in the context of the two-party

37. Green and Herrnson (2002).
38. See Green and Coffey (2006).

system. Here our findings have important implications for the culture war debate. On one hand, the religion-based divisions among party elites in 2004 fit reasonably well with the culture war argument. But on the other hand, it is far from clear that this result was inevitable or based on deep public divisions over religion or moral values. In these matters, as in other aspects of politics, there is an element of choice. The party elites in 2004 certainly displayed political "responsibility" in one sense of the term, but it remains to be seen if they can fulfill the other meanings of the term.

The Moral
Values Election?

Moral Values
Media, Voters, and Candidate Strategy

D. Sunshine Hillygus

The conventional wisdom about the 2004 presidential election is that the electorate voted on the basis of "moral values."[1] Journalists and pundits largely concluded that Bush won reelection because his stance on moral issues, especially gay marriage and abortion, coincided more closely than that of Kerry with the views of the American public.[2] The London *Times* reported that "Americans voted in record numbers for a Republican president primarily because they identified with his moral agenda."[3] Tony Perkins, president of the Family Research Council, insisted that same-sex marriage was "the hood ornament on the family values wagon that carried the president to a second term."[4] Some scholars have similarly concluded that the anti–gay marriage ballot initiatives contributed to Bush's victory,[5] although others have challenged the

1. This chapter is part of a larger project coauthored with Todd Shields.
2. Some journalists were skeptical of the moral values interpretation. For instance, "Moral Values Malarkey: CBS's Meyer Doesn't Buy the Big Post-Election Idea," *CBS News*, November 5, 2004 (www.cbsnews.com/stories/2004/11/05/opinion/meyer/main653931.shtml).
3. Harding (2004, p. 8).
4. Cooperman and Edsall (2004, p. A1).
5. Campbell and Monson (2005); Donovan and others (2005). See also chapter 7 by Campbell and Monson in this volume.

assumption that voters were primarily concerned about moral issues in the 2004 election.[6]

In this chapter, I evaluate the relationship between presidential vote choice and attitudes on gay marriage, abortion, and other prominent campaign issues. The findings suggest that the election was not primarily a referendum on gay marriage or abortion policy. Rather, as in most elections in the past, the economy and war appeared to be foremost on the minds of most voters. The results show that gay marriage and abortion had roughly the same effect on their vote as the issues of Social Security reform, the environment, education policy, and a minimum wage increase.

On the surface, this chapter may appear to run counter to the others in this volume. I conclude that the election was not fundamentally "about" the moral issues of gay marriage and abortion. At the same time, however, the analysis suggests that "matters of faith" might have influenced at least one aspect of the candidates' campaign strategies and policy appeals—their ground war communications. Religious fractures *within* the traditional party coalitions created incentives for candidates to appeal to narrow issue publics on wedge issues like abortion and gay marriage (among many others) while focusing the broader campaign, especially television advertising and news coverage, on Iraq and terrorism. The 2004 campaigns were able to use information and communication technologies to microtarget different issue publics with the specific policies that they cared about. Thus, although the analysis in this chapter suggests that most voters (or the average American voter) did not select a candidate on the basis of moral issues, it is important to recognize that a subset of voters cared about moral issues and that the Bush campaign was able to use direct mail, phone calls, and personal canvassing to emphasize issues like abortion and gay marriage for that subset of voters. (See chapter 7, by David Campbell and Quin Monson, in this volume.)

Assessing the Moral Mandate

Political scientists rarely engage in public debate with journalists and pundits—our efforts are more commonly devoted to topics of academic rather than popular appeal. Yet understanding the role of gay marriage and abortion in the 2004 election is important for both theoretical and practical reasons. For political scientists, evaluating the role of moral issues in 2004 contributes to our understanding of voter decisionmaking. Did moral issues trump the

6. Hillygus and Shields (2005); Burden (2004).

broader issues of the economy and war, which academics have for so long believed account for electoral success? Ken Mehlman, Bush's campaign manager, argued that "people now vote much more on their values."[7] Do political scientists need to update election forecasting models and theories of voter decisionmaking?

For policymakers, it is important to understand what an election is "about" in order to gauge the policy priorities of the electorate. Following the 2004 election, many political actors behaved as if Bush had won because of moral values. Christian conservatives were quick to claim responsibility for Bush's reelection, and they expected a specific policy agenda to be pursued following it. The Reverend D. James Kennedy, a broadcast evangelist, declared that "now that values voters have delivered for George Bush, he must deliver for voters. The defense of innocent unborn human life, the protection of marriage, and the nomination and confirmation of judges who will interpret the Constitution, not make law from the bench, must be first priorities come January."[8] Acting on the same assumption, Democrats fretted about how to bring the "values voters" back to the party. Senate Democrats selected a pro-life senator, Harry Reid, as their minority leader. Senator Hillary Clinton recently emphasized that it would be "a great disservice to dismiss" the concerns of Americans who were driven to the polls because of their opposition to issues like gay marriage.[9]

Did the American electorate give Bush a "moral mandate," or did its vote represent support for other public policies? Elections are a blunt instrument for assessing the preferences of the public, but they are our most fundamental mechanism for ensuring democratic accountability. Yet in an environment in which political parties are polarized across a number of different issues, it may be difficult to interpret the directive of the voters.

The media concluded that moral values drove the election results on the basis of the success of anti–gay marriage initiatives in eleven states, the ongoing assumption that there is a cultural divide between "red" and "blue" America, and a single exit poll question that found that 22 percent of respondents selected "moral values" as the most important issue when they voted for president. That conclusion is described more fully in the following chapter. A number of scholars and journalists have since pointed out various flaws in interpreting the poll question in this way, but the most basic is that it is not

7. Harris (2004, p. A35).
8. Eichel (2004).
9. Hernandez (2005).

clear what voters meant when they selected moral values.[10] However, the media have largely interpreted the term as reflecting preferences on gay marriage and abortion, a conclusion reinforced by Scott Keeter's analysis in this volume (see chapter 5). As one journalist wrote, "We all have a sense of what is meant by moral values in this election: gay marriage, stem cell research, late-term abortion, prayer in school and several other similar issues. What it really refers to is being against gay marriage, stem cell research and late-term abortion."[11]

The analysis here evaluates the effect of attitudes toward gay marriage and abortion; it does not try to gauge the influence of values more generally. Underlying values and ideological philosophies no doubt always shape the preferences and priorities of voters, but such values are much broader than the common interpretation of "moral values" in the 2004 election. Moreover, underlying values are much more difficult for both voters and scholars to conceptualize, operationalize, and evaluate. In contrast, political attitudes on specific issues can be more cleanly measured and are more proximate to choice of candidate.

To assess the influence of gay marriage and abortion on voter decision-making in 2004, it is necessary to account for other factors that might influence candidate selection. I evaluated the influence of gay marriage and abortion—controlling for other political issues, party identification, and relevant demographic characteristics—using data from a unique postelection survey of 2,800 respondents. The Blair Center 2004 Presidential Election Survey is nationally representative and randomly sampled from the Knowledge Networks (KN) Internet panel.[12] The KN panel consists of a national random sample of households recruited by random-digit dialing (RDD) who have been provided Internet access through their own computer or given a WebTV console in exchange for completing three or four surveys per month. Thus, although surveys are conducted over the Internet, respondents are representative of the U.S. population.[13] By using a probability sample for initial contacts and by

10. Fiorina (2005); Burden (2005); Hillygus and Shields (2005).

11. Meyer (2004a).

12. Independent comparison studies have found the KN sample representative of U.S. Census averages (Krosnick and Chang, 2001; Viscusi, Huber, and Bell, 2004). Krosnick and Chang (2001) commissioned a set of side-by-side surveys using a single questionnaire regarding the 2000 U.S. election from national samples of American adults. They found the KN survey comparable to the RDD telephone survey and representative of the U.S. population.

13. Detailed information on the KN methodology can be found on the KN website at www.knowledgenetworks.com/ganp/index.html. Research using the KN panel has been published in a number of academic journals, including *American Political Science Review, American Journal of Political Science,* and *Journal of Politics,* to name a few.

Figure 4-1. Importance of Issues

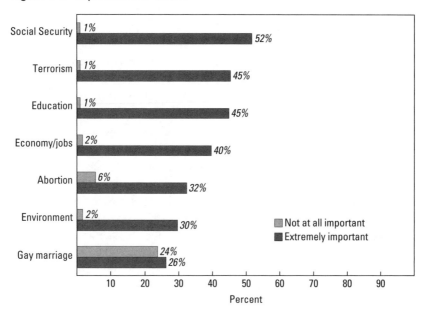

providing web access for respondents without it, KN overcomes the most common shortfall of other Internet surveys; the KN method eliminates non-Internet coverage bias and allows researchers to accurately gauge the potential for self-selection and nonresponse bias.[14]

Gay Marriage, Abortion, and the 2004 Election

I began by considering the importance voters placed on the specific issues of gay marriage and abortion relative to other political issues. Figure 4-1 reports responses to the request "Regardless of your position on the issue, please tell us how important the issue is to you personally." On average, gay marriage and abortion were considered less important than a number of other issues.[15] Only 26 percent of respondents considered gay marriage "extremely important"

14. For more elaborate comparison of probability versus volunteer Internet samples, see Pineau and Slotwiner (2003).

15. This is at the same time that a slight majority (54 percent) supported a constitutional ban on gay marriage.

and 24 percent (more than for any other issue) considered it to be "not at all" important. In contrast, nearly half of the respondents indicated that Social Security, terrorism, and education policy were extremely important.

Next I considered the relationship between the voters' preferences on these issues and their support for the presidential candidates. Which political issues were most strongly related to vote choice? If moral issues were the most important determinant of voter decisionmaking, they should do a better job than other issues of predicting vote choice. In other words, individuals who agreed with Bush on gay marriage and abortion should always have voted for Bush, while those who disagreed should always have voted for Kerry.

To evaluate the relationship between attitudes on gay marriage and abortion and vote choice, I estimated a multivariate logit model predicting a vote for Bush (over Kerry). This strategy makes it possible to compare the effect of the various issues while controlling for standard demographic and political variables, including income, gender, race, age, union membership, church attendance, interpretation of the Bible, party identification, and political ideology.[16] I also estimated the model separately for Independents, with the expectation that without partisan loyalties, Independents might be more open to selecting a candidate purely on the basis of issues.[17] The coefficients, standard errors, and model fit statistics are reported in the table in the appendix.

The substantive effects from this multivariate model are reported in figure 4-2. The bars map the change in predicted probability of a vote for Bush (over Kerry) between individuals who hold a conservative position on the issue compared with individuals who hold a liberal position.[18] The black bars display the results for all voters, while the gray bars reflect Independents only. The abortion bar, for instance, shows that the average pro-life voter was 15.1 percentage points more likely to vote for Bush than the average pro-choice voter. In comparing the various issue effects, I find that Iraq, terrorism, and the economy swamp the effects of gay marriage and abortion. In fact, the effects of gay marriage and abortion are roughly equivalent to the effects of the issues of Social Security reform, the environment, minimum wage policy, and the No Child Left Behind Act. Among Independents, I find that gay marriage and abortion had no effect on vote choice once other issues and factors were

16. These findings are robust to other specifications of the model, including omitting the church attendance and Bible measures, estimating gay marriage and abortion separately, and so forth.

17. These respondents might also be somewhat less prone to selecting an issue position on the basis of party identification or candidate support.

18. All other variables are held at their means.

Figure 4-2. Predicted Effect of Issues on Presidential Vote

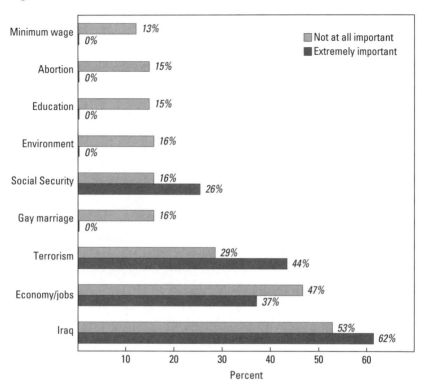

taken into account. (In other words, the coefficients on these variables were not statistically different from zero.) At the same time, the Iraq war, terrorism, and the economy had an even larger effect among political Independents than among the electorate as a whole. Among Independents, the issue of Social Security was the only other issue that had a statistically significant effect on voter decisionmaking.

Overall, then, gay marriage and abortion do not appear to have been the most important issues of the 2004 presidential election; Iraq, terrorism, and the economy had a much stronger impact on voter decisionmaking. Rather than a moral mandate, the electorate appears to have offered general support for an incumbent president on the basis of the status of the Iraq war and the economy. The finding that the war and economy were most strongly associated with presidential vote choice—despite media conclusions to the contrary— is perhaps not terribly surprising given that these issues accounted for most of the television advertising in the campaign and presidential debate coverage.[19] This finding also is consistent with the expectations of decades of political science research.[20]

Although the analysis here indicates that gay marriage and abortion were not the primary predictors of vote choice, it would be hasty to conclude that these issues played no role in the 2004 election. Even if the majority of the electorate did not vote on the basis of moral issues, they clearly were important to *some* voters, and those voters very well could have been decisive in a close race.

There also remains a lingering question about the so-called culture war. The media perception of a "moral mandate" resonated in large part because of a more general belief about the growing partisan and religious polarization in the country. As one journalist wrote, "The religion gap is the leading edge of the 'culture war' that has polarized American politics, reshaped the coalitions that make up the Democratic and Republican parties and influenced the appeals their presidential candidates are making."[21] Political commentator Michael Barone reflected the prevailing view in describing the religious and political divide between the religious red and the secular blue states: "One is observant, tradition-minded, moralistic. The other is unobservant, liberation-minded, relativistic."[22]

Although the empirical analysis suggests that moral issues were not foremost on the minds of most voters, there is a growing consensus that political elites in this country are more polarized on moral and cultural issues than at any time in recent history.[23] Democrats and Republicans in Congress more consistently oppose each other on legislation, the party platforms are more ideologically extreme, and party activists are more polarized across a variety of policy issues.[24] The Republican Party platform in 2004 asserts, "The unborn child has a fundamental individual right to life which cannot be infringed," while the Democratic Party platform proclaims, "Because we believe in the privacy and equality of women, we stand proudly for a woman's right to choose."

Although political elites are quite polarized along religious and partisan lines, the general public is much less divided. To be sure, there are differences

---

19. Kaid and Dimitrova (2005).
20. For example, Fiorina (1981).
21. Page (2004).
22. Littwin (2004, p. 1A).
23. Jacobson (2000); Abramowitz and Saunders (1998); Hetherington (2001).
24. Jacobson (2000); McCarty, Poole, and Rosenthal (2006); Layman (1999); Layman and Carsey (1999).

in the policy opinions of the devout and the nondevout, but religion has created divisions *within* the political parties, not just across them. In other words, many rank-and-file partisans in the electorate disagree with their affiliated political party on moral issues.[25] Among Republican identifiers in the electorate, 31 percent disagreed with the party's stance on abortion, 40 percent on stem cell research, and 14 percent on gay marriage. Among Democrats in the general public, 22 percent disagreed with the party's stance on abortion, 15 percent on stem cell research, and 40 percent on gay marriage. It is especially intriguing that, in contrast to the conclusions of pundits like Thomas Frank, partisans are actually more likely to be congruent with their party's stance on economic issues than on cultural issues.[26] Furthermore, as shown by John Green and John Jackson in chapter 3, divisions of this sort are also found among delegates to the party's conventions, suggesting that even party activists are not as monolithic as they often are portrayed to be.

Despite the conventional wisdom that the public is divided into God-fearing, church-going Republicans and godless, secular Democrats, the reality is hardly so stark. America is a quite religious society, and that is reflected in both party coalitions. When asked about their interpretation of the Bible, more Democrats (16 percent) than Republicans (7 percent) responded that the Bible was "written by men" and slightly more Republicans (44 percent) than Democrats (37 percent) responded that the Bible is the "literal word of God," but the modal response given by partisans of both stripes was that the Bible is the "inspired word of God" (47 percent of Democrats and 49 percent of Republicans). In looking at church attendance, the religious divide between partisans is also not as deep as is often assumed. Somewhat more Democrats (14 percent) than Republicans (9 percent) reported never attending church, while more Republicans (47 percent) than Democrats (30 percent) reported attending church at least once per week, but these differences are not nearly as deep as so often assumed.

Shown in figure 4-3 and 4-4 is the relationship between church attendance and cross-pressures for Democrats and for Republicans. As expected, devoutly religious Democrats were more likely to disagree with the cultural policy positions of the Democratic Party, while less religious Republicans were much more likely to disagree with the stated positions of the Republican Party on

---

25. The following numbers are calculated conservatively, with partisan leaners (people who say they lean toward one party) excluded and moderate issue responses coded as congruent with the party.

26. Treier and Hillygus (2005).

Figure 4-3. Moral Issue Cross-Pressures by Church Attendance among Democrats

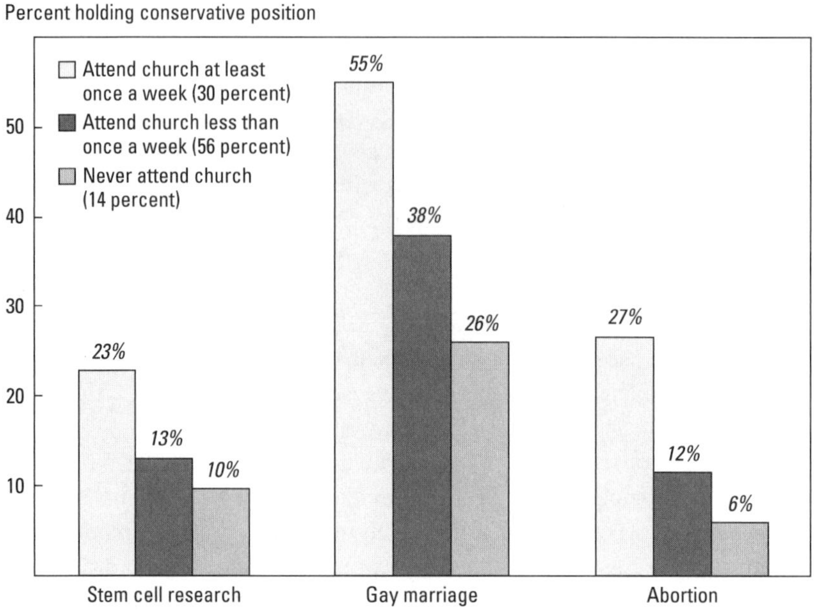

Percent holding conservative position

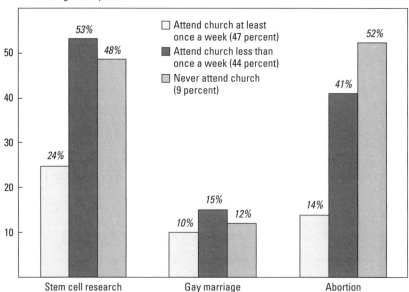

Figure 4-4. Moral Issue Cross-Pressures by Church Attendance among Republicans

Percent holding liberal position

the issues of gay marriage, abortion, and stem cell research. Of the Democrats who attended church at least once a week, a majority supported a ban on gay marriage, 27 percent were opposed to abortion, and 23 percent were opposed to stem cell research. Among Republicans who attended church less than once a week, 53 percent supported stem cell research, 15 percent supported gay marriage, and 41 percent supported abortion rights. Such cross-pressured individuals are more likely to feel that their affiliated party does not represent them well, and they are more likely to defect to the opposing party candidate on election day, even while maintaining their party affiliation.[27]

Although these descriptive comparisons do not do justice to the more nuanced religious landscape described in chapter 2, they do suggest that the divisions on religious and moral issues between Democrats and Republicans in the electorate are not as deep as so often assumed. Coalitional fractures on moral issues have long been apparent in the Democratic Party and have recently shown themselves in the Republican Party as well. Charlie Cook of the *National Journal* writes, "The Senate fight over filibustering President Bush's judicial nominations and, before that, the congressional intervention in the Terry [sic] Schiavo case expose a large and growing rift between the 'sacred' and 'secular' factions of the Republican Party."[28]

The Growing Elite-Electorate Gap

This analysis suggests that partisans in the electorate are much less polarized on moral issues than are the political parties and presidential candidates. Yet, according to political science research, vote-maximizing politicians are supposed to cater to the middle, not the extremes, in the electorate. What explains the apparent disconnect between the more extreme policy pursuits of political elites and the more moderate preferences of the American public? Although there is no definitive explanation, scholars have suggested a number of contributing factors, including the individual preferences of the candidates, the role of social groups, the influence of interest groups, the polarization of the media, growing income inequalities, the primary system, and strategic redistricting.[29]

In addition, the potential influence of microtargeting campaign strategies on candidates' positions should not be overlooked. New technologies have

27. Hillygus and Shields (2005).
28. Cook (2005).
29. Fiorina with Abrams and Pope (2005); McCarty, Poole, Rosenthal (2006).

allowed candidates to better identify specific issue publics within their potential constituencies; in response, candidates have emphasized explicitly issue-based campaign messages to try to appeal to them. In chapter 6 in this volume, Quin Monson and Baxter Oliphant provide a much more detailed descriptive analysis of microtargeting in the 2004 election. I would like to suggest that the ability of candidates to microtarget campaign appeals creates incentives for candidates to take positions on divisive political issues.

Using enormous databases of information about the voting public, candidates today are able to predict the probability that an individual is going to vote and the probability that he or she is going to vote for a particular candidate. They also can identify the political issues that the voter cares about. With that information the candidates can efficiently target mobilization efforts and messages. As one political consultant explained, "You don't have to shotgun anymore. You can now bullet."[30] Thus, a letter or e-mail highlighting a candidate's sporting policy will be sent to the registered Independent who owns a gun, while a message focused on gay marriage will be sent the evangelical Democrat. This fundamental strategy change was explained by one campaign consultant in the following way: "I think politics has always been driven by data; it's just that the data on the electorate was never very accurate. The reason traditional politics has been about class or race politics is because individual policy preferences could only be meaningfully categorized by class or race. Now I can differentiate between nine gradations of nose-pickers, and political culture produced over new media is going to have the same nuances . . . or is it fragments?"[31]

Political scholars have long recognized that technology can fundamentally alter political campaigns. Whereas the introduction of previous technology, especially radio and television, was once used to spread the message to a broader audience, technologies today are used to tailor the message to specific issue publics. These technologies have created incentives for candidates to make explicitly ideological and issue-based appeals to narrower portions of the public while ignoring those individuals with little chance of voting for them, either because they support other candidates or are unlikely to vote at all. As one consultant explained, "In previous campaigns Republicans would call potential voters with a tape-recorded message from Ronald Reagan or a similar personage on the generic importance of voting. In 2004 a voter concerned about abortion would hear 'If you don't come out and vote, the number of abortions next year is going to go up.'"

---

30. Milbank (1999, p. 23).
31. Howard (2003, p. 229).

It remains unclear whether the campaigns actually succeeded in mobilizing individuals with issue appeals. (Consider, for example, the 4 million "missing evangelicals" referred to by Karl Rove following the 2000 election.)[32] Does a single campaign mailer about gay marriage have an impact above and beyond the television advertising and the dozens of other mailers, phone calls, and front-door visits that bombard residents of battleground states? Ultimately, the effect of microtargeting on voter behavior might be less important than its impact on candidate behavior. Issue microtargeting is consequential because it shapes the policy promises that candidates make and determines the candidate's perceived constituency. And with a microtargeting strategy, candidates take more explicit and more extreme positions across a greater variety of issues than if they were targeting a broader audience. Their campaign promises then become their policy priorities if they are elected.[33]

To return to the original question about the role of gay marriage and abortion in the 2004 presidential election: the 2004 election was not a "moral mandate"— the average American appeared to be voting on the basis of economic considerations, war, and terrorism. Yet the story of the average voter does not fully capture the more nuanced campaign strategy of the candidates in 2004. Different groups of voters received different messages, tailored to their priorities. The White House political director, Sara Taylor, reported that the campaign identified thirty different target groups, including elderly investors, military families, small business owners, and Christian conservatives.[34] Each of these groups was told that its issue priorities were at stake in the election, and once the election was over, each of these groups expected President Bush to make its issue a high priority. Thus, the fragmentation of campaign promises not only makes it more difficult to interpret the meaning of the election outcomes, it may create a potential challenge to governance if the targeted groups find that the winning candidate is unable to fulfill the many different policy promises made during the campaign.[35]

32. Gilgoff and Schulte (2004, p. 42).
33. Han (2005).
34. Interview with author.
35. See, for instance, Mueller (1970).

Statistical Appendix

Appendix Table 4A-1. Multivariate Model of Presidential Vote[a]

	All voters		Independents	
Issue/variable	Beta	Standard error	Beta	Standard error
Party identification	3.65	0.32*		
Ideology	3.03	0.68*	3.85	1.30*
Iraq	2.45	0.27*	2.97	0.48*
Economic evaluation	2.13	0.31*	1.59	0.49*
Abortion	0.62	0.31*	0.75	0.50
Gay marriage	0.65	0.27*	−0.21	0.45
Terrorism approach	1.22	0.31*	1.91	0.49*
Education policy	0.62	0.27*	0.50	0.45
Social Security	0.65	0.28*	1.05	0.44*
Minimum wage	0.52	0.26*	0.61	0.45
Environment	0.65	0.25*	0.70	0.42
Female	0.03	0.23	−0.34	0.37
Black	−1.06	0.35*	−1.19	0.59*
Married	0.57	0.25*	1.31	0.41*
Income	0.66	0.57	0.43	0.95
Union household	0.40	0.27	−0.03	0.44
Age	0.00	0.01	−0.01	0.01
Bible interpretation	−0.45	0.21*	−0.35	0.33
Church attendance	−0.02	0.08	−0.02	0.13
Constant	−7.12	0.87	−5.46	1.40
Percent correctly predicted	92.5		89.1	
Proportional reduction in error	0.846		0.776	
N	1,788		462	

a. 1 = Bush, 0 = Kerry; *p < .05.

Issue Question Wording

Economy. "Would you say that over the past year the nation's economy has generally gotten better, or has it stayed the same or generally gotten worse?" (Much better, Somewhat better, Stayed about the same, Somewhat worse, Much worse)

Gay marriage. "Would you favor or oppose an amendment to the U.S. Constitution that would define marriage as being between a man and a woman, thus barring marriages between gay or lesbian couples?" (Completely favor, Somewhat favor, Neither favor nor oppose, Somewhat oppose, Completely oppose)

Abortion. "Which of the following opinions comes closer to your view about abortion? It should never be permitted; it should only be permitted when the woman's life is in danger; it should only be permitted if the woman's health or life is in danger; by law, a woman should always be able to obtain an abortion as a matter of personal choice."

Social Security. "Some people have proposed allowing individuals to invest portions of their Social Security taxes in the stock market, which might allow them to make more money for their retirement, but would involve greater risk than the current government-run system. Do you favor or oppose allowing individuals to invest a portion of their Social Security taxes in the stock market?" (Completely favor, Somewhat favor, Neither favor nor oppose, Somewhat oppose, Completely oppose)

Education. Average score of the following question: "Given what you know about the No Child Left Behind educational reform legislation, do you agree or disagree that the plan does each of the following: identifies weak schools that need to do better; improves learning by students; imposes a financial burden on local schools; encourages teaching for tests instead of knowledge." (Completely agree, Somewhat agree, Neither agree nor disagree, Somewhat disagree, Completely disagree)

Environment. "Do you favor or oppose relaxing some environmental standards to increase oil and gas production in the United States?" (Completely favor, Somewhat favor, Neither favor nor oppose, Somewhat oppose, Completely oppose)

Minimum wage. "Which of the following do you think should be emphasized more in an economic recovery plan: An increase in minimum wage? Or tax cuts for businesses?" Scale ranges from 1 = *Minimum wage increase more important* to 7 = *Tax cuts more important.*

Iraq. "Taking everything into account, do you agree or disagree that the war in Iraq has been worth the cost?" (Completely agree, Somewhat agree, Neither agree nor disagree, Somewhat disagree, Completely disagree)

Terrorism/international problems. "People have different views on the best way to solve problems, such as terrorism and the environment, that are of a more international nature. Some people think it is better for the U.S. to work with other countries through international institutions. Other people think that international institutions are slow and bureaucratic, so the U.S. should be prepared to solve such problems on our own. Still others have opinions somewhere in between these two. Where would you place yourself on the scale below?" Scale ranges from 1 = *U.S. should work through international institutions* to 7 = *U.S. must go it alone.*

Issue importance. "Regardless of where you stand on the following political issues, please indicate how important each issue or policy is to you personally." Issues were presented to respondents in random order. (Extremely important, Very important, Moderately important, Slightly important, Not at all important)

Evangelicals and Moral Values

Scott Keeter

On election night 2004 and in its immediate aftermath, much discussion focused on the importance of "moral values" as a basis for voter choice in the presidential race. Analysts, political activists, and pundits noted with evident surprise that a plurality of 22 percent of voters responding to the Election-Day voter survey of the National Election Pool (NEP) chose moral values (from a list of seven items) in response to a question asking, "Which *one* issue mattered most in deciding how you voted for president?" Subsequent commentary on the race argued that the Democrats (and the news media) had failed to appreciate the strength and fervor of "values voters" and that Democrat John Kerry had failed to close the "God gap" between his party and the rest of the country.

"This election is all about emerging voters whose primary concern is traditional religious values," according to Richard Land, head of the Southern Baptist Convention's Ethics and Religious Liberty Commission. The *Washington Times* editorial page argued that the Democrats and the liberal media did not even know what hit them: "In a Wednesday-morning chin-pulling session, CNN anchor Bill Hemmer turned to his ex-politico colleague Carlos Watson and asked earnestly, 'Why has the country gone so far in the conservative direction?' The truth is that the country was already there. It's just that the liberal media elites never realized it."

The apparent rush to interpret the election through the prism of a single exit poll question quickly led to warnings that too much was being made of this finding, including a caution from the chief pollster for one of the television networks that sponsored the exit poll. "A poorly devised exit poll question and a dose of spin are threatening to undermine our understanding of the 2004 presidential election," wrote Gary Langer.[1] Subsequent analysis by academics and other pollsters argued that the exit poll evidence was equivocal and could not be used to prove that the election hinged on issues such as gay marriage, abortion, and the like.[2]

But even if critics are right to question the simplistic conclusion that moral values—whatever they are—somehow arose from nowhere to swing the election to Bush, the impression left by the revisionist interpretations may also be misleading. Even if it did so inadvertently, the moral values polling item underscored the importance of a genuine group of values voters: white evangelical Christians.

This essay thus complements chapter 4, in which Sunshine Hillygus shows that, for most voters, moral values were not a primary factor in the 2004 election. But they did matter to a particularly critical constituency for George W. Bush—the white evangelicals whom Karl Rove said Bush needed to mobilize (see chapter 1). Despite his advantage on the critical issue of terrorism, Bush would have lost his reelection bid without a strong showing among white evangelicals.[3]

A key strategy of the Bush campaign for 2004 was to mobilize the "missing evangelicals" highlighted by Rove. Although the evangelical share of the voting population was not higher in 2004 than in 2000 (23 percent in both years), the proportion of evangelicals voting for the president did rise—from 68 percent in 2000 to 78 percent in 2004. Bush's margin among evangelicals grew more than his margin among all other groups in the population. While terrorism and Bush's response to it were a very important reason for support among evangelical voters, the cluster of considerations captured by the term "moral values" provided an additional edge, either as an explicit justification for voting for Bush or as a reason for the growing association of evangelicals with the Republican Party. Indeed, white evangelicals have become the bedrock of

---

1. Langer (2004).
2. Burden (2004); Hillygus and Shields (2005); Pew Research Center (2004d).
3. Pew Research Center (2005b); Hillygus and Shields (2005).

Table 5-1. Presidential Vote, by Issue of Most Significance, 2004[a]

Issue	All	Bush	Kerry
Moral values	22	35	8
Economy, jobs	20	7	33
Terrorism	19	32	6
Iraq	15	8	22
Health care	8	4	13
Taxes	5	6	5
Education	4	2	7
Don't know	7	7	7

Source: National Election Pool exit poll, 2004.
a. The exit poll question asked, "Which *one* issue mattered most in deciding how you voted for president?"

the Republican Party. In the 2004 election, they were the largest single demographic group among Bush voters, constituting fully 35 percent of his total. By comparison, African Americans—the most loyal of Democratic constituencies—constituted only about one-fifth (21 percent) of Kerry voters.

This analysis of the importance of the evangelical voter in the 2004 election and the controversy over the "most important issue" exit poll question draws on data from surveys conducted by the Pew Research Center from 1987 to the present as well as on exit polls conducted by Voter News Service, the National Election Pool, and the *Los Angeles Times*.

The Critique of NEP and the Rebuttal

Skepticism regarding the importance of moral values in the election centered on three related arguments. First, critics noted that, although "moral values" was the choice of a plurality (22 percent) in the NEP poll, it barely exceeded economy-jobs (20 percent), terrorism (19 percent), and Iraq (15 percent). Even taking moral values at face value, issues related to foreign and military policy (terrorism at 19 percent plus Iraq at 15 percent) easily outpaced it (see table 5-1 for the details). Second, they observed that the term "moral values" conflates issues and the personal qualities of the candidates, since the term could logically refer to the moral attributes of Bush or Kerry. Third, some critics argued that moral values was not a specific issue such as Iraq or gay marriage; instead, in the words of ABC's Gary Langer, "Moral values is a grab bag; it may appeal to people who oppose abortion, gay marriage, and stem cell research but, because it's so broadly defined, it pulls in others as well."[4]

4. Langer (2004).

While these objections have merit, they also have limits. Abortion might be a specific example of an issue within the catch-all category of moral values, but one could argue that other terms on the exit poll list are similarly broad. For example, the economy-jobs issue encompasses many specific issues, including the minimum wage, job training, economic development assistance to depressed areas, trade policy that affects the health of domestic manufacturing firms, and so forth. The omission of other issues related to the economy could also have distorted the results: Social Security was not even on the list, despite the president's expressed desire to introduce private accounts to the system and despite the fact that it was on the exit poll list in 2000 and was checked by 14 percent of voters.

Although moral values was indeed the choice of only a slim plurality in the NEP poll, it proved to be even more popular in the *Los Angeles Times* exit poll's expanded format (twelve options), which permitted respondents to choose more than one issue and also to choose among a mix of general and specific issues, as displayed in table 5-2. The *Los Angeles Times* exit poll found that moral-ethical values led the list in *both* 2000 and 2004. In 2000 it was checked by 35 percent overall and by 55 percent of Bush voters. In 2004 it was checked by 40 percent overall and by 54 percent of Bush voters. In both years, the list also included abortion (in 2000 as a separate item, which was checked by 14 percent, and in 2004 as a combined item labeled "social issues" such as abortion and gay marriage, which was checked by 15 percent). The fact that moral-ethical values led the lengthy *Los Angeles Times* list in both years—one election with and one without an overriding national security issue in play—strongly suggests that the term captures an ongoing and strong concern among a segment of voters.

The objection that the phrase "moral values" taps into opinions about the personal qualities of the candidates and not just issues is a reasonable one, although that was evidently true of only a minority of those choosing it. The question posed by the Pew Research Center (hereafter, Pew) probing the meaning of moral values among those who picked it (discussed in detail below) found that 23 percent explicitly mentioned some personal quality of the candidates.

Criteria for the Vote

Moral values were especially important to evangelical voters, whether in the NEP or Pew fixed-list question or in Pew's open-ended question, which allowed voters to mention anything they wished. Indeed, most of the voters in Pew's survey who mentioned moral values were white evangelicals, despite the fact that they constitute only about one-quarter of the voting population.

Table 5-2. Voting Behavior, by Two Issues of Most Importance,
2000 and 2004[a]

Issue	2000		
	All	*Bush*	*Gore*
Moral, ethical values	35	55	17
Education	25	20	31
Social Security	21	16	25
Taxes	17	25	9
Abortion	14	17	12
The environment	9	2	14
Health care	8	5	11
Medicare, prescription drugs	8	6	10
Budget surplus	6	6	6
Foreign affairs	5	5	5
None of the above	4	4	3
	2004		
	All	*Bush*	*Kerry*
Moral, ethical values	40	54	24
Jobs, economy	33	18	48
Terrorism, homeland security	29	45	13
Situation in Iraq	16	11	21
Education	15	12	18
Social issues such as abortion and gay marriage	15	14	15
Taxes	9	11	7
Health care	9	5	14
Foreign affairs	5	3	8
Social Security	5	3	7
Medicare, prescription drugs	3	2	4
None of the above	2	2	3

Source: *Los Angeles Times* exit poll, 2000 and 2004.

a. The exit poll question asked, "Which issues, if any, were most important to you in deciding how you would vote for president today?" Up to two replies accepted.

In its postelection survey, the Pew Research Center replicated the seven-item list of issues from the exit poll. From the close-ended list, 27 percent of all voters said moral values were the most important issue in their vote (slightly higher than the 22 percent who picked it in the exit poll).[5] Among white evangelicals, fully 55 percent picked moral values, and no more than 11 percent selected any other issue (terrorism) (see table 5-3). On its face, this sizable disparity between moral values and other issues signaled the

5. It is certainly possible that the choice of moral values was somewhat more popular in this postelection survey as a result of the widespread discussion of the exit poll finding, although the 5 point difference between the exit poll and the Pew poll barely exceeds the threshold for statistical significance.

Table 5-3. Gap between All Voters and White Evangelicals over the Issues That Matter, 2004

Percent unless otherwise noted

Issue	Fixed list[a]		Open-ended format[b]	
	All voters	White evangelicals	All voters	White evangelicals
Moral values (net)	27	55	14	42
Moral values	...	...	9	27
Social issues[c]	...	...	3	8
Candidate's morals	...	...	2	7
Iraq	22	9	25	14
Economy, jobs	21	10	12	6
Terrorism	14	11	9	9
Health care	4	5	2	2
Education	4	2	1	1
Taxes	3	0	1	1
Other	4	6	31	20
Honesty-integrity	...	...	5	5
Like or dislike Bush	...	...	5	4
Like or dislike Kerry	...	...	3	4
Direction of country	...	...	2	1
Leadership	...	...	2	1
Foreign policy	...	...	2	0
Don't know	1	2	5	5
Total	100	100	100	100
Number of respondents	567	150	569	129

Source: Pew Research Center postelection survey, November 2004.
... Not applicable.
a. First choice among the seven items on the exit poll list.
b. Unprompted verbatim first response to open-ended question.
c. Abortion, gay marriage, stem cell research.

importance of the concept for evangelicals. But a similar, and proportionally larger, disparity appeared even without the cue of the moral values terminology.

In Pew's open-ended version of the question, 42 percent of white evangelicals mentioned moral values explicitly (27 percent), a specific social issue such as abortion or gay marriage (8 percent), or the morality or religiosity of the candidates (7 percent). No other issue was cited by more than 14 percent of evangelicals. By contrast, only 14 percent of voters overall (or about 6 percent of non-evangelicals) mentioned moral values or a closely related topic. Far more—25 percent—mentioned the war in Iraq. Another way to look at the experiment is to consider that twice as many evangelicals as voters as a whole selected moral values from the exit poll list; in the open-ended version, without the cue, three times as many evangelicals mentioned something within the moral values framework. This strongly suggests that, while the exit poll list may have inflated the number concerned about moral values, it did so more for the public in general than for evangelicals.

Defining Moral Values

Voters who were given the fixed list of issues (which corresponded to the choices on the exit poll) were asked to describe, in their own words, "What comes to mind when you think about 'moral values'?" Among voters who chose moral values as most important from the list of seven issues, about half gave a response that mentioned a substantive issue. More than four in ten (44 percent) defined the phrase specifically in terms of social issues (as did 51 percent of evangelicals), including abortion (28 percent), homosexuality and gay marriage (29 percent), and stem cell research (4 percent). A few other issues also were mentioned, including poverty, economic inequality, and the like. Table 5-4 presents the details.

But the meaning of "moral values" was not limited to substantive policies. Nearly a quarter of respondents (23 percent) who cited moral values as important explained their thinking in terms of the personal characteristics of the candidates, including honesty and integrity (9 percent). Almost one in five (18 percent) explicitly mentioned religion, Christianity, God, or the Bible.

Table 5-4. The Meaning of "Moral Values" for Those Choosing and Not Choosing Moral Values as the Most Important Issue, 2004[a]

Percent unless otherwise noted

Issue	Moral values the most important issue	Moral values not the most important issue
Social policies	44	18
Gay marriage	29	11
Abortion	28	8
Stem cell research	4	3
Other policies	9	8
Candidate's qualities	23	17
Religious references	18	11
Traditional values	17	35
Negative responses	1	12
Other (volunteered response)	4	6
Means nothing or don't know	2	15
Number of responses	205	362

Source: Pew Research Center postelection survey, November 2004.
a. The question asked, "What comes to mind when you think about 'moral values'?"

Another 17 percent answered in terms of traditional values, using language such as family values, right and wrong, or the way people live their lives.

Individuals who did *not* choose moral values from the list of issues were also asked what the term meant to them. Their pattern of responses was quite different from that of individuals who said that moral values were an important consideration. Fewer mentioned a specific issue, candidate quality, or general religious theme; more answered in general terms, and 12 percent explicitly protested the imposition of others' values on them, said the idea was being used as a "wedge" against Democrats, or otherwise expressed a negative reaction to the phrase.

The Partisan Realignment of Evangelicals

The issue of moral values has garnered greater attention not just because of the exit poll question in 2004 but because of the growing alignment of moral values voters—evangelical Christians—with the Republican Party. Evangelicals have long been concerned about the cluster of issues related to moral values, but only in the past decade or so have their political values been so aligned with their partisan affiliation (and voting behavior).

There is a widespread belief that evangelicals are a growing proportion of the American public, but this is incorrect. The rising political clout of evangelical Christians is the result not of their growing numbers, but rather of their increasing cohesiveness as a key element of the Republican Party. The percentage of the population who are white evangelicals has changed very little (19 percent in 1987; 21 percent now) and what growth there has been occurred in the late 1980s and early 1990s.[6]

However, in 1987, white evangelical Protestants were closely divided in their partisan attachments, with 34 percent identifying as Republicans and 29 percent as Democrats. Today, Republicans outnumber Democrats within this group by more than two to one (49 versus 22 percent) and hold a lead of 60 versus 30 percent when partisan "leaners" are included. Given the relative stability in the party affiliation of other religious groups in the population— and the population as a whole—this is a remarkable degree of change.[7] Although Republican Party identification among both evangelicals and

6. Pew defines white evangelical Protestants as non-blacks who identify as Protestant or other Christian (but not Catholic) and answer yes when asked, "Would you describe yourself as a 'born again' or evangelical Christian, or not?"

7. Green, Palmquist, and Schickler (2002).

non-evangelicals increased slightly in the year following the September 11 attacks, it has since fallen back to pre-9/11 levels for non-evangelicals. Among evangelicals, it has continued to inch up.

This shift toward Republican identification among white evangelicals occurred in two stages. In the late 1980s, white evangelicals in the South were still mostly wedded to the Democratic Party, while evangelicals outside the South were more aligned with the GOP. But over the course of the next decade or so, the GOP made gains among white southerners generally—and evangelicals in particular—nearly eliminating this regional disparity.

The second stage began in 2000, coinciding with Bush's election. In polling conducted by Pew in 1999, Republicans outnumbered Democrats among white evangelicals (39 versus 26 percent); in 2000 the gap was even wider (42 versus 26 percent). Since then, there has been growth in Republican identification among *both* southern and non-southern evangelicals. Nationwide, Republican identification among white evangelicals reached 49 percent in polling conducted in 2006, when white evangelicals made up 21 percent of the population and constituted nearly four out of every ten Republicans (37 percent).

Presidential Vote, 2000 and 2004

The growing political solidarity of evangelicals is even more evident in presidential voting than in partisan affiliation. Very few demographic groups vote overwhelmingly for one party or the other. African Americans have been nearly unified in their support of the Democratic Party since voting rights legislation promoted by President Lyndon Johnson expanded the franchise to blacks living in the South, drawing them away from the party of Abraham Lincoln. In presidential elections over the past thirty years, their level of support for the Democratic candidate has varied between 83 and 91 percent.

But white evangelicals are approaching this degree of political solidarity with the GOP. In the 2004 presidential race, George W. Bush received 78 percent of the vote among white evangelicals, up 10 percentage points from 2000. This was the highest level of support for Bush among any religious group (or, indeed, any demographic or social group other than Republican Party identifiers) and represented the largest increase of any group compared with 2000. Table 5-5 displays the comparisons between 2000 and 2004.

President Bush significantly increased his margin among evangelicals but also made gains among other religious groups. Bush's overall gain from 2000 to 2004 was 3 percentage points: 5 percentage points among Catholics,

Table 5-5. Presidential Vote, by Religion, 2000 and 2004

Percent unless otherwise noted

Indicator	2000 VNS exit poll		2004 NEP exit poll		Bush gain
	Bush	Gore	Bush	Kerry	
Total	48	48	51	48	+3
Protestant	56	42	59	40	+3
White	62	35	67	33	+5
Evangelical	68	30	78	21	+10
Mainline	53	43	55	45	+2
Black	7	91	13	86	+6
Catholic	47	50	52	47	+5
White, non-Hispanic	52	45	56	43	+4
Hispanic	33	65	39	58	+6
Jewish	19	79	25	74	+6
Other religion	28	62	23	74	−5
Secular	30	61	31	67	+1
Protestant					
Attend church weekly or more	64	34	66	33	+2
Attend church less often	48	49	52	47	+4
Catholic					
Attend church weekly or more	53	44	56	43	+3
Attend church less often	42	54	49	50	+7
Church attendance					
More than once a week	63	36	64	35	+1
Once a week	57	40	58	41	+1
Few times a month	46	51	50	49	+4
Few times a year	42	54	45	54	+3
Never	32	61	36	62	+4

Source: Evangelical-mainline division in 2000 estimated from Pew's final preelection poll. All other estimates based on Voter News Service (VNS) and National Election Pool (NEP) exit polls. (Pew's final preelection poll in 2004 estimated that 79 percent of evangelicals would vote for Bush, virtually the same margin as in the NEP.) Pew trends include Hispanics in the designation of white Protestants; the exit poll figures have been adjusted to fit this definition.

6 percentage points among Jews, and 6 percentage points among black Protestants. But he did not improve this much among all groups. He gained 2 points among mainline Protestants and 1 point among voters who identified with no religious tradition. Among religious voters outside the Judeo-Christian religious traditions, he lost vote share (down 5 percentage points).

Still, it is interesting that Bush gained as much among the less observant Judeo-Christian voters as among the more observant. Among voters who never attend religious services, Bush's support was up 4 points (and was up a similar amount among those who only occasionally attend). His gains were greater among both Protestants and Catholics who attend church less than weekly than among those who attend weekly or more often. The chapter in this volume by Geoffrey Layman and Laura Hussey explores in depth Bush's gains specifically among less committed evangelicals.

Voter Turnout in 2004

Even though voter turnout was up significantly in 2004, there is no indication that religiously committed voters in general—or white evangelicals in particular—boosted their level of participation more than other groups in the population. According to a comparison of exit polls and Pew surveys in 2000 and 2004, white evangelicals constituted the same percentage of voters in both years: 23 percent. Overall, there was remarkable stability from 2000 to 2004 in the religious composition of the voting population.

White Protestants constituted nearly half of voters (45 percent), divided almost evenly between mainline and evangelical Protestants (22 and 23 percent, respectively). White, non-Hispanic Catholics were a similar percentage (21 percent). Other religious groups, including black Protestants, Hispanic Catholics, and others, were nearly one-quarter (24 percent). Avowedly secular individuals constituted 10 percent of the population who voted, although 15 percent of voters said they never attend religious services and another 28 percent said they do so only a few times a year. Voter turnout, as reflected in the number of voters from each of these groups relative to 2000, was up among all of these segments, but no more by some than by others.

Although not more religious, the voting population was more Republican and conservative in 2004 than in 2000. In 2004 the number of Republicans matched the number of Democrats (37 percent each), compared with 39 percent Democrat and 35 percent Republican in 2000. The percentage of self-identified conservatives rose 4 percentage points (from 30 to 34 percent).

Conservative gains were about the same among less frequent churchgoers (up 2 percent) as among those who attend church at least once a week (up 1 percent). Similarly, turnout among Republicans who do not attend church weekly was up at least as much as among those who go more often.

Discussion

Evangelical Christians have been a powerful force in American politics at many points in the nation's history. They played a key role in the rise of the abolitionist movement, in the triumph of the progressive movement, and more recently in the rise of the religious right in the 1970s and 1980s. Despite considerable ambivalence about engaging in politics, many American evangelicals have come to believe that participation in politics is necessary to defend their values and promote their vision of society.[8] Their growing solidarity with the Republican Party has been critical in the party's electoral successes of the past decade and promises to keep the party competitive for the foreseeable future. John Petrocik argues that this shift has made the American party system more like that of other Western democracies: "The mobilization of the religious impulse by the GOP has created a Republican coalition that is highly similar to the coalitions that support Christian Democratic parties through much of the rest of the world. Its impact on American electoral politics is to make cultural and moral issues a centerpiece of party conflict, often able to trump economic concerns and major international events."[9]

The 2004 election was unusual insofar as the campaign was dominated by the issue of terrorism and related judgments about the war in Iraq. It was also a remarkably candidate-focused election, with public opinion highly polarized around President Bush and, by extension, his signature policies. In this environment, there was less room than usual for other issues to play a decisive role in voter choice.

Still, the election was very close, especially in key states, and many other factors, including moral values, may have played a role in tipping the balance, especially insofar as they served to mobilize conservative evangelical Christians. The issue of gay marriage, for example, may have helped the Bush campaign in the linchpin state of Ohio, where a ballot initiative banning gay marriage was thought by many observers to have boosted turnout among religious conservatives. Although some analysts doubt whether the ballot initiative was decisive in swinging Ohio, and thus the election, to Bush,[10] there can be little doubt that the issue was important to some voters, especially evangelicals. For instance, Gregory Lewis's extensive analysis of state-level polling concluded, "Same-sex marriage mattered in the 2004 election, less than some issues but more than most."[11] The chapter by David Campbell and Quin Monson shows that gay marriage mattered most of all to white evangelicals, precisely the group most concerned about moral values.

As we look forward to future elections, it is important to remember that evangelicals are not a monolithic group. Although they exhibited impressive

8. Layman (2001).
9. Petrocik (2006), p. 295.
10. Freedman (2004).
11. Lewis (2005), p. 197.

political solidarity in the 2004 election and have become a significant part of the Republican Party, evangelicals remain a diverse group in many respects. Their strong support for George W. Bush reflects a combination of factors that may not always be present in future elections: great personal affinity for the presidential candidate himself; heightened concerns about foreign and security policy tied, at least in part, to the Middle East and to Israel; and the elevated prominence of social issues such as gay marriage. Pew's typology of the American electorate revealed that evangelicals are not concentrated in a wing of religious conservatives but instead constitute a sizable segment of each of three distinct Republican groups. White evangelicals are 43 percent of the aptly named "social conservatives," but also 34 percent of the business-friendly "enterprisers," and 37 percent of the "pro-government conservatives."[12]

The latter is an economically struggling bloc of voters who could defect from the party over bread-and-butter issues. Other kinds of issues could split evangelicals from the party as well. Although their support for a muscular foreign policy is solid right now, evangelicals could conceivably form alliances with liberal internationalists and oppose Republican Party doctrine with respect to the human rights policies of U.S. allies. And there have been interesting alliances between evangelicals and environmentalists in certain parts of the country. But as long as the issue of moral values remains on the political agenda, and the GOP is identified as the party most supportive of the evangelicals' interpretation of it, their attachment to the party is likely to remain strong.

12. Pew Research Center (2005a).

Mobilizing the Faithful

Microtargeting and the Instrumental Mobilization of Religious Conservatives

J. Quin Monson and J. Baxter Oliphant

Previous chapters have shown that religious conservatives—evangelicals especially—were subject to intense mobilization efforts in 2004.[1] This chapter demonstrates the mechanics of this mobilization, specifically the method and messages that Republicans used to rally their religiously conservative base.

One example provides a taste of how this was done. Consider the 2004 contest between former Senate minority leader Tom Daschle and John Thune, one of the most expensive and hotly contested races in the country. Within the context of South Dakota's conservative and very religious culture, this high-stakes U.S. Senate race yielded some jarring examples of how religion is appropriated in politics. For instance, while South Dakota did not vote on a gay marriage ballot proposition in 2004, gay marriage was a topic in the campaign. Thune supported a federal constitutional amendment to ban gay marriage, while Daschle left the issue to the states to decide. Bumper stickers

---

1. Except when we cite other work, the term "religious conservative" is used throughout the chapter to encompass "conservative Christian," "conservative Protestant," and "evangelical Protestant." While most religious conservatives are conservative Christians or evangelical Protestants, the label "religious conservative" can extend beyond those labels to encompass others who might respond to similar campaign appeals.

sent anonymously to churches statewide said, "Vote for Daschle & Vote <u>for</u> SODOMY." The mailer gave Daschle's campaign headquarters as the return address.[2] Other issues, especially abortion and school vouchers, were the topic of voting guides and other communications aimed at religious voters, including rallies attended by James Dobson of Focus on the Family and statements by Bishop Carlson of the Catholic Diocese of South Dakota about life and abortion that pushed voters away from Democrats and toward Republicans.[3]

The mobilization of religious conservatives went far beyond South Dakota in a presidential election year that pitted an evangelically minded Protestant against a progressive Catholic. Evidence of such mobilization in 2004 includes Republican attempts to obtain church lists for inclusion in their nationwide database of registered voters,[4] considerable publicity regarding the many Catholic bishops and archbishops whose public statements equated the support of pro-choice candidates with sin,[5] the presence of gay marriage bans on the ballot in eleven states,[6] and the well-documented activities of conservative religious interest groups such as the Christian Coalition and Focus on the Family. In addition, the direct mail campaigns of the Republican Party provide ample evidence of its mobilization strategy. One Republican Party mailer sent to households in Arkansas and West Virginia asserted, "Liberals want to impose their values on Arkansas," presenting the image of a Bible with "banned" stamped across it and the warning, "This will be Arkansas . . . if you don't vote," ominously displayed next to an image of one man proposing to another.[7] Most communications were less direct, but clearly the Republican Party and the Bush campaign actively pursued religious conservatives through a variety of means.

The activities of the Republican Party are particularly noteworthy because, unlike in previous elections, in which the Christian Coalition and other groups played leading roles, the mobilization of religious conservatives in 2004 was dominated by the Republican National Committee (RNC). The RNC's messages were not explicitly religious, but they were dominated by abortion, gay marriage,

2. Sanderson (2004); Smith and Braunstein (2007, p. 61).

3. Sanderson (2004); Shouse (2004); Smith and Braunstein (2007, pp. 61–62).

4. Cooperman (2004b); Kirkpatrick (2004c).

5. Kirkpatrick and Goodstein (2004); Goodstein (2004). For example, Archbishop John Donoghue of Atlanta was quoted on the front page of the *Atlanta Journal Constitution* as saying, "You have an erroneous conscience if you think there is some case in which you can vote for a pro-abortion candidate. . . . You're wrong as far as church teaching is concerned. . . . [Catholics may debate other issues, like war or capital punishment], but there's no debate about abortion. It is intrinsically evil. It is way above other issues as far as evil is concerned" (White 2004, p. A-1).

6. Campbell and Monson (2005); see also their chapter in this volume.

7. Kirkpatrick (2004d).

judicial appointments, and family values generally. Many of the top issues were mentioned together in the same piece of mail. The RNC invoked religion instrumentally in its political mail to win elections and maintain the Republican hold on the presidency.

The overwhelming presence of the RNC in the religiously oriented campaign communications during the 2004 election validates the prediction of John Green and his colleagues that the consistent involvement of religious conservatives, particularly the Christian Right, on behalf of Republican candidates would eventually lead to their assimilation into the Republican Party.[8] Our purpose in this chapter is to show *how* the GOP mobilizes religious conservatives. This includes the mechanics of identifying religious conservative voters, especially the specifics of "microtargeting," in which large voter databases are matched to consumer databases in an effort to target messages to individual voters. It also includes the process of communicating with these voters.

Previous Research

Political scientist Kenneth Wald offers three explanations for how evangelical Protestants are mobilized: social influences, institutional influences, and values. The first two influences tend to ebb and flow as institutions and social connections shift between high and low involvement in political contests and social issues. These forces provide motivation when they are activated; on their own, they do not impel political participation and consequently are less likely to create long-term mobilization trends. Values, however, have an independent effect on political activity, especially when individuals with strong religious commitments become more willing to use their religious beliefs and values to inform their political ideology and behavior.

Few groups are as susceptible to values-based mobilization as evangelical Protestants, who have a long history of pressuring governments, traditionally state and local units, when they perceive threats to their traditional values and morals. John C. Green and others have described such pressure as "demand" for traditional values in the political marketplace. Traditionalists, because of changes in society, demand that candidates and parties defend their values, and political actors frequently respond to this demand in an effort to obtain support from religious voters. This mobilizing influence, much like consumer

---

8. Guth and Green (1988); Green, Guth, and Hill (1993). According to Green's terminology, the mail related to religion sent by the RNC represents an instrumental use of religion by the Republicans to win elections and maintain their hold on the presidency (Green 2000a).

demand, is an internal impulse that is influenced by larger societal trends, not political actors; therefore, it has great staying power.[9]

The process of social categorization is central to values-based mobilization. Social categorization defines issues in terms of right and wrong and is often accompanied by efforts to establish one side of an issue as morally righteous and the other as morally bankrupt.[10] This process extends the realm of politics beyond its traditional bounds of economics and class and turns morality and values into legitimate political considerations. This development, in turn, motivates increasing numbers of religious conservatives to vote on Election Day and to become involved with a variety of political causes.

Among evangelical Protestants, this process of defining the issues initially drew heavily on religious imagery. Over time, however, the language of values-based mobilization has changed. To overcome opposition from the Republican establishment, especially from moderates and secular conservatives who are uneasy with religious political rhetoric, in the early 1990s conservative Christian activists began to advocate religious causes in secular terms.[11] This shift away from religious imagery and language and toward more secular arguments may account for much of the success of the Christian Coalition in the early 1990s under Ralph Reed.

A number of studies have analyzed subsequent efforts to mobilize religious conservatives. For example, James Guth and his coauthors find that the efforts of the religious right to mobilize evangelicals in 1996 were quite successful, especially when they involved direct contact with voters by religiously oriented interest groups or informal discussions about politics with associates at church.[12] They also find similar, although slightly smaller, effects in the 2000 election.[13] However, their analysis focuses on mobilization through informal discussions at church, activity of the clergy, and religiously oriented interest groups and has little to say about the religiously oriented activities of the political parties.

9. Wald (2003, pp. 217–23); Green, Guth, and Hill (1993).
10. Guth and others (2002, p. 14).
11. Fowler, Hertzke, and Olson (1999, p. 146); Wilcox and Larson (2006, p. 48).
12. Guth and others (1998).
13. Guth and others (2002). They also acknowledged that repeated efforts by the Christian Right on behalf of GOP candidates could result in a partisan transformation of religious conservatives that might obscure the impact of religion in statistical analysis. As more religious conservatives move into the Republican camp, the "indirect effect" of religious mobilization will be measured by a respondent's partisan identification, leaving little to be explained by religious affiliation.

In contrast, other research has given significant attention to the relationship between political parties and the mobilization of religious conservatives. In his 2001 book *The Great Divide: Religious and Cultural Conflict in American Party Politics,* Geoffrey Layman provides clear evidence regarding the extent of the realignment of evangelical Protestants as part of the Republican coalition, calling evangelicals "the religious core of the Republican Party" and noting their switch from strongly Democratic to strongly Republican as "the clearest change in the relationship between religious orientations and partisan loyalties over the last thirty years."[14] He suggests that these changes are elite driven or a mass-level response to conflict and change at the elite level. In another study, David Leege and his coauthors provide the theoretical mechanism for this change by identifying the psychological mechanisms that political elites use to mobilize at the mass level. They explain that the growing proportion of evangelical Protestants in the Republican coalition can be attributed to the Republican Party's increased use of religious issues at an emotional or even visceral level to motivate evangelicals to political participation.[15]

Given its increasingly important role in defining the coalitions of the two parties, especially the place of social conservatives in the Republican Party, religion was poised to be an important factor in voter mobilization in 2004. Accounts leading up to the 2004 election and early postelection analysis focused heavily on the efforts of the Republican Party to reach out to religious conservatives and mobilize them through interactions with clergy (both Catholic and Protestant), religious interest groups, and the party itself. These efforts included a videotaped speech from the White House to the annual conventions of the Southern Baptist Association and the Knights of Columbus and even outreach to select African American pastors.[16] But the efforts of the RNC and the Bush campaign to mobilize religious conservatives went beyond speeches and symbolic meetings. Sensing concerns from clergy members that politics would distract them from their religious mission, the Bush campaign and the RNC sought to recruit lay religious conservatives as "team leaders" using the label "faith and values."[17] Team leaders were given specific tasks to accomplish, including talking "to your pastor about holding a citizenship Sunday and

14. Layman (2001, p. 229).
15. Leege and others (2002).
16. Kirkpatrick (2004a, 2004b); Cooperman (2004a).
17. Separate teams exist for Catholics as well as secular teams for young voters, women, Hispanics, African Americans, and so on.

voter registration drive," recruiting others at church to volunteer for the campaign, and placing reminders to vote in the church bulletin the Sunday before the election.[18]

Microtargeting Religious Conservatives in 2004

The targeting of appeals to religious conservatives in 2004 was more sophisticated than ever before, owing largely to the efforts of the Republican National Committee. Building on the mobilization techniques developed by labor unions in the late 1990s, the RNC underwent a transformation in the 2002 election, creating the 72-Hour Task Force to increase personal contact with voters and boost Republican turnout.[19] These efforts expanded dramatically in 2004, and religious conservatives were a significant part of that expansion; as Bush campaign deputy strategist Sara Taylor said, "Our union is the Christian evangelical vote."[20]

The mobilization of religious conservatives in 2004 included a new development that has been referred to as "microtargeting."[21] The microtargeting process involves the use of large sample surveys mixed with consumer marketing data for individual-level targeting rather than more traditional demographic or geo-demographic targeting based on precinct characteristics and past voting patterns. Techniques, such as sifting through lists of subscribers to religious magazines or purchasers of Christian pop music, make it possible to identify a religious conservative living in an urban area who is surrounded by Kerry-supporting neighbors.

The process of microtargeting voters in a particular state is as follows:

—Begin with the statewide registered voter file and whatever data are available on individual voters. Voter file data usually include date of birth, party registration, gender, and past turnout.

—Append to this file any proprietary data available from the state or national party, including party registration or identification information, if available. This information might include the results of a phone canvass from a prior election.

18. Cooperman (2004b).
19. Monson (2004).
20. Magleby, Monson, and Patterson (2007, p. 23).
21. Gertner (2004). This section is similar to material presented in Magleby, Monson, and Patterson (2007) and draws heavily on an interview by David Magleby and Quin Monson with Alex Gage and his associates at TargetPoint consulting in December 2004.

—Add "customer information" in the form of consumer data. This includes purchasing information for a variety of products, subscription lists, mortgage information, and car registration information.

—Conduct a survey using a random sample of 5,000 to 10,000 names from the file. The survey obtains or confirms party identification and likely vote choice and then proceeds through a long list of issue questions. The sample size is large enough to facilitate detailed examination of small subgroups of the population.

—Model political behavior in the survey as a function of the consumer variables available for all voters. The political variables (especially party iden-tification and vote choice) from the sample survey are dependent variables, and consumer data (available for every voter in the database) are independent variables.

At this point, the results from the models are used to divide the database into segments using consumer variables that significantly predict vote choice and party identification. This is not a deeply theoretical exercise. If a consumer variable predicts well in the modeling and is widely available for voters in the file, it becomes a valuable means of identifying and contacting voters. How-ever, there is some art to creating these segments. Table 6-1 lists a sample of segments for microtargeting efforts in the fictitious state of "Republicana." They were obtained from Alex Gage, a Republican consultant who worked closely with the RNC on microtargeting efforts. The segments are given names that reflect group characteristics and are ranked in descending order of strength of "GOP base" or Republican partisan identification. The other figure listed is the percentage of the segment that expressed a preference for Bush. It is noteworthy that "religious conservative Republicans" top the list in terms of their Republican Party identification, followed by "conservative Republican families." Segments one through twelve will likely receive appeals to turn out to vote, the middle group (segments thirteen through eighteen) will likely receive persuasion-oriented communications, and the remaining segments will likely be ignored.

The final step in the process involves analyzing the detailed issue questions for each segment so that messages can be crafted and designed to appeal to each group. Table 6-2 presents a demographic profile of the religious conservative Republicans as well as their issue positions, as shared by Alex Gage. The data highlight some large and not particularly surprising differences between polit-ical attitudes statewide and within the religious conservative segment. Com-pared to the statewide population, much larger proportions of the religious conservative segment *strongly* oppose gay marriage, *strongly* support parental

Table 6-1. Republican Microtargeting Segments in the Fictional State of "Republicana," 2004

Segment	Group characteristic	Number of persons	Percent identifying with the GOP	Percent expressing a preference for Bush
1	Religious conservative Republicans	37,145	87	86
2	Conservative Republican families	53,082	86	96
3	Younger Republicans	122,335	85	92
4	Motivated Republicans	164,204	83	89
5	High-turnout Republicans	35,878	82	92
6	Older reliable Republicans	133,191	80	83
7	Limited-government conservatives	34,630	78	85
8	Culturally conservative independents	69,667	78	80
9	Socially moderate Republicans	275,542	75	68
10	Education-oriented Republican families	94,475	74	76
11	Unreliable Republican voters	130,245	74	80
12	Pleased weak Republicans	31,700	71	82
13	Secular Republicans	44,266	58	51
14	Pro-Bush antitax swing voters	42,133	50	79
15	Secular independent singles	56,580	48	59
16	Conflicted male voters	39,243	41	56
17	White liberal independents	44,382	33	42
18	Low-turnout pro-Bush male Democrats	120,595	33	57
19	Average-turnout weak male Democrats	41,597	27	27
20	Secular younger females	280,716	24	38
21	Young unreliable social liberals	174,993	18	37
22	Liberal Democrats	335,889	14	21
23	High-turnout female Democrats	235,019	9	17
24	Minority Democrats	425,646	4	10
	Total	3,023,153	. . .	. . .

Source: Based on hypothetical information obtained by authors from Alex Gage, TargetPoint Consulting.
. . . Not applicable.

notification laws, and *strongly* oppose partial-birth abortion. Moreover, the strong opinions of religious conservatives extend beyond social issues and include taxes and terrorism.

Detailed profiles for each segment are given to the RNC staff and consultants who create campaign communications. They then use the profiles to target messages to the voters who are most likely to receive them positively. In the case of direct mail, every registered voter in the state is assigned to a segment, and the mail and other communications directed toward each segment are created after closely consulting its issue profile has been consulted.

Table 6-2. Demographic Characteristics of a Hypothetical Microtargeting Segment of Religious Conservatives, 2004

Percent

Characteristic	Statewide population	Religious conservative Republicans[a]
Party		
GOP base	43.0	87.0
Democratic base	27.0	4.0
Independent	30.0	9.1
President in 2004		
Committed to Bush	55.0	86.0
Committed to Democrats	45.0	14.0
Motivation		
Highly motivated	34.0	37.0
Gender		
Male	49.0	51.0
Female	51.0	49.0
Religion		
Attend church weekly	31.0	61.0
Protestant	37.0	45.0
Catholic	28.0	25.9
Jewish	4.0	4.2
Age (years)		
18–34	18.0	4.0
35–44	19.0	7.0
45–64	42.0	49.0
65+	21.0	40.0
Union		
Union household	28.0	14.0
Nonunion household	72.0	86.0
Race		
White	84.0	91.0
Black	2.0	0.0
Hispanic	9.0	3.9
Work status		
Working full time	48.0	23.0
Working part time	6.0	6.0
Unemployed	1.9	0.0
Retired	33.2	68.0
Homemaker	6.1	2.4
Role of government		
Limited government	29.0	47.0
Expanded government	17.0	5.0
Mixed view	25.0	21.2
More-services Republican	32.0	29.8
Less-government Democrat	41.0	53.3
Turnout		
Reliable (deciles 7–10)	40.3	82.0
Unreliable (deciles 4–6)	29.6	17.0
Suspect (deciles 1–3)	30.2	1.0

Source: Based on hypothetical information obtained by authors from Alex Gage, TargetPoint Consulting.

a. Segment 1 from table 6-1, which consists of 37,145 persons constituting 3.8 percent statewide.

Table 6-3. Attitudes of a Hypothetical Microtargeting Segment
of Religious Conservatives, 2004

Percent

Attitude	Statewide population	Religious conservative Republicans[a]
Strongly opposes gay marriage	44	86
Strongly favors parental consent for abortion	47	92
Strongly opposes tax increases	36	57
Worries about the influence of the religious Right	31	12
Strongly opposes affirmative action	30	37
Strongly opposes gun control	31	45
Strongly opposes activist judges	60	70
Worries about the cost of health insurance	56	44
Is angry about Internet pornography	57	82
Strongly supports increased military funding	34	49
Strongly favors increased intelligence funding	38	43
Worries about job losses	40	16
Is angry about no weapons of mass destruction in Iraq	33	32
Strongly supports president's actions in war on terror	45	62
Strongly supports Republican tax cuts	39	76
Strongly supports No Child Left Behind Act	38	32
Strongly opposes partial-birth abortion	36	77
Strongly favors curbs on frivolous lawsuits	41	48

Source: Based on hypothetical information obtained by authors from Alex Gage, TargetPoint Consulting.
a. Segment 1 consists of religious conservative Republicans (from table 6-1).

The traces of this process are readily apparent when we compare the descriptions of some RNC mail pieces in table 6-8 with the key issues in table 6-3. At times it is as if the creator of the mail piece simply cut and pasted the list of issues from the profile to the mailer.

2004 Campaign Communications Survey

We next turn to some data that will help to answer questions about the mobilization of religious conservatives in 2004. In particular, we can accurately assess the extent of religiously oriented messages in campaign communications and identify the organizations that sent the most mail with a religious or moral focus. We also can assess the issue, content, and partisan bent of the mail pieces and examine the mail for explicitly religious language or symbols.

To answer the question of who sent religiously oriented mail and to examine the content of those communications, we use the 2004 Campaign Communications Survey (CCS) conducted by the Center for the Study of Elections and Democracy (CSED) at Brigham Young University. The CCS consists of a mixed-mode mail and telephone survey of registered voters nationwide with an oversample in Florida and Ohio.[22] The sample was drawn from the registered voter database of the Democratic National Committee (DNC), which contains all of the registered voters in the country.[23] The survey design was pilot-tested in a special election in 2002 and then used in four statewide samples in 2002 before being employed nationally in 2004. Fieldwork was handled by the Social and Economic Science Research Center at Washington State University.

Respondents were asked to complete a questionnaire booklet that included space to note political contacts (mail, e-mail, phone calls, and personal contacts) they had during the three weeks before Election Day. They collected and sent in their political mail, permitting content analysis of the mail pieces they received. Respondents were contacted multiple times by telephone and mail during the four weeks leading up to and immediately after Election Day to request their participation, answer questions, and remind them to be diligent in collecting the necessary information.[24]

For this chapter we focus on communications that are not broadcast. Broadcast communications are much more open to public scrutiny and, if cast in terms that are too narrow, risk being largely ineffective or, even worse, motivate the opposition as well as supporters. As a result, broadcast communications often focus only on very broad and general issues, and studying them exclusively can miss some issues that are very important to the campaign, yet less conspicuous. Communications that are not broadcast improve the campaign's ability to focus on specific subgroups of voters with specific messages, maximizing the effectiveness and minimizing the risk of offending those who do not share the point of view expressed in the communication. While the survey collected information on telephone calls and in-person contacts, we focus entirely on the mail because it is more accurately and readily coded for religiously oriented content. In addition, the mail pieces all contain return addresses, making identification of the sponsor simple. In-person contacts, especially telephone calls, rely on the respondents' descriptions, which can be less accurate or in some cases never provided or missing.

22. The survey was funded by a grant to the Center for the Study of Elections and Democracy at Brigham Young University from the Pew Charitable Trusts.

23. We thank Lina Brunton of the DNC, who was extremely helpful in drawing the sample.

24. The survey design benefited greatly from advice given by Don Dillman of Washington State University based on his work in mail surveys (Dillman 2000). Ashley Grosse, then at Washington State University, was also instrumental in the survey design, fieldwork, and initial coding of the data. Additional details regarding sampling, response rates, questionnaires used, and other aspects of the survey methodology are available from the authors upon request.

To measure the extent to which candidates, political parties, and interest groups used religion and values in campaign mail, we counted two distinct aspects of the political mail. First we measured how many different or unique mail pieces in the survey contained references to religion. We refer to these throughout the analysis as "unique mailers." Every unique mailer has a different design or message than the others, even though they might be produced by the same candidate or organization. This measurement aimed to capture the diversity of messages being disseminated to voters and infused into the campaign. It also helped to measure the number of groups and campaigns that used religion or religiously informed issues to further their interests and agenda. The second measure is the total number of copies of each piece of unique mail received by the survey respondents. This offers a relative measure of how many copies of each unique mail piece were sent out or the volume of circulation. We refer to this measure throughout the analysis as "mail pieces" or "number of mail pieces." Full details about coding decisions are presented in the appendix to this chapter.

One caveat is important to offer at this point: quantity may not trump credibility. In other words, a voter who receives ten professionally designed mail pieces from the RNC may briefly examine each of them in the few seconds it takes to walk from the mailbox to the trash can. However, a lower-production-quality mail piece arriving from Focus on the Family or National Right to Life may receive more attention because it is from a trusted source. Perhaps the voter is a dues-paying member of the organization. In this case, the mail may be read in its entirety, and the message will be allowed to exercise its full potential impact. However, for some voters, the Republican Party has achieved a high level of credibility on these issues, and a few seconds of reading before the piece is discarded may be enough exposure, especially if the message is delivered repeatedly.

Source and Content of Religiously Oriented Mail in 2004

Our findings shed further light on the uses of religion and religiously informed values in political campaigning and mobilization. Table 6-4 lists the top ten conservative and liberal organizations, respectively, that sent religious or values-based mail during the survey's three-week field period. The table presents two measures of activity. The first is the total number of religious mailers received by the respondents from each organization. The second is the total number of unique mailers received from each organization. According to both measures, but especially the total mail received, conservative organizations

Table 6-4. Organizations Sending Mail about Religious, Moral, or Social Issues, 2004

Organization	Total pieces of mail[a]	Number of unique mailers[b]	Number of issues addressed[c]
Conservative organizations			
Republican National Committee	664	10	8
National Right to Life	121	7	2
Republican Jewish Coalition	46	2	1
Focus on the Family	17	5	3
Bush-Cheney '04	15	7	4
Christian Coalition	8	3	7
Susan B. Anthony List	8	3	2
Life Issues Institute	3	2	1
Traditional Values Coalition	3	2	8
Citizen Leader Coalition	2	2	6
Total	887	43	4.2[d]
Liberal organizations			
America Coming Together	49	4	3
American Federation of State, County, and Municipal Employees (AFSCME)	25	2	2
National Association of Abortion and Reproductive Rights Action League (NARAL) Pro-Choice America	20	4	2
Planned Parenthood	20	12	4
Democratic National Committee	19	3	2
Human Rights Campaign	14	3	2
National Organization of Women	5	4	2
People for the American Way (PFAW)	5	1	8
Democratic Senatorial Campaign Committee	4	1	1
Equality Florida Action Network	2	2	2
Total	163	36	2.8[d]

Source: 2004 Campaign Communications Survey (CCS).
a. The total number of mail pieces received by CCS respondents from the organization.
b. The number of unique mailers sent by the organization and received by respondents.
c. The total number of different issues that the organization addressed in its mailers. For example, the RNC sent 664 copies of ten unique mailers to CCS respondents that addressed eight issues (see table 6-5 for a list of issues).
d. Average.

were far more active than their liberal counterparts in sending mail pieces with religious or values-based content. This result is expected given the increasingly religious composition of the Republican coalition[25] and the conventional wisdom that religious and values-laden messages are more effective on the Right than the Left because they invoke stronger emotional reactions among conservatives than liberals. Survey respondents received a whopping 887 pieces

25. Layman (2001).

of religious mail from conservative organizations compared to a meager 163 from liberal groups. Conservative organizations also sent forty-three unique mailers, while liberal groups only sent thirty-six. Production of unique mailers on the Right and the Left reached relative parity, while the total number of mail pieces was very imbalanced.

The other major finding in table 6-4 is that the Republican National Committee sent considerably more values-based mail than any other group. The RNC accounted for most of the difference between liberals and conservatives. Removing the RNC from the conservative total balances the counts at 223 from conservative groups and 163 from liberal groups. Likewise with the RNC removed, the top ten organizations on the Left sent slightly more unique mailers (thirty-six) than the top nine conservative organizations (thirty-three). In sum, the RNC accounted for the vast majority of all values-based and religious-oriented mail, dwarfing the efforts of all other groups. We do not have comparable data for 2000 or earlier, but it is fair to say that these results support the prediction of Green and his colleagues that, with continued involvement of religious conservatives in GOP politics, the party would assimilate those attitudes and positions into its electioneering activities.[26]

We coded the content of each piece of mail for up to eighteen identifiable issues that could reasonably be related to religion or religious and moral values, ranging from abortion and gay marriage to general statements about faith to comments relating judicial nominations to these issues. Many of the most active organizations dealt with multiple issues in their mailers. Table 6-4 also summarizes the issues coded by group. Traditional single-issue interest groups, such as NARAL Pro-Choice America, and National Right to Life, addressed a small number of issues. Other groups, such as the RNC and People for the American Way (PFAW), dealt with eight of the eighteen coded issues; the RNC and PFAW had the most diverse issue content of the groups in the CCS. On average, conservative organizations advocated a slightly more diverse portfolio of issues than liberal organizations. Organizations on the Right dealt with an average of 4.2 issues per group, while those on the Left addressed 2.8. Again, the difference between the Right and Left is largely a result of the RNC's efforts.

Table 6-5 contains a breakdown of the eighteen issues coded by their frequency of appearance in the mail pieces of conservative organizations. Abortion was the most prominent issue for both conservative and liberal groups (not shown). Far more unique mailers dealt with abortion than with any

---

26. Guth and Green (1988); Green, Guth, and Hill (1993).

Table 6-5. Distribution of Issues in the Mail of Conservative Organizations, 2004

Issue	Total mail pieces[a] Number[c]	Total mail pieces[a] Percent of total (899)	Unique mailers[b] Number[c]	Unique mailers[b] Percent of total (66)	Number of organizations sending mailers that mention the issue
Abortion	673	75	52	79	15
Same-sex marriage	533	59	27	41	8
Nomination of judges	458	51	14	21	5
Family values	397	44	8	12	3
Boy Scouts	167	19	3	5	2
Faith	125	14	11	17	9
Faith-based initiatives	21	2	5	8	3
Gay rights	12	1	4	6	1
Separation of church and state	8	1	5	8	4
Gay adoption	7	1	2	3	2
Ten Commandments	6	1	3	5	2
Public decency	5	1	2	3	2
Prayer	3	0	3	5	2
GOTV	2	0	1	2	1
Traditional morality	1	0	1	2	1
Liberal religious values	1	0	1	2	1

Source: 2004 Campaign Communications Survey (CCS).
a. The total number of mail pieces received by CCS respondents that mention the issue.
b. The number of unique mailers sent by the organizations that were received by respondents.
c. Totals do not equal 887 or 43 for total mail pieces and unique mail pieces, respectively, by conservative organizations from table 6-4, because mailers dealing with more than one issue were counted for every issue that they mention.

other issue, but same-sex marriage also made a strong showing.[27] Conservative groups created fifty-two unique mailers addressing abortion, nearly double the twenty-seven that addressed same-sex marriage or marriage generally. However, those twenty-eight unique mailers were circulated almost as widely as the fifty-two abortion mailers. Nearly 60 percent (533) of the mail pieces

27. Coding choices affect which issue is the most common in table 6-5. References to same-sex marriage were often accompanied by references to support for tax breaks for families (increasing the child tax deduction and lowering or eliminating the marriage penalty), linking marriage and taxes to support for the institution of marriage; therefore, we combined references to marriage and family tax policy in our coding of same-sex marriage. Nearly all the mail pieces, especially the RNC's mail, mentioned both issues together. However, one RNC mailer mentioned President Bush's tax policies only and not same-sex marriage. The analysis presented here excludes this RNC mailer. If it is included, then slightly more mail pieces mentioned marriage and same-sex marriage (707) than abortion (673). However, we opted to exclude the RNC mail piece in the end because its main focus was not on values or religion.

received mentioned same-sex marriage, while 75 percent (673) addressed abortion. On average, about thirteen copies of each unique mailer that discussed abortion were received, while mailers mentioning marriage had an average circulation of about twenty copies each. We expected abortion to play a prominent role in the issue content of the mail, given its long-standing importance to religious conservatives. The total for marriage-related mail reflects the growing importance of the issue in recent years. It also reflects the appearance of eleven state ballot proposals to ban gay marriage in 2004.[28] Again, in support of the proposition that the Republican Party is assimilating religious conservative values and issues, CCS respondents received 458 pieces of mail from the RNC that addressed abortion and 489 pieces that addressed same-sex marriage. Thus for the RNC, same-sex marriage was a dominant issue, reflecting, as Campbell and Monson describe in their chapter, the instrumental use of gay marriage in 2004 to mobilize religious conservatives, especially in states with marriage propositions on the ballot. However, the RNC mail still prominently emphasized a pro-life position. In fact, most RNC mailers addressed same-sex marriage and abortion together, while a few focused exclusively on same-sex marriage. The older social issue of abortion was important, but RNC strategists probably saw a new issue to use in getting likely Republican voters to the polls. In light of the discussion of stem cell research in the chapter by Norrander and Norrander, it is interesting to note that this issue was rarely, if ever, broached in direct mail appeals.

The RNC accounted for the majority of mail pieces addressing same-sex marriage, while various groups accounted for a lot of the campaigning on abortion. Smaller groups like National Right to Life and the Traditional Values Coalition rarely, if ever, mentioned same-sex marriage; instead they relied heavily on abortion as the salient issue in their mailers. As table 6-5 indicates, nearly 80 percent of all unique mailers on the conservative side mentioned abortion, while only 41 percent mentioned same-sex marriage. Again, this suggests that the Republican Party used values more broadly in its communications and capitalized on the salience of the marriage issue to get the attention and votes of religious voters.

Some issues that we expected to appear frequently in conservative mail did not receive much attention. For example, religious liberty, often mentioned along with same-sex marriage in the media, was never mentioned by conservative organizations in the mailers. The top issues for the Right were abortion, same-sex marriage, the nomination of conservative federal judges, family val-

---

28. Campbell and Monson (2005); see also their chapter in this volume.

Table 6-6. Images and Language in the Mail of Conservative
Organizations, 2004

Image or language	Total mail pieces[a]	Total conservative mail pieces[b]	Unique conservative mailers[c]
Image			
Church	116	111	2
Cross	8	2	3
Pastor	5	0	2
Jewish icon	1	0	1
Bible	0	0	0
Language			
Bible	39	38	7
God	21	14	12
Other	11	9	3
Leader	3	3	3

Source: 2004 Campaign Communications Survey (CCS).
a. The total number of mail pieces received by CCS respondents that contained the image or language.
b. The total number of mail pieces received by CCS respondents from conservative organizations that contained the image or language.
c. The number of unique mailers from conservative organizations that contained the image or language.

ues, and the Boy Scouts (an issue in a number of RNC mailers trumpeting President Bush's conservative credentials). Most uses of the issues addressed were not explicitly religious. Table 6-6 presents a breakdown of the total number of mail pieces that contain religious symbols and language. The table shows that relatively few explicitly religious images and language were used by either side. Only the image of a church appears in more than 100 pieces of mail, and that is because an RNC mailer had the image of a church on the front. Even then, the image was a relatively ambiguous visual reference to religion; the image appears to be a church, but it lacks clear markings as such. The RNC mail piece elicited the underlying visceral emotions and thoughts of religion, as Leege and his coauthors suspected,[29] without explicitly drawing on religious imagery. These findings reinforce the concept that the uses of values in 2004 were primarily instrumental; few explicit appeals to religion were made, either visually or in language.

The rarity of explicitly religious references and images follows the findings on explicitly racial appeals that Tali Mendelberg reports in her book, *The Race Card: Campaign Strategy, Implicit Messages, and the Norm of Equality*.[30] She

29. Leege and others (2002).
30. Mendelberg (2001).

Table 6-7. Support for Presidential Candidates in Mail about Religious, Moral, or Social Issues, 2004

Position[a]	Mail pieces[b]		Unique mailers[c]	
	Number	Percent	Number	Percent
Pro-Bush/anti-Kerry	860	80	46	39
No position	81	8	36	30
Pro-Kerry/anti-Bush	131	12	37	31
Total[d]	1,072	100	113	100

Source: 2004 Campaign Communications Survey (CCS).
a. Position defined by explicit references to either candidate by name.
b. The total number of mail pieces received by CCS respondents that takes each position.
c. The number of unique mailers that takes each position.
d. Mail is not double-counted in the totals for mail pieces and unique mailers.

argues that sensitive issues are conveyed best through implicit communications dealing with topics informed by the controversies, but not explicitly about them. This tactic allows politicians to exploit a controversial or disfavored issue for electoral gain without paying the political price that explicit references would exact. Our findings suggest that most politicians have adopted this subtle approach when using religion in their campaigns. They address religiously informed issues widely, such as general values and political activities that affect those values, but are hesitant to introduce religion and faith directly as issues. For example, the RNC produced a number of mailers asserting that, if reelected, President Bush would nominate conservative judges to the federal judiciary. While not explicitly about religion, the message's underlying point is that President Bush would nominate judges who would side with religious evangelicals on issues such as abortion and same-sex marriage. Campaigns approach religion carefully, without explicit religious images or words, but they still seek to infuse their message with religiously informed issues.

Many election mailers not only used values extensively in 2004, but also were very explicit in endorsing candidates. And the mailers that endorsed candidates overwhelmingly endorsed President Bush or attacked Senator Kerry. Table 6-7 presents the breakdown of mailers that supported or opposed the presidential candidates. The pro-Bush/anti-Kerry mailers, while about the same in number, were distributed far more widely than the pro-Kerry/anti-Bush mailers. About 80 percent of all religiously oriented mail pieces were pro-Bush/anti-Kerry, while only 12 percent were pro-Kerry/anti-Bush, with the remainder having no discernible position. Nearly eight times more mail was received that attacked Kerry or supported Bush than attacked Bush or supported Kerry. The RNC and other Bush supporters were far more active, and effective, in disseminating their values-based messages.

Most of the pro-Bush/anti-Kerry mailers focused on values instead of explicitly on religion; the message of many mailers was essentially that President Bush shares the values of the conservative religious community. The Left framed the issues more frequently in the context of social policy, avoiding the language of right and wrong and instead focusing on what the government should and should not do within a public policy framework. Liberal organizations avoided the language of values in general and focused on the issues they addressed as policy judgments. Conservative organizations accompanied their references to many of the same issues with the language of values. For example, RNC mailers contained statements like "John Kerry claims to represent your values," "Give your values a voice," "Fighting for our values," and "George Bush: Working to protect our values." Conservative organizations were more willing to address issues as matters of right versus wrong by appealing to voters' opinions about values, morality, and life and by evoking the emotional reactions that are informed by religious beliefs.[31]

Table 6-8 lists the top ten most widely distributed mailers. Of these, nine are from the Right and five are from the RNC. The top RNC mailers all deal with same-sex marriage and abortion, issues that Republicans saw as working in their favor among religious conservatives. The four most common mail pieces were RNC mailers, and the next two were National Right to Life mailers. The eighth most common mail piece was the first offering from a liberal organization. The one liberal mailer in the top ten only vaguely addressed religious and moral values by appealing to voters not to be distracted by unimportant issues (like values) to the detriment of important issues (like jobs and health care). This appears to be a response to the volume of values-based communications sent by Republican-affiliated groups.

Conclusions

Understanding microtargeting is critical to understanding the overall GOP strategy in 2004. Other groups campaigned on values-related issues, but the RNC took the lead, especially in volume of mail sent but also in diversity of messages addressed. In part as a result of such efforts, evangelicals and other

31. Leege and others (2002).

Table 6-8. Top Ten Mail Pieces about Religious, Moral, or Social Issues, 2004

Rank	Organization	Number of mail pieces	Description
1	Republican National Committee	147	Mentions abortion, same-sex marriage, and nomination of conservative judges. Criticizes Kerry for claiming to represent conservative values when he is associated with or supported by prominent liberals such as Michael Moore, Jane Fonda, Michael Dukakis, and Ted Kennedy.
2	Republican National Committee	111	Mentions abortion, same-sex marriage, family values, President Bush as a man of faith, and nomination of conservative judges. Main title: "This election is for families." Asks, "Who can you count on to support traditional values?"
3	Republican National Committee	93	Mentions abortion, same-sex marriage, nomination of conservative judges, and the Boy Scouts controversy. "John Kerry claims to represent your values . . . but in twenty years in Washington Kerry has voted 119 times *against* conservative values" [emphasis in original]. Lists ways in which Kerry's views differ from conservative values.
4	Republican National Committee	73	Mentions abortion, same-sex marriage, family values, the Boy Scouts, and nomination of conservative judges. Asks, "Who shares your values?" and then describes both candidates' positions on social and moral issues.
5	National Right to Life PAC	65	Mentions abortion and Supreme Court nominations. Gives a detailed breakdown on the candidates' positions on partial-birth abortion, abortion on demand, government funding of abortion, voting record on abortion, and Supreme Court appointments. Also gives short paragraphs on the positions of the vice presidential candidates.
6	National Right to Life PAC	32	Focuses exclusively on abortion. Shows a picture of a baby with the words, "This little guy wants you to vote for President Bush." On the back, summarizes the position of the presidential candidates on abortion. Top of back has a biblical quotation and in large print says, "Vote like life depends on it . . . it does."
7	Republican National Committee	30	Mentions same-sex marriage and family values. On the front cover, asks, "Where do the presidential candidates stand on protecting marriage?" On the inside, asserts that Kerry's actions show that he is against marriage. On the back cover, declares, "President George W. Bush strongly supports marriage."

Table 6-8. Top Ten Mail Pieces about Religious, Moral, or Social Issues, 2004 (*continued*)

Rank	Organization	Number of mail pieces	Description
8	America Coming Together	23	Deals with liberal religious values of jobs and health care as more important than other moral and social issues. Title: "Don't be distracted." Claims that Republicans are distracting voters with unimportant issues. Ends with plea: "If we stay focused on jobs, health care, and homeland security, we can get Ohio back on track."
9	Republican Jewish Coalition	23	Deals with abortion and stem cell research. Prominently features former New York mayor Ed Koch and highlights his disagreement with President Bush on abortion and stem cell research but says that he is supporting the president because of his strong position on security and Israel.
10	Republican Jewish Coalition	23	Deals with abortion by advocating that pro-choice Democrats vote for Bush because of his support for Israel and strong stance against terrorism.

Source: 2004 Campaign Communications Survey (CCS).

religious conservatives have become an important part of the Republican base, but whether the alliance is permanent remains to be seen. Some within the party are uncomfortable with the shift toward values. They think the strategy is mortgaging future success for wins today by making the party too reliant on an overly targeted message that attracts some voters at the expense of alienating many others. Others in the Republican Party, however, believe that the political mobilization of religious conservatives is permanent because the cultural issues they are concerned about show no signs of going away. As long as those issues remain on the political horizon, the Republican Party is likely to continue using them instrumentally to convince religious conservatives to participate in elections.

But the rise of microtargeting also has implications beyond its impact on the GOP. Microtargeting represents a significant innovation in how messages are disseminated in modern elections. As campaigns have developed into highly professional and mass-marketed affairs, mobilization strategies have shifted away from community-based or grassroots volunteers (and thus away from community-based messages) and toward centralized mass marketing that disseminates broader messages. As Putnam has asserted, "Financial capital—the wherewithal for mass marketing—has steadily replaced social capital—

that is, grassroots citizen networks—as the coin of the realm."[32] Microtargeting represents a shift back toward community messages but delivers these messages through the tools of mass marketing. It represents a new development in method, not style. Highly targeted messages were the norm in earlier eras because they were distributed by highly targeted means (campaign volunteers, neighborhood party workers). Now similarly targeted messages can be delivered in bulk.

While these new tactics mimic the social capital–intensive methods of the past, they may threaten the social capital that elections produce. Political scientists have suggested that elections are unifying events that build social capital in a community because they reinforce the mutual obligations of the community through the social interactions they create.[33] The ritualistic aspect of elections thus reinforces community standards and symbols. However, microtargeting could pose a risk to this process because it divides the community into different subgroups and attempts to make the election about different issues for different community members. This division is particularly potent when infused with the political charge of religiously oriented issues. Instead of being a reaffirmation of shared democratic beliefs, an election becomes a plebiscite on private beliefs, which can cause failure at the polls to be seen as a challenge to deeply held values and the people who hold them. The "non-bargainable" nature of religious and cultural issues can tax and even shut down democratic discourse, thus curtailing the gains in social capital created by elections.[34]

32. Putnam (2000, pp. 39–40).
33. Rahn, Brehm, and Carlson (1999, p. 115).
34. Leege and others (2002, p. 29).

Appendix. Campaign Communications Survey Coding Criteria

The first step in the coding was to identify whether a mailer contained any references to religion or religious issues. A preliminary list of issues and references was compiled from issues we thought likely to appear in the mail; this list consisted of abortion, same-sex marriage, school prayer (and any other mentions of prayer), religious liberty, faith, separation of church and state, and family values. As the mail was coded, other issues were identified and added to the list. For example, after noticing that many religiously themed mailers mentioned the nomination of conservative judges, we added the nomination of judges as an issue and then reviewed what had previously been coded for other mentions of the issue. As the coding proceeded, the following issues were added: culture of life, support for marriage independent of same-sex marriage, reproductive health, Boy Scouts, liberal religious values (health care, welfare, and so forth in light of religious values), gay rights, faith-based initiatives, gay adoption, the Ten Commandments, morality, public decency, and get-out-the-vote. These categories were not mutually exclusive; mailers could have been coded with one or all of these categories.

We also coded the mail for the appearance of religious imagery and the use of religious language. The use of religious language and religious imagery was considerably less prevalent than the appearance of religious issues, so we had fewer categories. The codes for images included church, the Bible, cross, pastors or clergy, and an "other" category. The codes for language included mentions of God, the Bible, religious leaders, and an "other" category.

Below are the categories of issues, language, and images that were coded. Accompanying each is a short description of the types of statements and phrases that were coded as falling under the category.

Issues

Abortion. Explicit statements on the issue of abortion. Also any reference to the partial-birth abortion ban was coded under this category.

Boy Scouts. Statements of support for the organization as a whole and for its right to use public buildings and facilities. Also included were criticisms of opponents for not supporting the organization.

Faith. Statements about faith, particularly statements about the need for faith or statements about a candidate's faithfulness or lack of it.

Faith-based initiatives. Statements of support for or opposition to the president's proposals to allow religious organizations to use government funds in their provision of social services.

Family values. Explicit uses of the phrase "family values."

Gay adoption. Statements in opposition to gay couples' having the legal ability to adopt children.

Gay rights. Statements in support of or opposition to gay rights, excluding marriage, which was classified as an independent category because of its salience during the 2004 elections. Most statements dealt with discrimination in housing, employment, and such. Adoption by gay couples was classified separately.

Get-out-the-vote. Religious mailers that dealt with religious individuals' need to vote and the legal limits on what religious leaders can do to mobilize their congregations.

Liberal religious values. The values often espoused by liberal people of faith— that is, health care, welfare, social policies to benefit the poor, and peace discussed through a religious paradigm.

Prayer. Mostly statements dealing with school prayer but also the subject of prayer in general.

Public decency. Statements about the public display or dissemination of sexually explicit materials.

Religious liberty. Statements dealing with the free exercise of religion.

Reproductive health. Discussion of social issues along the lines of a woman's right to choose when, how, and why to have a family, including access to birth control, reproductive health services, and so forth. Also included were mentions of opposition to stem cell research, support for the Unborn Victim of Violence Act (Laci and Connor's Law), overall statements about support for life of the unborn, and statements about preventing the extension of legal rights to fetuses.

Same-sex marriage. Explicit statements dealing with marriage as only between a man and a woman; support for or opposition to the Federal Marriage Amendment, Defense of Marriage Act, or any other legal issue dealing with same-sex marriage; statements about "marriage equality"; statements about support for the institution of marriage without explicit mention of the debate about same-sex marriage. Also included were statements dealing with a candidate's support for ending the marriage tax penalty, which often accompanied other statements about abortion, judicial nominations, and so forth.

Separation of church and state. Discussion of the issue of the Establishment Clause of the Constitution and the separation of religion and public policy. The issue was generally addressed by groups left of center.

Ten Commandments. Statements of support for the public display of the Ten Commandments and their application in public life.

Traditional morality. Making an issue of traditional morals and, particularly, sexual mores.

Language

Bible-themed. Use of the Bible as a source of authority for political positions; direct quotations of scriptures from the Bible; any mention of the Bible.

God. Use of the word "God" in any context; appeals to divine authority to support or oppose a position.

Other. Uses of religious language such as *sacred* and *religious.*

Religious leader. Quotations from religious leaders; statements of support or opposition from prominent religious leaders and figures; testimonials from pastors, bishops, or other clergy members who were less prominent, but whose status as a religious leader was emphasized.

Images

Bible. Pictures of books obviously identifiable as the Bible.

Church. Images easily identifiable as a church or another religious building.

Cross. Use of the cross in any way, either in graphics or in photographs.

Jewish. Use of Jewish iconography such as yarmulkes, menorahs, or other obviously Jewish images. The one instance found was a yarmulke prominently displayed on a man's head.

Religious leaders. Images of individuals easily identifiable as a religious leader or a member of the clergy. For example, one mailer showed a man with a pastor's collar.

The Case of Bush's Reelection
Did Gay Marriage Do It?

David E. Campbell and J. Quin Monson

In the case of George W. Bush's reelection, did gay marriage do it? One storyline of the 2004 election, widely repeated in the immediate wake of the contest, went something like this: Bush returned to the White House because he capitalized on many voters' concerns about moral values. Specifically, he rode a groundswell of opposition to same-sex marriage in those eleven states that held referenda on gay marriage simultaneously with the presidential election. Voters who otherwise would have stayed home on Election Day turned out to thwart gay marriage and, while at the polls, also cast a ballot for Bush. This story stands in contrast to the traditional account of a president's coattails, whereby congressional candidates benefit from their association with a popular presidential candidate who is of the same party. It is better labeled a *reverse* coattail effect.

Earlier chapters have shown that the hue and cry about moral values in the immediate wake of the election was overblown. As Sunshine Hillygus shows, for most voters the 2004 contest centered largely on their attitudes about the economy, the war in Iraq, and which candidate they felt was better able to keep the country safe from terrorism. However, as Scott Keeter illustrates, moral values *did* matter to a well-defined subset of the population: religious traditionalists, particularly evangelical Christians. Further probing reveals that for these voters the term "moral values" often connotes issues like gay marriage. In other words, while gay marriage may not have mattered much to most voters, it mattered a lot to a few voters. And in a close election, that may have been enough to tip the scales in favor of Bush.

Of course, in a close election almost any issue or group can be said to have been decisive. As in any investigation, to solve the case of Bush's reelection, the suspect must be shown to have had the *motive, means,* and *opportunity,* all of which are necessary, but none of which is sufficient to close the case. Forensic evidence is the clincher. The remainder of the chapter, therefore, is laid out accordingly. We begin by considering Bush's motive for capitalizing on gay marriage, how the issue came to represent an opportunity for his reelection bid, and the means employed by his campaign to benefit from the issue among social conservatives, without incurring a backlash from social moderates who supported Bush for other reasons. We then turn to the forensic evidence regarding the role of gay marriage in the reelection of George W. Bush.[1]

Motive

Having lost the 2000 popular vote and won the White House only by way of a controversial Supreme Court decision, George W. Bush had a strong motivation to boost support wherever he could in preparation for his reelection bid. His reelection rested on widening, even if only slightly, his electoral coalition. As has been noted in previous chapters, Karl Rove identified evangelicals as a group among whom Bush needed to shore up support—the now famous comment about the 4 million "missing evangelicals." This was not an obvious group for Rove to target for growth, as conservative Protestants had supported Bush overwhelmingly in 2000. As Green and his coauthors report in chapter 2, 87 percent of traditionalist evangelicals voted for Bush in the 2000 election.[2] It is not clear how Rove arrived at the precise figure of 4 million missing evangelicals, but given that Rove is in the business of winning elections, not providing transparent analysis of election data, its provenance is largely irrelevant.

---

1. For other scholarly analysis of the role of gay marriage in the 2004 election, see Abramowitz (2004); Burden (2004); Hillygus and Shields (2005); McDonald (2004); Smith, DeSantis, and Kassel (2005).

2. Throughout this chapter, we use the terms "conservative Protestants" and "evangelicals" interchangeably. We recognize that, technically, not all conservative Protestants are evangelicals and not all evangelicals are conservative Protestants. However, the two groups overlap to a great extent, and the distinctions scholars draw among conservative Protestants—evangelicals versus fundamentalists, for example—are too nuanced for our empirical analysis.

What matters is that Rove saw energizing the evangelical base of the GOP as an important component of winning reelection. He did not say there was a need to *persuade* evangelicals to support Bush, as they were squarely in the center of the GOP tent. Rather, he said that there was a need to *mobilize* them to turn out to vote. As David Leege and his colleagues argue in *The Politics of Cultural Differences,* Republicans have become adept at building presidential campaigns around moral issues, such as gay marriage, precisely to ensure the mobilization of voters with whom such issues resonate.[3] Winning elections not only entails bringing new supporters over to your side; it also involves getting longtime supporters to the polls.

In short, if we are to believe Bush's most prominent political adviser—and we have no reason not to—the Bush campaign team saw potential for mobilizing conservative Protestants, particularly evangelicals. The Bush team thus had a motive for finding issues and campaign themes that would appeal to this constituency and spur them to the polls.

Opportunity

Since the emergence in the late 1970s and early 1980s of what has come to be called the New Christian Right, the movement has coalesced around a bundle of issues that includes opposition to abortion, support for traditional gender roles, support for restrictions on pornography, and resistance to homosexual rights.[4] While some recent elections have featured more attention to some of these issues than others, the general area of cultural issues has been a recurring motif. Abortion is a perennial hot-button issue, while other controversies come and go. The issue of gay marriage, for example, simmered for about a decade before emerging on the national stage.

During this period, supporters of gay marriage found sympathy in courts of law but opposition in the court of public opinion. In 1996 a lower court in Hawaii ruled that a prohibition on gay marriage violated the state's constitution. In response, Congress passed (overwhelmingly) and President Bill Clinton signed (publicly) the Defense of Marriage Act (DOMA). DOMA enshrines in federal law the principle that marriage is between one man and one woman and says that states which do not want to recognize homosexual marriages performed in other states are not required to do so. In addition to DOMA, there have been a number of referenda on whether a gay marriage

3. Leege and others (2002).
4. Wilcox and Larson (2006).

ban should be written into the state's constitution, and, in each case, the amendment has passed by a wide margin. This set of cases includes Hawaii, home to the first pro–gay marriage ruling, and Alaska, home to the second. It also includes California, which because of its national prominence and the size of its homosexual community, drew national attention for a 2000 initiative on gay marriage. Proposition 22 maintained the winning streak, however, as Californians also endorsed a statutory ban on homosexual nuptials. Similar gay marriage bans were written into the state constitutions of Nevada and Nebraska after statewide referenda, and twenty-three other states have enacted statutory prohibitions on homosexual marriages.

While gay marriage was losing at the polls, in 1999 it did win a victory in the courts. In that year, the Vermont Supreme Court ruled that same-sex couples could not be denied the benefits granted to heterosexual married couples, although it stopped short of saying that they should be permitted to marry. Shortly thereafter, the Vermont legislature recognized "civil unions" for homosexual couples, which grants them the same benefits as marriage. Governor Howard Dean signed the bill into law, but he did so with no public ceremony. Presumably, he decided to sign the bill privately because, even in socially liberal Vermont, legal recognition of homosexual unions is unpopular. Dean's national political ambitions undoubtedly were a factor also, as a photo of himself signing the nation's first law formally recognizing homosexual relationships surely would be fodder for opponents during a presidential run.

For roughly a decade prior to the 2004 election, marriage for homosexual couples was an issue that sporadically caught the public's attention but did not dominate the national agenda, even among social conservatives. That changed in late 2003 and early 2004, when events transpired to focus attention on gay marriage, just as the 2004 presidential election season was beginning. The Massachusetts Supreme Judicial Court ruled in November 2003 that the state's law against gay marriage violated the Massachusetts constitution and gave the state legislature 180 days to change the law to permit same-sex couples to be married. In the wake of that decision, the mayor of San Francisco, Gavin Newsom, began issuing marriage licenses to homosexual couples. From February 12 to March 11, thousands of licenses were issued, and the news media featured many stories showcasing newly "married" gay couples. A media frenzy began as gay marriage became the issue du jour. A few other communities soon followed San Francisco's example, and local officials in New York and New Mexico began issuing marriage licenses to gay couples, drawing still more attention to same-sex marriage. The issue remained on the front pages when all of these marriage licenses were later ruled invalid by the state attorney general (New Mexico) or the courts (California, New York). Gay marriage attracted still another wave of attention as the Massachusetts court's 180-day deadline arrived, and the first legally recognized homosexual marriages were performed in Cambridge in May of 2004.

Figure 7-1 underscores just how prominent gay marriage became in the early months of 2004. The figure displays the number of stories in newspapers and broadcast media that mentioned gay marriage or its synonyms from 1998 to 2004. The huge spike in news media attention in early 2004 overwhelms the previous upticks in attention to gay marriage. Same-sex marriage was no longer simmering; it had boiled over.

George W. Bush was not the reason that gay marriage became such a salient issue so quickly. Nonetheless, the issue presented an opportunity for him to take a stand popular among his conservative Protestant base of supporters. As indicated by the winning streak of gay marriage referenda, Americans generally oppose permitting homosexual couples to wed. However, opposition to gay marriage runs especially deep among conservative Protestants. For example, the

Figure 7-1. Media Coverage of Gay Marriage

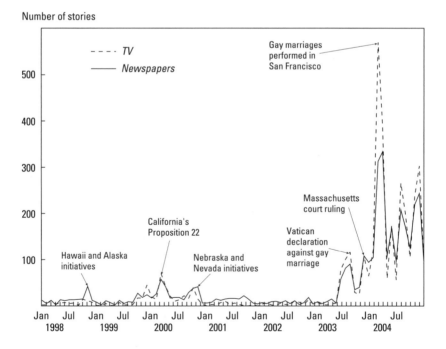

Number of stories

2004 Election Panel Study (details below) found that 65 percent of evangelicals oppose gay marriage, compared to 38 percent of all Americans. If Bush needed an issue to mobilize evangelicals, gay marriage was a prime candidate. It was not surprising, therefore, that Bush publicly opposed homosexual marriages in his 2004 State of the Union address and later supported an amendment to the federal Constitution that would limit marriage to heterosexual couples.

Owing to all the public attention to the issue and particularly the Massachusetts court ruling in favor of gay marriage, by the spring of 2004 campaigns were being launched in various states to put gay marriage bans (GMBs) on the ballot. The specifics varied, but they all sought to write a prohibition against homosexual marriage into the state constitution. We have found no evidence that these campaigns were orchestrated by Bush's strategists.[5] Once under way, however, they presented an opportunity for the Republicans and their allies to emphasize Bush's opposition to gay marriage. Eventually, GMBs were on the ballot in thirteen states in 2004. Eleven of these referenda coincided with the presidential election, while two were held in conjunction with earlier contests. Table 7-1 lists the states and the final share of the vote taken by the GMB initiative in each one.[6] In many of these states, the results of the presidential election were hardly a matter of suspense; Karl Rove did not stay up nights worrying about Bush's support in deep-red states like Utah, Montana, and North Dakota. Among the GMB states, however, were a few states that were going to be competitive, like Michigan and Missouri. Most important, a GMB was on the ballot in Ohio, a battleground state where, in the end, the election was decided.

Means

The Bush campaign had the motive for finding a way to mobilize Bush's evangelical base, and gay marriage presented just such an opportunity. But did Bush make use of the issue during the campaign? And if so, how? In other words, by what means was gay marriage a factor in the 2004 presidential race?

Based on the intensive discussion of moral values and gay marriage following the 2004 contest, one might conclude that Bush made opposition to

5. Obviously, the absence of evidence does not prove that it did not happen, and so we hold open the possibility that further research will uncover evidence that these campaigns were coordinated by the Bush team.

6. The table does not include Louisiana and Missouri, which held referenda on gay marriage in 2004, but prior to the November balloting. In Missouri 71 percent voted to ban gay marriage, while in Louisiana 78 percent did so.

Table 7-1. Percentage of Voters in Favor of Gay Marriage Ban, November 2004

State	Percent of voters for gay marriage ban	Change in Bush's vote share regressed on percent of voters for gay marriage ban		
		Coefficient	Standard error	P value
Arkansas	75	0.192	0.050	0.000
Georgia	76	0.246	0.036	0.000
Kentucky	75	0.014	0.042	0.746
Michigan	59	0.021	0.036	0.571
Mississippi	86	0.293	0.062	0.000
Montana	67	−0.025	0.048	0.598
North Dakota	73	0.031	0.061	0.613
Ohio	62	0.162	0.028	0.000
Oklahoma	76	0.186	0.067	0.008
Oregon	57	0.076	0.039	0.061
Utah	66	0.029	0.053	0.591

Source: Authors' calculations based on data from the respective secretary of states' offices.

gay marriage a centerpiece of his reelection campaign. He did not. In fact, throughout 2004 gay marriage was mentioned infrequently by the president or other administration officials. It was never the subject of a media blitz in the same way as other signature issues of the Bush administration, such as education reform, privatization of Social Security, homeland security, and the war in Iraq. There were no speeches, photo ops, or town meetings devoted to the subject. Even the public references Bush made to gay marriage were subdued. His allusions to gay marriage in the State of the Union address and at the 2004 Republican convention were relatively brief and focused on "activist judges" more than homosexuality. Here is an illustrative quotation from the 2004 State of the Union address:

> Activist judges, however, have begun redefining marriage by court order, without regard for the will of the people and their elected representatives. On an issue of such great consequence, the people's voice must be heard. If judges insist on forcing their arbitrary will upon the people, the only alternative left to the people would be the constitutional process. Our nation must defend the sanctity of marriage.

Bush's most extended remarks on gay marriage came amid the national brouhaha on the subject, in February 2004, and consisted of a brief speech after which he took no questions.[7]

---

7. All of these statements from the president can be found at www.whitehouse.gov.

Given that mobilization of evangelicals was a key aspect of the strategy to reelect Bush and that opposition to gay marriage runs deep among conservative Protestants, it may seem puzzling that Bush did so little to exploit the issue. In reality, however, Bush simply could not rely on evangelicals alone, or even a larger coalition of religious traditionalists, to win in 2004. His coalition needed to include a sizable proportion of social moderates. Outside of evangelicals, opposition to gay marriage is better described as broad than deep. For example, while only 31 percent of Americans endorse the Massachusetts model of full marriage rights for homosexuals, another 31 percent support the Vermont model of civil unions—marriages in all but name. When you combine support for the Massachusetts and Vermont models, outright opposition to homosexual unions is a minority position. Just as Bush's campaign strategists undoubtedly knew the depth of conservative Protestants' opposition to gay marriage, they certainly also knew that a sizable portion of the electorate is ambivalent about the issue. Highlighting Bush's opposition to gay marriage risked a backlash among the socially moderate voters Bush needed to win and who were inclined to support him on other issues, particularly national security.

There is a parallel between the potential for a backlash from emphasizing gay marriage and the consequences of using racial imagery in campaign advertising and rhetoric. Tali Mendelberg makes a convincing case that racially moderate voters respond to racially themed campaign appeals as long as the racial content of the appeal is submerged—featuring African Americans in campaign advertising, for example, but not explicitly drawing attention to the fact that they are black.[8] If the racial content of such appeals is publicized, racial moderates react by pulling their support from the sponsor. Even the hint of racism is radioactive. Similarly, riding the coattails of opposition to gay marriage required Bush to tread carefully lest he alienate social moderates.

The socially conservative bona fides of the Republican Party, and George W. Bush in particular, meant that the president did not *need* to talk much about gay marriage to cement his opposition in the minds of voters. In the language of John Petrocik, the GOP "owns" socially conservative issues like gay marriage.[9] Having spent a generation building an infrastructure within the evangelical community and courting support from traditionalist Catholics as well, the Republican Party is widely identified as the party of social conservatism. Opposition to gay marriage thus fits naturally into the GOP's bundle

8. Mendelberg (2001).
9. Petrocik (1996).

of issues. Technically John Kerry opposed gay marriage too, but it strains credulity to think that many Americans saw the Democratic Party as the home of opposition to gay marriage or John Kerry as a candidate who would work actively to prevent widespread legal recognition of gay marriages. For one, Kerry's position was characteristically nuanced. He opposed only gay *marriages,* not the legal recognition of same-sex relationships, having publicly endorsed civil unions for homosexuals during the 2004 campaign. Prior to 2004, Kerry opposed an amendment to the federal Constitution that would ban gay marriage, and he was one of only fourteen senators to vote against the Defense of Marriage Act in 1996. In 2002 he signed a public letter indicating his opposition to efforts under way in Massachusetts to enact a state constitutional amendment outlawing gay marriage.[10]

Because emphasizing gay marriage ran the risk of turning moderates off while turning evangelicals out, Bush had to channel any campaign advertising that mentioned gay marriage to social conservatives—evangelicals specifically. Consequently, the Bush campaign steered clear of television advertising that mentioned gay marriage, since television is better suited to campaign messages for the masses rather than a select constituency. In Ohio, where the Bush campaign spent $50 million on television advertising and a GMB initiative was on the ballot, the Bush team and its allies did not run a single television ad on the subject of gay marriage.[11] The same story was repeated around the country; the Republicans did not feature gay marriage in their television advertising on Bush's behalf. For that matter, neither did the Democrats feature gay marriage in their advertising.

The avoidance of gay marriage in television advertising is not surprising. Other potentially explosive social issues, notably abortion, were also kept off the airwaves, so as not to alienate social moderates. Yet this hardly means that such social issues were ignored. Instead, they were made the subject of more targeted appeals, notably direct mail, which can consist of customized appeals tailored to the interests of a specific household. As detailed by Quin Monson and Baxter Oliphant in chapter 6, the 2004 campaign saw the most sophisticated data collection efforts ever undertaken by the parties, especially the Republicans. Whereas it was once the precinct captain who knew the background and interests of voters in the precinct, now the parties can purchase that information from firms that collect consumer data. The parties have

---

10. Associated Press (2004); Toner (2004).

11. These statements about television advertising during the 2004 election are based on data from the Campaign Media Analysis Group (CMAG). Details are available upon request.

developed massive databases of voters in an effort to identify the issues that will both persuade potential supporters and mobilize their base.

In sharp contrast to its invisibility in the Bush campaign's television advertising, gay marriage—or its opposite, traditional marriage—was frequently mentioned in direct mail supporting Bush. Gay marriage–related appeals were targeted toward social conservatives, many of whom were evangelicals. In an example of how microtargeting operates, one Republican campaign strategist noted in an interview that subscribers to religious magazines were selected to receive mail that mentioned moral issues, like gay marriage.[12] In some states, Republican operatives even collected church directories in an effort to identify voters amenable to morality politics.[13]

Using the Campaign Communications Survey (CCS), described more fully in chapter 6, we are able to test the effectiveness of these efforts by tracking the incidence of direct mail that mentioned gay marriage. Especially revealing is a comparison between two battleground states: Ohio (which had a GMB initiative on the ballot) and the equally competitive state of Florida (which did not). While mentions of gay marriage appeared in the mail used within both states, they were more common in Ohio. In Ohio, twenty-five unique pieces of mail linked Bush with opposition to gay marriage, compared to sixteen in Florida. Demonstrating the targeted nature of this communication, the voters most likely to receive mail that mentioned gay marriage in the context of supporting Bush's reelection were self-described members of the "religious right" in Ohio.[14] In other words, gay marriage was mentioned more frequently in Ohio than in Florida—owing to Ohio's GMB—and such appeals were steered toward social conservatives.

To bolster our claim that the Bush campaign was wary of a backlash from social moderates responding negatively to the perception of intolerance toward homosexuals, consider the language contained within the direct mail ads that did mention gay marriage. Targeting is an inexact science, and so a

12. Interview conducted by J. Quin Monson and David B. Magleby with Alexander Gage, Brent Seaborn, and Michael Myers (president, vice president, and vice president, respectively), TargetPoint Consulting; December 15, 2004.

13. Interview conducted by J. Quin Monson and David B. Magleby with Terry Nelson, political director, Bush/Cheney '04, January 5, 2005.

14. In Ohio, people who identify with the religious right received 1.4 pieces of mail mentioning gay marriage, compared with 0.9 for everyone else, a difference that is statistically significant at 0.05 (one-tailed test). Religious right identifiers in Florida also received 0.9 pieces of gay marriage–related mail, which is significantly different than the average for the religious right in Ohio ($p < 0.10$, one-tailed test).

campaign cannot be sure who is going to receive its advertising, let alone what will be featured in the news media. As a consequence, direct mail must be designed so as to avoid causing collateral damage should it end up in the "wrong" hands. In the case of gay marriage, this means that the issue was not framed as "Bush Opposes Homosexual Marriage" but instead as "Bush Supports Traditional Marriage," leaving the voter to deduce that supporting traditional marriage is the flip side to opposing homosexual marriage. Figure 7-2 displays a typical example of a direct mail piece that refers to marriage. In addition to the positively phrased text, note the subtle imagery of a church and a young, smiling family. This is not incendiary material likely to trigger a backlash from voters wary of supporting a candidate who appears intolerant toward homosexuals.

On the other end of the partisan spectrum, very little direct mail supporting John Kerry mentioned gay marriage. Of the ten most common pieces of mail in Ohio that mentioned gay marriage, only one was in support of John Kerry. And that single piece of mail hardly put the issue front and center; it was a flyer from the Ohio Democratic Party that listed a single oblique reference to gay marriage with a "NO on Issue 1" recommendation as one line of a large sample ballot. Democrats' relative silence regarding gay marriage is not surprising, given that Kerry's ostensible opposition to gay marriage was not going to mobilize core Democratic supporters, while his support for civil unions was unlikely to win over social conservatives. The most prudent strategy for Kerry was simply to avoid the issue.

In Ohio, most of the direct mail advertising that mentioned gay marriage came from the presidential campaigns, not the groups organized to support or oppose the ballot initiative (Issue 1). The Bush campaign and the pro–Issue 1 campaign thus had a symbiotic relationship. Bush benefited from the fact that Issue 1 had the potential to boost the number of social conservatives who went to the polls. The Issue 1 campaign benefited from the deep pockets of the Bush campaign, ensuring that the most sophisticated campaign tools available were enlisted in the cause of writing a ban on homosexual marriage into the state constitution.

While direct mail was an important means through which targeted advertising was directed toward the most receptive constituency, it was not the only channel of communication. There are numerous reports of voter mobilization within evangelical churches—a tactic long practiced by African American churches, but relatively new to white evangelicals, for whom the most common way in which politics works its way into the pews is through the distribution of voter guides from an organization like

Figure 7-2. Example of Direct Mail in Support of Bush

the Christian Coalition.[15] Messages delivered through church-based networks (or, in some cases, from the pulpit) are likely to be narrowly targeted since, almost by definition, the audience shares a common set of values and opinions.

To this point, we have seen three streams of evidence suggesting that gay marriage played a decisive role in the reelection of George W. Bush. First, Bush had the *motive* to maximize turnout among evangelicals. Second, the rise of gay marriage as an issue on the 2004 agenda provided the *opportunity*. Third, we have learned of the *means* by which gay marriage was cited in campaign appeals. Does the confluence of these streams lead to the conclusion that gay marriage was decisive? The answer rests on sifting through the forensic evidence from Election Day 2004. As detailed in the next section, the evidence supports the conclusion that there was a reverse coattail effect: Bush picked up votes from evangelicals in states with a gay marriage ban on the ballot.

Forensic Evidence

We begin with the question of whether the ballot initiatives on gay marriage gave Bush a boost at the polls. If Bush was helped by the GMBs, he should have done better in places where there was greater opposition to gay marriage. Thus for each of the eleven states with a GMB on the November ballot, we test whether there is a relationship at the county level between the share of the vote garnered by the GMB and the change in Bush's share of the presidential vote from 2000 to 2004 (subtracting 2000 from 2004, so that a positive number means an increase). We focus on the change in support for Bush because it best tests the claim that the gay marriage bans led Bush to do better than he otherwise would have. However, the results are comparable when we examine Bush's share of the vote in the 2004 election.

When the change in Bush's vote share from 2000 to 2004 is regressed on the percentage of each county voting for the GMB, we find that in ten of the states there is a positive relationship, although not all of the relationships reach statistical significance, owing to the small number of counties in some states. Only in Montana does the relationship appear negative, but with a *p* value of 0.598, it is better described as no relationship (and, visually, appears as essentially a flat line). For the coefficients, standard errors, and *p* values for each state, see

15. Chaves (2004).

table 7-1 on page 126. Thus, with the exception of Montana, which was a lock for Bush anyway, Bush saw a bigger gain in his vote share where there was greater opposition to gay marriage. Even in states that Bush took handily in 2000, like Georgia, Oklahoma, and Utah, he was able to squeeze out even more support where the GMB did better. In particular, the slope of the regression line in Ohio is among the steepest. In other words, in Ohio there is a particularly strong relationship between the vote share of the GMB and the increase in Bush's support from 2000 to 2004.

These bivariate results are suggestive but leave the possibility that other factors explain the gain in Bush's vote share from 2000 to 2004 and that the effect of the GMBs is illusory. To see whether the relationship between the GMB vote share and Bush's vote gain is spurious, we turn to multivariate regression and control for a host of other county characteristics. Those control variables include the following:

—Percentage of college graduates,

—Mean family income (logged),

—Percentage of African Americans,

—Degree of urbanization,

—Change in the unemployment rate from October 2003 to October 2004, and

—Whether the county is in a presidential battleground state.

The key independent variable, of course, is the percentage voting for the gay marriage ban (percent GMB), coded 0 for all counties in states that did not have a GMB on the ballot. We also include a binary variable indicating whether the state had a GMB. The model accounts for the fact that counties within a state are more alike than counties in different states by clustering the standard errors by state.

Column 1 of table 7-2 displays the results. Even when controlling for these other potentially confounding variables, many of which are themselves related to Bush's gains, percent GMB is positive and statistically significant ($p < 0.05$). Its coefficient of 0.087 means that, for every percentage point of support for the GMB, on average Bush gained 0.087 percentage point of support in 2004 over his share of the vote in 2000. This may not sound like much, but it can add up to a sizable margin.

This model of county-level returns is evidence that support for the GMBs was positively related to Bush's gains in 2004, but it still leaves open the question of whether those gains came from evangelicals—the group targeted by the Bush campaign. To test whether evangelicals were, in fact, responsible for the upsurge in support for Bush, the model in column 2 of table 7-2 includes

Table 7-2. Change in Bush's Vote Share: Results from Linear Regression[a]

Indicator	Model 1	Model 2 with percent evangelical
Percent GMB	0.087***	0.039
	(0.030)	(0.032)
Percent evangelical	. . .	0.056***
		(1.343)
Percent college graduates	−0.249***	−0.225***
	(0.026)	(0.021)
Mean family income	0.066**	0.078***
	(0.029)	(0.026)
Percent African American	−0.012	−0.020
	(0.012)	(0.013)
Percent urban	0.024***	0.023***
	(0.024)	(0.004)
Unemployment rate, October 2004	−0.152***	−0.116**
	(0.053)	(0.056)
Change in unemployment rate	−0.151	−0.063
	(0.097)	(0.087)
GMB state	−6.689***	−3.359
	(2.026)	(2.193)
Constant	4.414***	2.301*
	(1.286)	(1.180)
Number of observations	3,220	3,220
R^2	0.28	0.28

Source: Authors' calculations based on data from the respective secretary of states' offices and the U.S. Census Bureau.
. . . Not applicable.
* $p < 0.10$.
** $p < 0.05$.
*** $p < 0.01$.
a. Numbers in parentheses are robust standard errors, with clustering by state.

the percentage of evangelicals in each county.[16] If Bush's gain in vote share is due to increased support among evangelicals who also voted in favor of the GMB, we should find two pieces of evidence. First, the coefficient for percent evangelicals should be positive (and statistically significant). Second, the impact of percent GMB should be wiped out.

Both pieces of evidence are observed. The percentage of evangelicals in a county is positively related to Bush's gain in vote share—for every percentage point of the evangelical share of a county's population, Bush gained 0.056 percentage point of the vote. In a county with the average percentage of evangelicals among the GMB states (28 percent), this translates into a gain of roughly

16. For the specific denominations classified as evangelical Protestant, consult the American Religion Data Archive (www.thearda.com), which relies on a denominational classification system that parallels the one used by John Green and his coauthors in chapter 2 and by Geoffrey Layman and Laura Hussey in chapter 10 of this volume. See also Steensland and others (2000).

1.6 percentage points. In a county with 50 percent evangelicals, it means a boost of just under 3 percentage points. Given the close margin of the 2004 contest, these are meaningful gains. While percent evangelicals has a positive and significant impact on Bush's vote share, it also soaks up the impact of percent GMB. The coefficient for percent GMB drops to 0.039, about the same size as its standard error (0.032); it is thus statistically insignificant.

In sum, while we do not have the proverbial smoking gun, there is probative evidence that the more votes garnered by a ballot initiative to ban gay marriage, the more votes Bush gained over his total in 2000. Furthermore, those gains appear to have come largely from evangelicals.

We acknowledge that aggregate data are always subject to the ecological fallacy, whereby aggregate-level patterns obscure individual-level relationships.[17] In this case, however, we have confidence in the inference that evangelicals were voting for both the GMB and Bush. As noted, the mobilization of evangelicals was a publicly stated objective of the Bush campaign, while evidence from direct mail shows that evangelicals were more likely to receive mail that mentioned gay marriage as an issue. Furthermore, individual-level analysis by Todd Donovan and his colleagues shows that voters in states with a GMB on the ballot were more likely to identify same-sex marriage as an important issue and that, where people were thinking about gay marriage, Bush picked up votes.[18] While the Donovan study does not include religious affiliation in its analysis, the intensity with which evangelicals oppose gay marriage suggests that they were especially amenable to prioritizing the issue.

Fortunately, we can employ individual-level data to test these aggregate-level results by drawing on data from the 2004 Election Panel Study (2004 EPS), collected as a collaborative project between the Center for the Study of Elections and Democracy at Brigham Young University and the Wisconsin Advertising Project at the University of Wisconsin. The sample design includes an oversample of voters in the states that had the most competitive presidential and senatorial contests, while still including enough respondents in the remaining states so that inferences can be drawn about the national population.[19]

Recall the earlier point that winning an election requires a candidate both to persuade and to mobilize. We thus test for both effects. In other words, we

---

17. King (1997); Robinson (1950)
18. Donovan and others (2005).
19. The "battleground" states that were oversampled were Arkansas, Arizona, Colorado, Florida, Iowa, Louisiana, Maine, Michigan, Minnesota, Missouri, New Hampshire, New Mexico, Nevada, Ohio, Oregon, Pennsylvania, Washington, Wisconsin, and West Virginia.

ask first whether the gay marriage referenda affected the choices voters made and then whether they increased turnout. Vote choice is modeled with a binary dependent variable: a vote for Bush is coded as 1, and a vote for anyone else is coded as 0.[20] To test whether opposition to gay marriage helped Bush more in states with a GMB, we have created an interaction between evangelicals and residence in a state with a gay marriage ban on the ballot (evangelical * GMB state).[21] In operational terms, if gay marriage opponents were more likely to vote for Bush in states with a GMB on the ballot, this interaction will be positive. Because American evangelicalism spans multiple denominations and includes many people with no denominational affiliation at all, previous research has developed different analytical strategies to identify evangelicals. Our method relies on respondents' self-report of whether they consider themselves to be a born-again or evangelical Christian, similar to the technique employed by Christian Smith in his seminal book *American Evangelicalism: Embattled and Thriving.*[22] Because of sharp social and political differences between white and African American Protestants, we combine this question about being born again and one about racial identification to isolate white evangelical Protestants. An alternative method of identifying evangelicals entails classifying people on the basis of their denominational affiliation.[23] The denominational affiliation method has much to recommend it but is not available for the EPS since the survey did not include a detailed set of denominations. Since previous research has generally found the denominational system to have more analytical leverage than a question about being a born-again or evangelical Christian, we assume that any inferences we draw about evangelicals would be stronger if we could identify evangelicals by their denominational affiliation. Similarly, the EPS did not ask respondents about their frequency of church attendance (or any other measure of religious participation, devotion, or orthodoxy). Owing to the "devotional divide" within the American electorate, this is lamentable.[24]

20. 2.9 percent of EPS respondents reported voting for a candidate other than Bush or Kerry. They are coded as 0.

21. It is not clear whether the two states with gay marriage bans on the ballot prior to the November election—Louisiana and Missouri—should be considered GMB states for the purposes of this analysis. We have opted to classify as GMB states only the eleven states with gay marriage measures on the November ballot, but when the models are reestimated with Louisiana and Missouri classified as GMB states, the results are substantively identical.

22. Smith (1998).

23. Kellstedt and others (1996); Steensland and others (2000).

24. Kohut and others (2000).

The model also contains a number of control variables, to ensure that we do not conflate any gains among evangelicals with other factors influencing the vote. At the state level, we account for whether the respondent lives in a battleground state, since that is where presidential campaigns concentrate their resources. We also account for southern states, as this is the region with the highest concentration of evangelicals and social conservatism more generally. At the individual level, we control for education level, gender, race (African American), Hispanic ethnicity, and age.[25] Additionally, we include a measure of whether the respondent opposes gay marriage[26] and another indicating that George W. Bush "shares my values."[27] Including both enables us to separate the impact of opposition to gay marriage from a more general affinity for Bush's social conservatism and to distinguish both from evangelicalism. We also control for the degree to which the respondent was the subject of persuasion attempts with an index of political mobilization[28] and for partisanship with a binary measure of whether the respondent is a strong Republican. Given that evangelicals have increasingly found a home in the Republican Party, including partisanship in the model is a substantial hurdle to clear. The estimator is probit analysis, since the dependent variable is dichotomous. We estimate robust standard errors and allow for clustering by state, since variance is likely less within a state than between states. The data have been weighted to reflect U.S. population demographics and to account for the complex sample design.[29]

As shown in column 1 of table 7-3, notwithstanding the other influences of the vote reflected in the model, evangelicals were more likely to vote for

25. Coded as two dummy variables for people under thirty and those over sixty.

26. Opponents of gay marriage are identified as people who, when asked a close-ended question about their opinion on gay marriage, chose "There should be no legal recognition of gay marriage" (against gay marriage).

27. "Think of George W. Bush. In your opinion, does the phrase 'shares my values' describe George W. Bush extremely well, quite well, not too well, not well at all?" Respondents were also asked about other phrases, including "cares about people like me," "is a strong leader," "changes his mind too often," "does not tell the truth," "will keep America safe."

28. This is an additive index of responses to the following question: "Now we have a series of questions about any contact you may have had during the last week of the election from the two parties or campaign organizations on behalf of any candidate. Please tell us whether you were contacted in this way during the last week of the campaign. Did you: Receive a letter or mail piece from a campaign? Receive a request to donate money to a campaign? Have a face-to-face conversation or contact with someone from a campaign? Receive a phone call from a campaign? Receive an e-mail from a campaign; Hear a radio ad from a campaign?"

29. For more details regarding the sample design and post-stratification weighting, see csp.polisci.wisc.edu/BYU_UW/sampling.asp [December 2006].

Table 7-3. Vote Choice and Turnout in the 2004 Election: Probit Results[a]

Indicator	Vote for Bush	Vote for Bush (with weak Republicans)	Turnout
Evangelical*GMB state	0.473**	0.290	0.777*
	(0.236)	(0.280)	(0.428)
Strong Republican	1.153***	1.415***	...
	(0.207)	(0.219)	
Weak Republican	...	0.992***	...
		(0.197)	
Strong partisan	...	...	0.430*
			(0.239)
Evangelical	0.063	0.079	0.295
	(0.152)	(0.160)	(0.227)
GMB state	−0.284	−0.205	−0.280
	(0.216)	(0.234)	(0.220)
Against gay marriage	0.062	0.015	−0.278
	(0.131)	(0.137)	(0.211)
"Bush shares my values"	1.191***	1.107***	0.143
	(0.080)	(0.082)	(0.092)
Mobilization index	0.020	0.0276	0.426***
	(0.046)	(0.044)	(0.077)
Education	−0.017	−0.0170	0.086*
	(0.037)	(0.037)	(0.054)
Female	0.067	0.096	−0.497**
	(0.130)	(0.136)	(0.186)
African American	−1.150***	−0.978***	0.533*
	(0.300)	(0.342)	(0.296)
Hispanic	−0.157	−0.100	−0.376
	(0.342)	(0.314)	(0.239)
Married	0.088	0.028	−0.064
	(0.141)	(0.146)	(0.163)
Under 30	0.073	−0.021	−0.119
	(0.255)	(0.260)	(0.249)
Over 60	−0.284**	−0.271**	0.464***
	(0.135)	(0.138)	(0.157)
Battleground state	−0.181	−0.168	−0.002
	(0.160)	(0.175)	(0.179)
South	0.031	0.042	0.208
	(0.199)	(0.231)	(0.156)
Constant	−2.973***	−2.994***	−0.396
	(0.353)	(0.383)	(0.387)
Pseudo R^2	0.60	0.63	0.24
Observations	1,234	1,234	1,339

Source: Authors' calculations based on the 2004 Election Panel Study.
... Not applicable.
* $p < 0.10$.
** $p < 0.05$.
*** $p < 0.01$.
a. Numbers in parentheses are robust standard errors.

Bush in states with a gay marriage ban on the ballot (that is, the interaction between evangelical and GMB state is positive and statistically significant). When all other variables are held constant at their mean, evangelicals were roughly 7 percentage points more likely to vote for Bush in states where a GMB appeared on the ballot.

Column 2 of table 7-3 suggests the source of those votes. Recall that, to control for partisanship, the first model includes a measure of whether the respondent is a strong Republican. In other words, the "extra" evangelicals who were persuaded to vote for Bush in GMB states are not disproportionately strong Republicans. Given that the 2004 election was so polarized, this is not surprising—strong Republicans essentially voted monolithically for Bush. A more plausible hypothesis is that Bush picked up votes from evangelicals who were inclined to vote for him but needed a push, precisely the profile of the evangelicals Rove said the Bush campaign needed to win in 2004. Column 2 adds a control for weak Republicans, who are GOP supporters but lack the intensity of people who identify strongly as Republicans. Upon controlling for weak Republicans, the coefficient for evangelical * GMB state drops considerably in magnitude (from 0.473 to 0.290) and slides far past any conventional standard for statistical significance ($p = 0.30$). To put this more intuitively: Bush's evangelical gains in GMB states came from weakly attached Republicans.

Gay marriage primed evangelicals to support Bush once at the polls, but did it spur them to be at the polls in the first place? Rove's stated modus operandi was less about persuasion than mobilization—maximizing turnout among the 4 million missing evangelicals in 2000. Is there evidence that turnout among evangelicals was higher in GMB states? To test whether this was so, column 3 of table 7-3 displays a model of voter turnout. The model of the mobilization hypothesis mirrors the test of persuasion, only with a binary dependent variable measuring whether the respondent reported turning out to vote (probit is again used as the estimator).[30] The control variables are identical to those used in the persuasion models, with one exception. We have created a dummy variable indicating whether the respondent is a strong partisan on either side of the political spectrum (that is, either a strong Republican or a strong Democrat), since previous research has shown that it is the strength and not the direction of partisanship that affects turnout.[31]

---

30. "In talking to people about the elections, we often find that a lot of people were not able to vote because they weren't registered, they were sick, or they just didn't have time. How about you? Did you vote in the elections this November?"

31. Verba, Schlozman, and Brady (1995).

The model shows that, even in the high-turnout election of 2004, evangelicals in GMB states were more likely to show up at the polls (evangelical * GMB state is positive and significant, $p = 0.069$).[32] The substantive impact was modest, as the increase was roughly 2.5 percentage points but, when coupled with the generally high level of support for Bush within the evangelical community and the fact that evangelicals spurred to vote for a gay marriage ban were likely to support Bush as well, the bulk of this boost in turnout would have redounded to Bush's benefit.

Thus concludes the evidence uncovered in the investigation of the role of gay marriage in the 2004 election. Before we render a verdict, a brief summation of the evidence is in order. First, within the counties of the GMB states, Bush's vote gains from 2000 to 2004 were closely related to the share of the vote taken by the GMB. Furthermore, those gains came largely from evangelicals, the very group that Karl Rove singled out as in need of greater-than-usual courting. Individual-level data from the 2004 EPS, in turn, support these inferences and provide the detail missing in aggregate analysis. Evangelicals were persuaded to vote for Bush in states with a GMB on the ballot, with the increase coming from weak Republicans—evangelicals who identify with the GOP, but not strongly. Fulfilling Rove's stated objective of bringing more evangelicals to the polls in 2004, turnout among evangelicals in GMB states was up—not by a lot, but perhaps by enough.

The Verdict

We have laid out the evidence in favor of the claim that ballot initiatives to ban gay marriage helped George W. Bush to pick up votes in 2004 and that those votes came largely from evangelicals. Bush's campaign had the *motive* to target evangelicals in order to shore up the GOP base, the *opportunity* to do so because the issue of gay marriage thrust itself on the issue agenda in early 2004, and the *means* to capitalize on the issue without alienating socially moderate voters. This is not merely a circumstantial case, though, as the forensic evidence is consistent with the claim that the GMBs boosted support for Bush among evangelicals.

Even if one is convinced that the GMBs did win Bush support from evangelicals, many will want to know whether these gains were sufficient to tip the election in Bush's favor. In a close election, isolating a single element of the

32. Two-tailed test. Since we have a directional hypothesis, we could defensibly use a one-tailed test, which would cut the p value in half.

election as decisive is a fool's errand, as one can point to almost any group as *the* determinative factor. Political strategists do not think in terms of mono-causal explanations for an election victory, and neither should we. Elections are won by amassing a coalition, consisting of different groups who are attracted to a candidate for different reasons. Gay marriage mattered, but so did many other issues. In 2004 evangelicals were squarely at the heart of George W. Bush's coalition—above and beyond their already high level of support for him in 2000—and the evidence supports the conclusion that many cast their ballot for Bush because of his opposition to gay marriage. Whether the reverse coattail effect was enough to sway the election is the wrong question. It is better to ask whether it, among other factors like concern over terrorism, allowed Bush to improve on his performance at the polls in 2000. The answer to that question is clearly yes.

In the case of George W. Bush's reelection, did gay marriage do it? The best available evidence says yes, but it did not act alone.

Stem Cell Research

Barbara Norrander and Jan Norrander

At the 2004 Democratic convention, Ron Reagan, the son of the former president, took the podium to call for increased federal funding for stem cell research. Nancy Reagan also publicly supported stem cell research in the hope that some day this research could help to cure the Alzheimer's disease that had stricken her husband. Meanwhile in California, Republican governor Arnold Schwarzenegger supported Proposition 71, which would provide $3 billion in state aid for stem cell research. Yet despite support from some prominent Republicans, President George W. Bush generally opposed stem cell research due to ethical concerns over the destruction of human embryos. In August 2001 he had limited federal funding for such research to the existing sixty cell lines. In contrast, Democratic presidential nominee John Kerry promised a four-fold increase in federal funding.

The question remained whether stem cell research would become a decisive issue in the 2004 election. Various reasons existed to suspect that it would not. Voters were probably less aware of this issue than of more long-standing or common issues, such as the state of the economy. Voters also were receiving mixed signals as to the partisan content of the issue. On the one hand, voters' opinions on the stem cell issue might overlap with other moral issues, such as abortion, causing stem cell opinions to supplement, but not change, existing patterns of political preferences. On the other hand, stem cell research was a debated topic during the campaign, and positions on the issue might not line up directly with attitudes on other moral issues.

In investigating these questions, the chapter proceeds as follows. We begin with a brief overview of the science behind stem cell research and then turn to an analysis of whether opinions on stem cells had any impact on the 2004 presidential vote. We conclude with a discussion of whether stem cell research is likely to become the "new abortion"—a long-standing issue that divides the parties.

The Science of Stem Cell Research

The politics of stem cell research plays out against a backdrop of the science of stem cells.[1] Fully understanding the politics, therefore, requires a familiarity with the science involved. We begin with a brief "backgrounder" on what scientists know about stem cells, which, in turn, explains why they hold such promise and why they engender such controversy.

The cells that constitute the various tissues and organs of the body have specific structures and functions. For example, cardiac muscle cells have little structural or functional similarity to liver cells. The cells that carry out the functions of our tissues and organs are said to be specialized, differentiated cells. They express only a specific subset of their genes, resulting in cells that are tailor-made to carry out the tasks required for the normal functioning of the tissue or organ in which they reside. Most functional cells of the body are terminally differentiated and, as such, are not normally capable of becoming a different type of cell. For example, a cardiac muscle cell does not decide one day to become a liver cell.

Stem cells are unspecialized, undifferentiated cells that are capable of dividing and therefore of renewing themselves. They are also capable of differentiating to form various specialized types of cells. All specialized cells arise from the differentiation of stem cells. Which specialized cell type a stem cell will ultimately become depends on the physiological conditions to which it is exposed. Exposure to these factors causes a stem cell to "commit" to becoming a specialized cell type.

Human stem cells can be grown in vitro (outside a living organism) and induced to differentiate into specialized cell types. Potential uses for this

1. For some in-depth background on this research, see National Institutes of Health, *Stem Cell Basics*, 2006 (http://stemcells.nih.gov/info/basics).

technology include studies aimed at better understanding the molecular processes involved in the division, differentiation, and development of cells—critical processes that sometimes go awry. Cancer cells, for example, result from uncontrolled, abnormal division of cells, and many birth defects arise from errors occurring early in development. Stem cells could also be used to provide specialized cell types for drug and toxicity testing. But the most widely publicized application is their potential use in cell-based therapies. Some specialized cells, such as cardiac muscle cells, are incapable of division. As a result, cardiac muscle damaged or lost due to myocardial infarction is never replaced. Newly formed cardiac muscle cells, produced in vitro or in vivo (inside a living organism) from stem cells, could potentially be used to repair such tissue damage. Other possible targets of cell-based therapies include Parkinson's disease, diabetes, and paralysis due to spinal cord injuries. An obstacle that will have to be overcome is the need to ensure that the transplanted cells survive and are not attacked by the immune system. In addition, the transplanted cells must become properly incorporated into the patient's tissues and be able to function normally.

There are three classes of stem cells: totipotent, pluripotent, and multipotent. A totipotent stem cell has the ability to give rise to all the cell types; an example of a totipotent stem cell is a fertilized egg. Pluripotent stem cells can give rise to all cell types except those required to develop a fetus; embryonic stem cells are pluripotent. Multipotent stem cells can give rise to some, but not all, cell types in the body; adult stem cells are thought to be multipotent.

Most controversy arises from the use of embryonic stem cells. Embryonic stem cells are isolated from embryos arising from human eggs that have undergone in vitro fertilization as part of fertility treatments. Since many more embryos typically result from this procedure than are required for implantation, unused embryos may be donated for research purposes with the informed consent of the egg and sperm donors. Four to five days after fertilization, cells can be removed from the embryos and grown in laboratory culture dishes.

Under specific conditions, human embryonic stem cells proliferate but remain undifferentiated in vitro. If these conditions are not maintained, the stem cells will spontaneously differentiate into specialized cell types. To make embryonic stem cells useful for cell-based therapies, it is necessary to control which specialized cell type they will form, a process called directed differentiation. Directed differentiation can be achieved by adding growth factors and other substances into the culture medium.

Adult stem cells are undifferentiated cells present in low numbers in many adult tissues and organs. When specialized cells of an organ are lost or damaged, the adult stem cells present in that organ will divide and differentiate into specialized cells. Thus adult stem cells are the source for the renewal of specialized adult cells. Adult stem cells are generally thought to be multipotent and only differentiate into the cell types present in the tissue where they reside. To date, no pluripotent adult stem cells have been identified. However, recent experiments have suggested that some of the adult stem cells from one tissue may be able to differentiate into specialized cells of a different tissue, a process known as transdifferentiation or plasticity. Plasticity of adult stem cells would greatly increase their usefulness in cell-based therapies.

Blood-forming (hematopoietic) adult stem cells, isolated from the bone marrow, are currently the only stem cells routinely used in the treatment of disease. These cells have been used to treat diseases such as leukemia and lymphoma. There is some evidence to support the efficacy of adult stem cells in the treatment of other human diseases, including diabetes and kidney cancer, but these studies are in the early stages.

While the use of adult stem cells is less controversial than the use of embryonic stem cells, some aspects of adult stem cells may make them less valuable. The process of isolating and purifying adult stem cells is complicated by the fact that they are only present in tissues in very small quantities. There is evidence to suggest that some may not proliferate in vitro as readily as embryonic stem cells and therefore may not provide the numbers necessary for many therapeutic uses. There is also the possibility that the DNA of these "older" cells will contain mutations. One advantage to using adult stem cells is the potential for the donor also to be the recipient of the specialized cell type, eliminating the risk of transplant rejection.

Whether embryonic or adult stem cells will be the most useful for research and therapeutic applications will ultimately be determined by fostering both lines of inquiry. Federal funds for human embryonic stem cell research have only been available since August 9, 2001, and this funding is limited to the use of cell lines developed prior to that date. Thus the development of new lines of embryonic stem cells requires private funding or funding by individual states. The use of private funds for embryonic stem cell research limits the capacity for governmental oversight, and the restrictions on federal funding run the risk of losing both the economic benefits resulting from new discoveries and the presence of top researchers, who may choose to pursue their work in countries with more flexible policies.

The Political Debate over Stem Cell Research

The dominant political argument in support of further funding for stem cell research is the potential to cure diseases such as Alzheimer's and Parkinson's as well as conditions such as spinal cord injuries. Celebrities making the case for additional funding have included Christopher Reeve, who was paralyzed after falling from a horse in 1995, and Michael J. Fox, who suffers from Parkinson's disease. Advocates argue that more than 100 million Americans could benefit, as stem cell research could produce therapies for combating heart disease, autoimmune disease, diabetes, osteoporosis, cancer, and severe burns.[2] While recognizing the existence of an ethical concern, supporters of stem cell research argue for a balance between concerns over potential life and cures for human disease. They also note that in nature many embryos do not develop into fetuses.[3]

While it is not a dominant argument among the general public, some state officials include an economic component to their argument for government funding of stem cell research. Arnold Schwarzenegger supported Proposition 71 on this basis.[4] New Jersey provided $6.5 million in state funds as seed money for stem cell research, expecting to benefit from an additional $20 million in grants. Additionally, some American scientists fear that, without increased funding for stem cell research, they will not remain competitive with scientists in other countries.

Political opposition to stem cell research focuses on the destruction of potential life, the view that therapeutic cloning will lead to reproductive cloning, and the link between stem cell research and pro-life attitudes toward abortion. Opponents to stem cell research also challenge the potential benefits of stem cell research, arguing that advocates inflate the likelihood that such research will produce the desired medical benefits. Still other opponents argue that stem cell research could endanger and exploit women, with risks involved in the removal of eggs and concerns that poor women would be encouraged to sell their eggs.

Ethical concerns over the destruction of potential human life, however, are the most frequently cited reasons for opposition to stem cell research. In his 2001 prime-time television address, President Bush expressed such

---

2. The 100 million figure, used by Kerry in his campaign, came from the Coalition for the Advancement of Medical Research. They computed the figure based on the number of Americans suffering from a host of diseases and chronic conditions (Rosenbaum 2004).

3. Hansen (2004).

4. Ritter (2004); Hansen (2004).

concerns: "Research on embryonic stem cells raises profound ethical concerns, because extracting the stem cell destroys the embryo and thus destroys its potential for life."[5] Arguments against stem cell research often are intertwined with concerns over abortion. Both are elements of a "culture of life" advocacy.

Religious groups have adopted various positions on the stem cell issue. Evangelical Christian and Catholic Church leaders oppose stem cell research on ethical grounds. The Catholic Church argues that an embryo from the moment of fertilization is a human life that must be protected.[6] Many evangelical leaders were upset with President Bush for supporting research on existing stem cell lines.[7] Other denominations, such as the Episcopal Church, support stem cell research using donated embryos that otherwise would be discarded after in vitro fertilization efforts.[8] With denominations taking different stances on the issue, highly religious individuals may be divided in their support of or opposition to stem cell research.

Prior to the 2004 election, the public showed varying levels of attention to the stem cell debate and grasp of some of the major political arguments.[9] A slim majority (51 percent) of respondents to a 2001 Kaiser poll knew that the destruction of human embryos is a major source of the controversy. In that year, the public appeared to understand the complexity of balancing ethical concerns with medical necessity, with about one-third of respondents in a Gallup poll viewing stem cell research as morally wrong but necessary, another third not viewing the research as morally wrong, and one in five viewing such research as morally wrong and unnecessary. Public support for stem cell research varies with the source of the embryos, with higher support given when a survey question indicates surplus embryos from fertility clinics as the source. While the viewpoints of Americans on therapeutic cloning are variable and complex, their opinions on reproductive cloning are consistent and negative. Overwhelming majorities reject cloning for human reproduction.

The political debate over abortion has been prominent on the American political agenda for nearly four decades. Public attitudes on abortion have influenced support for presidential candidates.[10] Moreover, abortion attitudes have reshaped voters' core political identities. In a process known as

5. Quoted from White House, Office of the Press Secretary (2001).
6. Pontifical Academy for Life (2000).
7. Masci (2001).
8. Episcopal Church (2003).
9. Nisbet (2004).
10. Abramowitz (1995).

issue evolution, a significant number of voters have realigned their partisan preferences to match their attitude toward abortion.[11] Religion plays a role in the public's attitudes on abortion. Catholics and evangelical Protestants hold more conservative positions than mainline Protestants. Jews and those with no religious preferences are the most liberal in their abortion attitudes.

Stem cell attitudes are linked strongly with abortion attitudes, but the two are not identical.[12] Moreover, for most Americans the abortion issue provokes a complex set of opinions that lead many Americans to support abortion in certain circumstances and not in others. Rather than being pro-choice or pro-life, many Americans fall in between. Such nuances in abortion attitudes leave room for other moral issues, such as stem cell research, to play a role in influencing electoral choices.

Stem Cell Research and Voters in the 2004 Presidential Election

As described in earlier chapters, the media interpreted the 2004 presidential election exit polls as indicating that moral issues dominated voters' concerns. As Sunshine Hillygus shows in chapter 4, however, moral values were not at the top of most voters' lists of concerns. This includes stem cell research, which was not a priority for many voters at all.

In a preelection, October 2004, Pew Research Center poll, respondents were asked how important a variety of issues would be to their presidential vote. Table 8-1 lists the percentage of respondents who answered "very important" for each issue. The economy, terrorism, education, Iraq, and health care were judged to be the most important issues. Moral values ranked eighth out of sixteen issues. Stem cell research had the second lowest ranking, with 43 percent responding that this issue would be very important to their vote choice. However, stem cell research did outrank the other widely debated moral issue of 2004: gay marriage. In a postelection Pew Research Center survey, respondents were asked an open-ended question: "What *one* issue mattered most to you in deciding how you voted for president?" Table 8-1 lists these results and shows that, once again, the Iraq war and the economy topped the list of concerns. Moral values fell in a second tier of concerns, along with terrorism and candidate honesty. Only 1 percent of respondents mentioned stem cell research.[13]

11. Adams (1997).
12. Nisbet (2005).
13. For the preelection survey report and questionnaire, see Pew Research Center (2004c); for the postelection survey, see Pew Research Center (2004d).

Table 8-1. Importance of Various Issues to the 2004 Presidential Vote

Preelection, sequential questions		Postelection, open-ended	
Issue	Percent considering the issue very important	Issue	Percent mentioning the issue
Economy	78	Iraq	27
Terrorism	77	Economy, jobs	14
Jobs	76	Moral values	9
Education	75	Terrorism	9
Iraq	74	Honesty	5
Health care	73	Health care	3
Social Security	65	Abortion	3
Moral values	63	Direction of country	2
Taxes	59	Candidate religion	2
Budget deficit	57	Leadership	2
Energy	54	Foreign policy	2
Environment	53	Gay marriage	2
Abortion	47	Status quo	2
Gun control	45	Social Security	1
Stem cell research	43	Taxes	1
Gay marriage	32	Environment	1
		Stem cell	1
		Supreme Court	1
		Gun control	1
		Education	1

Source: Pew Research Center, October 20, 2004, and November 11, 2004, surveys.

Similar results were found in other surveys. An October 2004 *Newsweek* poll found 14 percent indicating that stem cell research would be a very important determinant of their presidential vote. A Kaiser Foundation poll from October 2004 indicated that stem cell research was not even the most frequently cited medical concern for the American electorate. While almost one-third of respondents were extremely concerned about the cost of health care, lack of health insurance, or the cost of prescription drugs, only 17 percent cited stem cell research as extremely important to their voting decision.[14]

Notwithstanding the public's relative lack of attention to the issue of stem cell research, even a small number of voters who care passionately about an issue can have a disproportionate influence in a razor-thin election, as noted in several other chapters in this volume. It is thus worth digging deeper to see if attitudes on stem cells had an impact on the 2004 presidential vote.

Even though stem cell research was not cited as a dominant issue in the 2004 presidential election, the public's awareness of the positions of the two

14. Blendon and others (2005).

presidential candidates was fairly high. In an October 2004 Pew Research Center poll, 59 percent identified Kerry as favoring federal funding for stem cell research, while 8 percent named Bush, 11 percent said both or neither, and 22 percent indicated that they did not know.[15] Across four different polls, on average, half the public selected Kerry as better able to handle the issue of stem cell research, while one-third named Bush.[16] Stem cell research was an issue that most American voters correctly identified as being more strongly supported by Kerry and an issue on which more Americans favored Kerry over Bush. Thus stem cell research could be an issue that advantaged Kerry in the 2004 presidential election.

Neither the National Election Pool national exit poll nor the American National Election Survey included a stem cell question in the 2004 questionnaire. Thus we use data from an August 2004 Pew Research Center poll to judge the influence of this issue on presidential preferences.[17] (This is the Pew survey closest to the election that elicited respondents' position on the stem cell issue.) The poll asked respondents, "All in all, which is more important: conducting stem cell research that might result in new medical cures [OR] not destroying the potential life of human embryos involved in this research." Overall, 61 percent of respondents selected the option of conducting research for medical cures, while 40 percent selected the option of not destroying potential human life.

Table 8-2 shows how a variety of measures of religion and religiosity influenced public attitudes on stem cell research. Jews were the most supportive of stem cell research for potential medical cures. Those with no religion also heavily supported using stem cells for medical research. Protestants were divided into two categories based on their responses to a second survey question asking whether they considered themselves to have been "born again." Protestants indicating having been born again were the most conservative on the stem cell issue, while other Protestants supported stem cell research for medical progress. Catholics more closely resembled these other Protestants than the more conservative Protestants, despite the Vatican's opposition to stem cell research. Mormons were the group closest to born-again Protestants in their opposition to stem cell research.

Religiosity also influenced the public's viewpoint on stem cell research. Attendance at religious services was associated with support for or opposition to stem cell research. Only 28 percent of those who attend religious services

15. Pew Research Center (2004b).

16. The polls were *Newsweek,* July 31, 2004; ABC News/*Washington Post,* August 30, 2004; ABC News, October 8, 2004; and CNN/*USA Today*/Gallup Poll, October 11, 2004.

17. Pew Research Center (2004a).

Table 8-2. Percent Supporting Stem Cell Research, by Denomination and Religious Attendance

A. Denomination

Denomination[a]	Percent supporting stem cell research	Number of cases
Jew	82	45
No religion	79	316
Other religion	76	63
Other Protestant	72	682
Catholic	61	676
Mormon	51	63
Born-again Protestant	41	903

a. $F = 14.42$; $p < 0.01$.

B. Level of attendance

Level of attendance[a]	Percent supporting stem cell research	Number of cases
Never	78	315
Seldom	79	415
A few times a year	69	582
Once or twice a month	64	425
Once a week	50	721
More than once a week	29	386

a. $F = 23.92$; $p < 0.01$.

C. Religious denomination and attendance

Religious attendance	Born-again Protestant	Other Protestant	Catholic
Never or seldom	53	84	76
Yearly or monthly	53	72	68
Once a week	42	64	47
More than once a week	26	46	32
Difference between those attending more than once a week and those attending never or seldom	27	38	44
F	5.48	4.30	6.51
Significance	0.00	0.01	0.00
Number of observations	393	333	298

Source: Pew Research Center, August 2004 survey.

more than once a week supported stem cell research, compared to more than three-quarters of those who never or infrequently attend services. Those who attend religious services weekly were equally divided on the issue, with half supporting and half opposing stem cell research.

The third component of table 8-2 combines denominational divisions and religious attendance. Religious attendance appears to have had the least influ-

ence among born-again Protestants, as this is the group for which we observe
the smallest difference (27 percentage points) in support for stem cell research
between those who attend religious services more than once a week and those
who never or seldom attend. The lesser influence of attendance on conservative Protestants' stem cell attitudes is derived, in part, from the finding that,
as a group, born-again Protestants were quite conservative in their opposition to stem cell research. In contrast, frequency of church attendance appears
to have been the most important for Catholics, with a difference in support
of stem cell research equal to 44 percentage points between the most frequent
and the least frequent church attendees.

Various other attitudes and characteristics were related to people's views
on stem cell research (results not shown). Those with higher levels of education and higher incomes were more supportive of stem cell research. No differences existed between men and woman or across different racial or ethnic
groups. Democrats and liberals were more likely to support stem cell research,
while Republicans and conservatives were more likely to oppose it. Attitudes
on stem cell research overlapped other moral issues, such as support for or
opposition to gay marriage. Finally, those who had heard more about the stem
cell issue were more likely to support research for medical purposes.

Table 8-3 provides results from logit analyses of presidential preferences,
using data from the same August 2004 survey. Opinions on stem cell research
are added, along with traditional demographic and attitudinal explanatory
variables. Various denominational categories are used as independent variables, with Catholic as the excluded category. Thus each denominational coefficient indicates whether adherents of the denomination differed significantly
from Catholics in their presidential vote. Religiosity is included by using the
survey question on worship service attendance. It also is possible that religious
and stem cell beliefs might interact. One might expect that highly religious
individuals who opposed stem cell research would have been strong supporters of President Bush's reelection. However, other highly religious individuals may have supported stem cell research and been led to support Kerry. Thus
model B in table 8-3 includes an interaction term between opinions on stem
cell research and religiosity.

The logit models are set up to predict a vote to reelect President Bush. Attitudinal variables are coded so that higher values indicate more conservative
or Republican positions. The economy variable runs from a low value for a
worsening economy to a high value for a better economy. Religiosity is coded
so that higher values indicate greater attendance. The stem cell research question has a higher code to indicate opposition.

Table 8-3. Explaining Presidential Candidate Preferences

Variable	Model A		Model B	
	Coefficient[a]	Significance level	Coefficient[a]	Significance level
Female	0.43	0.27	0.45	0.26
	(0.40)		(0.39)	
Black	−1.05	0.19	−1.16	0.16
	(0.80)		(0.82)	
Hispanic	−1.25*	0.10	−1.32*	0.09
	(0.77)		(0.78)	
Age	−0.01	0.30	−0.01	0.28
	(0.01)		(0.01)	
Education	−0.20	0.15	−0.21	0.14
	(0.14)		(0.14)	
Income	0.19*	0.06	0.19*	0.07
	(0.10)		(0.11)	
Veteran	0.56	0.26	0.62	0.20
	(0.50)		(0.48)	
Labor union	−1.24**	0.01	−1.23***	0.01
	(0.49)		(0.49)	
Partisanship	1.23***	0.00	1.26***	0.00
	(0.12)		(0.11)	
Ideology	−0.03	0.89	−0.09	0.72
	(0.25)		(0.25)	
Economy	0.36	0.22	0.39	0.18
	(0.29)		(0.29)	
Iraq	2.55***	0.00	2.47***	0.00
	(0.43)		(0.42)	
Gay marriage	0.70***	0.00	0.68***	0.00
	(0.22)		(0.23)	
Other religion	−0.74	0.36	−0.88	0.24
	(0.80)		(0.76)	
Jew	−0.47	0.45	−0.83	0.21
	(0.62)		(0.65)	
Born-again Protestant	−0.78	0.17	−0.77	0.15
	(0.56)		(0.54)	
Other Protestant	−0.39	0.44	−0.49	0.34
	(0.50)		(0.51)	
No religion	−0.34	0.67	−0.39	0.63
	(0.81)		(0.80)	
Mormon	−0.33	0.80	−0.24	0.86
	(1.29)		(1.35)	
Religiosity	0.06	0.66	−0.13	0.44
	(0.15)		(0.16)	
Stem cell	0.56	0.21	−1.25	0.24
	(0.45)		(1.07)	
Religiosity*stem cell	. . .	. . .	0.49*	0.08
			(0.28)	
Constant	−8.54***	0.00	−7.73***	0.00
	(1.15)		(1.16)	
Wald χ^2	238.33***	0.00	236.71***	0.00
Pseudo R^2	0.76		0.77	
Number of cases	857		857	

Source: Pew Research Center, August 2004 survey.
. . . Not applicable.
* $p < 0.10$.
** $p < 0.05$.
*** $p < 0.01$
a. Numbers in parentheses are standard errors.

As one would expect, partisanship and opinions on the Iraq war influenced preferences for the 2004 presidential candidates. Partisanship had a particularly strong effect: moving from a weak Democrat to a weak Republican changed the probability of voting for Bush by 0.59.[18] Moving from a strong Democrat to a strong Republican changed the probability of voting for Bush by 0.83. Switching from disapproval of the Iraq war to approval increased the probability of support for the president's reelection by 0.47. In addition, opinions on gay marriage played a role, although the effect is smaller, with a switch from strong approval to strong disapproval changing the probability of supporting Bush by 0.27. In general, demographic factors did not have independent effects on voters' choices, beyond what is subsumed under differences in issue position across groups. In an exception, union members were more likely to support Kerry.

None of the denominational categories is statistically significant. This means that none of these groups differed from Catholics in their support of President Bush's reelection. Stem cell beliefs and religiosity also did not have simple direct effects on the choice of presidential candidate. However, the effects of these two variables may be intertwined in an interaction effect. The effects of stem cell attitudes may depend on the level of religiosity and vice versa. The interaction term in model B suggests that such a relationship does exist, at least at the .10 percent significance level. Among those who favored stem cell research, as religiosity increases, support for Bush declined. Among those who opposed stem cell research, those who attend worship services more frequently were more likely to support Bush's reelection.

While denomination did not have a direct effect on voters' presidential preference, it is possible that the relationship between stem cell attitude and religiosity might vary across denominations. Given the public stance of the Catholic Church on stem cell research, as well as abortion, one might suspect that more observant Catholics would have been more likely to vote for Bush if they opposed

---

18. Changes in probabilities are calculated on the basis of model B, which includes the interaction component. The values of the independent variables were set as female, neither black nor Hispanic, neither a veteran nor a labor union member, high school graduate (three on a seven-point scale), income of $40,000 to $50,000 (five on a nine-point scale), independent (four on a seven-point scale), moderate (three on a five-point scale), "only fair" economy (two on a four-point scale), Iraq war was the "right decision" (versus "wrong decision"), and oppose gay marriage (three on a four-point scale). All the religious denomination dummy variables were set to 0, which makes the predictions based on a Catholic identity, attends religious services a few times a year (three on a six-point scale), favors stem cell research (0), and with the interaction term set to 0 (value for those who favor stem cell research). Probabilities were calculated through the use of CLARIFY (King, Tomz, and Wittenberg 2000; Tomz, Wittenberg, and King 2001).

stem cell research. However, for those Catholics who did not share the church's position on stem cell research, frequent church attendance could show that their position did not match that of the church or that of President Bush. This group of Catholics might be strong supporters of Kerry instead.

Table 8-4 examines the influence of religiosity, stem cell opinions, and other factors contributing to candidate preferences in the 2004 election for three major denominational groups. Among born-again Protestants, religiosity and stem cell opinions did not influence their candidate preferences. Born-again Protestants as a group were the most unified in opposition to stem cell research, with 59 percent opposed, compared to the national average of 40 percent. They also were the second strongest supporters of President Bush, behind Mormons. With a consensus among born-again Protestants on presidential support and stem cell research, little variation exists within the group to be revealed in a multivariate model. A model run without an interaction term also confirms no statistically significant effects for religiosity or stem cell opinions among born-again Protestants. Among other Protestants, religiosity had a significant effect on presidential preferences, but stem cell opinions (and any interaction between the two independent variables) had no influence.

It is among Catholics that stem cell opinions mattered (at the .10 percent significance level), but they did so through a relationship that is intertwined with religiosity. Figure 8-1 illustrates the effects of religiosity, stem cell opinions, and the interaction between the two for Catholics' choice of presidential candidate. Among those who accepted the church's doctrine on stem cell research—39 percent of Catholics—increasing attendance at religious services enhanced the probability that they supported President Bush's reelection. In contrast, those Catholics who disagreed with the church's position on stem cell research were more likely to vote for Kerry as their church attendance increases. Frequently attending Catholics who opposed the church's position on stem cell research may have developed a closer affinity with a fellow Catholic—Kerry—who also rejected the church's position.

Conclusions

Stem cell research was not the dominant issue of the 2004 elections. Traditional concerns over the economy and split public opinion over the course of the Iraq war were the most important short-term factors shaping the vote in these elections. The 2004 election, as was true for the 2000 election, was a highly partisan event. Democrats overwhelmingly voted for Kerry, and Republicans overwhelmingly voted for Bush. With partisanship, the Iraq war, and the

Table 8-4. Explaining Presidential Candidate Preferences across Three Types of Religious Denominations

Indicator	Born-again Protestant		Other Protestant		Catholic	
	Coefficient[a]	Significance	Coefficient[a]	Significance	Coefficient[a]	Significance
Female	2.46** (1.28)	0.05	0.55 (0.75)	0.46	-0.28 (0.87)	0.75
Black	-3.89** (1.72)	0.02	-2.50** (1.19)	0.04	2.33 (2.31)	0.31
Hispanic	0.79 (1.06)	0.46	-0.09 (0.93)	0.92	-1.72** (0.77)	0.03
Age	0.03 (0.03)	0.26	-0.05* (0.03)	0.07	-0.02 (0.03)	0.49
Education	0.22 (0.46)	0.63	-0.35 (0.27)	0.19	-0.18 (0.23)	0.45
Income	-0.08 (0.20)	0.69	0.02 (0.19)	0.90	0.41 (0.36)	0.25
Veteran	-1.56 (1.28)	0.22	-0.40 (0.70)	0.57	2.00** (0.89)	0.02
Labor union	-2.23 (1.37)	0.11	-3.44*** (0.86)	0.00	-0.84 (1.19)	0.48
Partisanship	2.21*** (0.55)	0.00	1.76*** (0.35)	0.00	1.83*** (0.62)	0.00

	(1)		(2)		(3)	
Ideology	−0.24	0.76	1.26	0.17	0.55	0.36
	(0.77)		(0.93)		(0.60)	
Economy	−0.57	0.49	1.44***	0.00	0.79	0.12
	(0.84)		(0.49)		(0.50)	
Iraq	6.01***	0.00	4.60***	0.00	2.50**	0.02
	(1.95)		(1.39)		(1.11)	
Gay marriage	0.94	0.17	0.16	0.78	1.09***	0.01
	(0.69)		(0.55)		(0.40)	
Religiosity	−0.03	0.95	0.82**	0.02	−1.07**	0.05
	(0.54)		(0.36)		(0.54)	
Stem cell research	−3.18	0.35	−2.80	0.40	−6.87*	0.07
	(3.43)		(3.31)		(3.76)	
Religiosity*stem cell	0.65	0.37	0.38	0.62	2.17*	0.09
	(0.73)		(0.78)		(1.29)	
Constant	−15.59***	0.01	−15.07***	0.00	−11.89***	0.00
	(5.53)		(4.05)		(4.14)	
Wald χ^2	34.63***	0.00	57.83***	0.00	59.48***	0.00
Pseudo R^2	0.86		0.84		0.81	
Number of cases	297		220		217	

Source: Pew Research Center, August 2004 survey.

* $p < 0.10$.

** $p < 0.05$.

*** $p < 0.01$.

a. Numbers in parentheses are standard errors.

Figure 8-1. Probability of Supporting Bush for Different Levels of Religiosity and Views on Stem Cell Research among Catholics

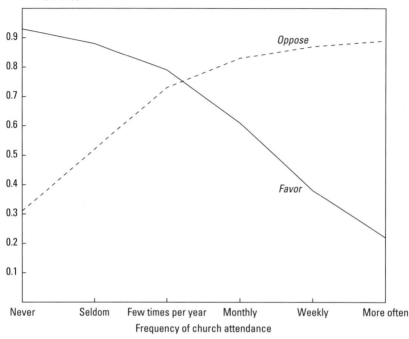

Source: Pew Research Center, August 2004 survey.

economy at the forefront of voters' decisionmaking, other issues vied for an also-ran spot. Yet positions on stem cell research do help to explain candidate preferences in the presidential contest.

Religious beliefs and practices are one explanation for voters' opinions on stem cell research. Not all voters follow the edict of their faith's religious leaders. In particular, Catholics were not generally much more opposed to stem cell research than other Christians. Born-again Protestants and Mormons were the most likely to oppose stem cell research. Jews and those with no religion were the most supportive. While Catholics as a group were not distinctive from other religious groups, such as mainline Protestants, divisions among Catholics made cultural issues decisive in their choice of presidential candidate. If a culture war did exist in the 2004 election, it was fought among Catholics. Born-again Protestants were firmly in the Republican camp, such that opinions on cultural issues did not have separate, identifiable influences on their vote choice. Mainline Protestants disagreed over cultural issues, with 72 percent favoring stem cell research but 66 percent opposing gay marriage. However, these cultural issues had little saliency among mainline Protestants, as neither of the cultural issues shaped their candidate preference. Among Catholics, however, with clear cues from the church hierarchy, both cultural issues mattered. Those who accepted the church's conservative position on these issues moved into the Republican camp, while Catholics in opposition to the church's position found an affinity with fellow Catholic John Kerry, who held positions similar to their own.

While stem cell research was not a dominant issue for most Americans in the 2004 presidential election, some, such as *Newsweek* columnist Jonathan Alter, expect the debate to play a more predominant role in future elections.[19] Alter argues that the issue will be framed as a "pro-cure movement," attracting the support of those who are stricken by the illnesses that have potential new therapies from stem cell research or who have relatives with such ailments. Stem cell research already is being debated at the state level. In 2005 fourteen state legislatures tackled the question of stem cell research, with approval of further spending the topic in some states and bans considered in others.[20]

Will stem cell research prove to be the "new abortion," an issue that sharply divides the electorate (or at least the most politically active members of the electorate) and, thus, Democratic and Republican presidential candidates? Thus far, stem cell research has proven to be a point of disagreement among many leading Republican presidential hopefuls. In the lead-up to the 2008 presidential primaries, potential Republican candidates have taken divergent positions on the issue. John McCain has changed his stated position from opposition to support of further research, while Mitt Romney has changed his position from support to opposition.[21] Therefore, in spite of its potential to take on the contours of the abortion issue, thus far stem cell research appears as likely to engender divisions within a party—particularly the Republican Party—as between the parties. Nonetheless, the fact that religious involvement is a dividing line on opinions about stem cell research—particularly among Catholics—suggests that stem cell research could become a new front in the "culture war." Such a development seems especially likely if advances in the science of stem cells continue to raise the issue's profile.

19. Alter (2005).
20. Associated Press (2005); Fineman and Lipper (2005).
21. Fineman and Lipper (2005); Greenberger and Phillips (2005).

Religious
Constituencies

The Changing Catholic Voter

Comparing Responses to John Kennedy in 1960 and John Kerry in 2004

J. Matthew Wilson

When John Fitzgerald Kennedy received the Democratic nomination for president in 1960, there was palpable excitement among America's Catholic community. Only one Catholic—Al Smith in 1928—had ever headed a major-party ticket, and his was a long-shot, ultimately unsuccessful candidacy on behalf of what was clearly the country's minority party. Kennedy, however, was seen as a much more viable candidate from what had become (Eisenhower's successes notwithstanding) the majority party in America. As such, he offered Catholic voters a real opportunity to see a fellow Catholic in the Oval Office. Catholic voters across the nation rallied to Kennedy's cause in overwhelming numbers, so much so that the perceived liability of his religion became an electoral asset, helping him to carry critical states like New York, Pennsylvania, and Illinois. According to one credible scholarly study, Catholic enthusiasm for the Kennedy campaign was sufficiently great that Kennedy's religion can be credited for a net gain of at least ten electoral votes.[1] In any event, American Catholics saw Kennedy's ultimate victory as a "triumph," a "breakthrough," a vindication of Catholicism as a legitimate American religion.[2]

1. Pool, Abelson, and Popkin (1965).
2. Byrnes (1991); Hennesey (1981); Prendergast (1999).

After Kennedy's assassination in 1963, it would be forty-one years before another Catholic would seek the presidency as the nominee of a major party. Despite the passage of time, in many ways John Forbes Kerry in 2004 was a strikingly similar candidate to John Kennedy in 1960. Both were Democratic senators from Massachusetts who had served with distinction in the military. Both were Catholics, although neither was particularly noted for his theological interests or personal piety.[3] Both were children of privilege and thus somewhat atypical reflections of the Catholic experience in America. Both faced a Protestant Republican opponent with little or no record of military service, and both chose a Protestant, Anglo Southerner as a running mate to balance their ticket. For the political analyst, this stunning range of similarities is a great boon, as it limits variation on some of the myriad factors that can explain voter reactions to a candidate's presidential bid.

Yet in one critical respect, the two candidacies were not at all similar: the way in which they were received by the Catholic electorate. The enthusiasm that greeted Kennedy's bid in 1960 was nowhere to be found in 2004. In fact, Kerry ultimately *lost* the Catholic vote to his Protestant opponent, George W. Bush. To be sure, some of the differences in Catholic responses to the two candidacies can be explained by factors other than religion: Kerry lacked Kennedy's charisma and decisiveness, Bush had the advantage of being an incumbent in wartime, and the Catholic electorate was more affluent and assimilated in 2004 than in 1960. Much more profoundly, however, the very nature of the relationship between religion and political choice, and even the nature of Catholic identity itself, had shifted over the intervening decades. The candidacies of Kennedy and Kerry, so similar in many superficial respects, serve to bookend and highlight this fundamental change.

In this essay, I use the radically different responses of American Catholics to two of "their own" as a vehicle for exploring the changing role of religion as a force in American politics. Catholicism, once an ascriptive, sociological category with little issue-specific political content in the American context, has become much more about support for a particular position on highly salient moral controversies, at least among those who take their faith most seriously. "Is he one of us?" has been replaced with "Does he believe as we

---

3. In fact, most people believed that both were more specifically *Irish* Catholics. While this was clearly true in Kennedy's case, John Kerry's ethnic ancestry was the subject of considerable confusion. Despite many claims to the contrary (including, at times, by Kerry himself; see Phillips and Mooney 2003), Kerry admitted during the course of the campaign that he was not aware of any Irish heritage and that part of his lineage was actually European Jewish (Ferdinand 2003).

do?" as the critical question motivating political choice for most observant Catholics. An examination of the forces driving support for (or opposition to) Kennedy and Kerry among Catholics clearly reveals the changed nature of this relationship and tells us much about the likely contours of American Catholic electoral politics in the future.

Kennedy, Kerry, and the Church

In order to understand how Catholic laity responded to John Kennedy and John Kerry, it is instructive to look first at how the two men positioned themselves vis-à-vis the institutional church and its hierarchy. For Kennedy in 1960, the challenge was clear: to convince a sufficient portion of non-Catholic America that he would not be beholden to the dictates of clergy or "foreign potentates." This task was made somewhat easier by the fact that, unlike his predecessor Al Smith, Kennedy was not a particularly pious or devout man. He was variously described during the course of the campaign as "a rather irregular Christian,"[4] "spiritually rootless and almost disturbingly secular,"[5] and one who "wore his religion lightly."[6] Kennedy actually staked out positions contrary to the preferences of the hierarchy on some questions, opposing both federal aid to church-related schools and the idea of sending a U.S. ambassador to the Vatican.[7] Of course, some of this apparent secularism and distance from the church was carefully cultivated as a political necessity for someone seeking to become the first Catholic president of the United States. America's Catholic clergy, moreover, warmly embraced Kennedy's candidacy despite these points of disagreement and did so in exactly the way that Kennedy wanted—with virtually no public statements, but with quiet support behind the scenes.[8] Anecdotal evidence suggests that students enrolled in Catholic schools in 1960 were left with little doubt as to whom the priests and nuns who taught them believed Catholics should support for president.

When John Kerry sought the presidency in 2004, he did so in a dramatically different religious-political landscape. The political focus of Catholic

4. Van Allen (1974, p. 133).
5. Hennesey (1981, p. 308).
6. Fuchs (1967, p. 182).
7. Prendergast (1999).
8. The only notable instance of anyone in the Catholic hierarchy challenging Kennedy was New York's Francis Cardinal Spellman, who expressed consternation that Kennedy had bucked the church's position on federal aid to parochial schools (see Marlin 2004). This criticism was not politically consequential, however, in part because Nixon held a similar position on the issue.

clergy and the institutional church had shifted away from parochial concerns like money for Catholic schools and toward broad social questions of moral import like abortion, nuclear weapons, poverty, and the nature of marriage.[9] In addition, recent decades had seen the rise of a plethora of lay Catholic organizations, many of them very conservative, that sought actively to promote a political agenda that they believed stemmed from Catholic orthodoxy. Like Kennedy, Kerry parted ways with the hierarchy on several political questions. Unlike Kennedy, he was not given a pass on those disputes because of his Catholicism.

Kerry's disagreements with church teaching were more politically consequential not only because of the clear moral import of the issues, but also because of the tone and fervor of his dissent. Not only did he support a constitutional right to abortion; he did so with gusto. At a 2003 National Abortion Rights Action League dinner, he declared, "I will not overturn *Roe* v. *Wade;* I will not appoint judges hostile to choice; I will allow poor women to have free abortions; I will never outlaw abortion; I will increase American taxpayers' dollars on population control efforts around the world."[10]

As a member of the Senate, Kerry opposed a ban on "partial-birth" abortion and a proposal to criminalize transporting minors across state lines to evade abortion restrictions, and he consistently supported federal funding for abortion. This record led him to be characterized as one of "the two most ardent supporters of abortion in the Senate."[11] In addition, Kerry not only opposed a constitutional amendment defining marriage as the union of one man and one woman, but also was one of only fourteen senators to oppose a similar statutory protection, the Defense of Marriage Act. Finally, Kerry dissented from the position of the church hierarchy on a range of other issues as well, including embryonic stem cell research, school vouchers, and voluntary school prayer.

As a result, the response to Kerry from Catholic elites was much different than that which had greeted John Kennedy. Almost from the outset of his campaign, he was dogged by public repudiations from church officials. Two archbishops and ten bishops stated publicly that they would deny the Eucharist to Catholic politicians who supported abortion rights, and several referenced Kerry specifically by name.[12] Kerry was vilified in the publications and web

9. Byrnes (1991).
10. Kralis (2004).
11. Duin (2003).
12. Kralis (2004); Duin (2004a).

pages of various conservative Catholic organizations and was formally charged with heresy by a Catholic lawyer within his own archdiocese.[13] While not all Catholic leaders shared this level of hostility, there was clearly none of the enthusiasm from the institutional church that had accompanied John Kennedy's presidential bid. Kerry's deviations from church positions were seen not as necessary and minor political expediencies, but as unpardonable departures from basic values. As Steven Waldman, founder of the religious website Beliefnet.com, put it, "Maybe the Kerry campaign is learning the wrong lesson from the 1960 presidential campaign. They figured that if Kennedy emphasized separation of church and state, that's the way we will do it, too. At the time, the question was whether Kennedy was too influenced by the church. The question now is whether Kerry is influenced too little."[14]

Catholic Voters and the Changing American Politics

Clearly, Catholic opinion leaders, both clerical and lay, gave John Kerry a much cooler reception than they gave John Kennedy. The virtually universal support among Catholic elites that Kennedy enjoyed had given way, in Kerry's case, to responses ranging from ambivalence to hostility. Elites, however, do not determine the outcomes of elections—at least not directly. Was this dramatic shift in approach by church leaders reflected in the Catholic mass public as well? Had the American Catholic electorate undergone a similarly profound change in its attitude toward one of its own seeking the presidency? If so, how and why? The remainder of this chapter seeks to answer these questions.

The first systematic, social-scientific accounts of American voting behavior described the nation's electorate in the 1940s and 1950s. These studies, most prominently those of the "Columbia school," posited what could be called an ethnocultural model of political choice.[15] Based on the largely ascriptive identifications of race, ethnicity, class, region, religion, and so on, voters were held to associate themselves with one or the other political party in an almost tribal way. Even the "Michigan model,"[16] which modified this overwhelmingly sociological approach with a greater consideration of psychological factors and issue preferences, conceded that the most common basis for

---

13. Duin (2004b).
14. Duin (2004a).
15. See Lazarsfeld, Berelson, and Gaudet (1948).
16. Campbell and others (1960).

voter choice was a group-centered heuristic.[17] In these accounts, religion (and Catholicism specifically) was treated not as a set of beliefs that mapped onto specific issue positions in the political realm, but rather as a social tie that motivated political allegiances through group identification. To use language common in the sociology of religion, it was "belonging," not "believing," that motivated "behaving" in the political sphere. As a result, the fundamental religious divide in American politics was between Catholics and Protestants, an ever-present cleavage that was especially salient in the 1840s, the prohibition era, and, of course, the 1960 campaign.

Beginning in the 1960s, however, the issue matrix in American society began to change in a way that would have profound consequences for the relationship between religious identification and political choice. While partisan contestation in the New Deal era focused almost exclusively on the size and scope of the welfare state, the 1960s and 1970s saw the rise of the feminist and gay rights movements, the end of public school prayer, and the legalization of abortion. The resulting set of new political controversies gave rise to a "post-bourgeois" or "post-material" cleavage in American society, spurring the emergence of a "politics of cultural difference."[18] These new cleavages did not break neatly along the same lines as the economic and ethnocultural divides that had shaped partisanship in the New Deal. In the realm of religion, orthodox members of nearly all Judeo-Christian traditions were troubled by these challenges to established values, and many were galvanized to political action in defense of a moral order under attack. As a result, many of the traditional sectarian divisions in American society and politics began to decline in importance, with more committed, observant believers from a wide variety of denominational backgrounds pitted together in a "culture war" against secular Americans and more nominal members of their own religious tradition.[19]

In the case of evangelical Protestants, the political results were dramatic. Over the course of two decades beginning in the 1970s, they went from a politically divided group that leaned Democratic (especially in the South) to an overwhelmingly Republican bloc, perhaps the largest single element in the GOP coalition. For Catholics, however, the case is more ambiguous. While they have indisputably become less Democratic over time, it is unclear how

17. In Campbell and others' discussion of the "levels of conceptualization," the "group benefits" voters greatly outnumber any other category in the study.

18. Ingelhart (1971, 1977); Leege and others (2002).

19. Wuthnow (1988); Hunter (1991); Guth and others (2001). See also Green and his coauthors in chapter 2 of this volume.

much of the change has been due to increasing affluence and social integration and how much specifically to moral issues. Unlike evangelicals, Catholics as a whole continued to give majority or plurality support to Democratic presidential candidates up through the 2000 election. Moreover, scholars are also divided over the partisan and ideological implications of Catholic faith, with Andrew Greeley consistently making the case for a distinctively Catholic liberalism and others emphasizing a significant and accelerating Republican trend.[20] Finally, since Catholicism remains a minority religion in the United States and since most American Catholics have ancestors who came to this country after the Civil War (some long after), it is possible that elements of the old ethnocultural alignments—which tended to favor Democrats—might linger as well.

In this regard, the campaigns of 1960 and 2004 provide instructive points of comparison. If the same general patterns of Catholic voter support for a Catholic Democrat against a Protestant Republican opponent hold across the two elections, then this would support the ethnocultural or Catholic liberalism theses. If, conversely, the relationship between Catholic faith and support for the Catholic Democrat has changed significantly, this may mean that Catholics, like evangelicals, have become combatants in the culture war.

A Look at the Data

In comparing Catholic voter responses to the candidacies of John Kennedy and John Kerry, the challenge is to find data sources that contain the requisite questions on candidate preference, denomination, and religious observance and at least roughly comparable sets of demographic and general political items. While survey data for 2004 are varied and abundant, the range of options for 1960 is much more limited. Thus, all things considered, the best data source for this analysis is the 1960 and 2004 surveys of the American National Election Study (NES) series.[21] The disadvantages presented by the smaller-than-ideal sample of Catholics (about 25 percent of the total sample in each year) are ultimately outweighed by the quality and quantity of items tapping

20. Greeley (1977, 1989, 1990). On the latter, see, for example, Prendergast (1999).

21. The American National Election Study is administered by the Center for Political Studies at the University of Michigan, supported by grants from the National Science Foundation and the Russell Sage Foundation. Information on the series may be found at www. electionstudies.org/nesguide/nesguide.htm [December 2006]. Any opinions, findings, or conclusions expressed here are those of the author and do not necessarily reflect those of the funding agencies.

both political and (to a lesser extent) religious attitudes and by the continuity of questions even across this relatively large span of time.

As a first cut, it is instructive to examine the percentage of respondents supporting the Democratic candidate in each electoral cycle, by religious tradition, religious observance, and age. Clearly, we would expect more Catholics across-the-board to support Kennedy in 1960 than Kerry in 2004, if for no other reason than the well-documented diversification in Catholic baseline partisanship that occurred during the intervening decades. More interesting, however, is the relationship between religious observance and vote choice. If either the ethnocultural model or the Catholic liberalism thesis is operative, we would expect more committed Catholics to be more *Democratic* than their less observant counterparts, as greater commitment to the faith presumably would be associated with stronger group identity or more salient theological liberalism. Moreover, we would expect religious commitment to work differently among Catholics and Protestants, pushing them in opposite partisan directions. If, conversely, the culture war thesis is operative, we would expect more committed Catholics to be more *Republican,* rejecting their ideologically wayward co-religionists. In addition, we should find that religious commitment motivates Catholics and Protestants in the same partisan direction.

Table 9-1 reports levels of support for John Kennedy in the 1960 preelection study by age and frequency of church attendance for both Catholic and non-Catholic voters (among whites only).[22] Several patterns are immediately apparent. First, church attendance is a major predictor of candidate choice for both religious groups, but in opposite directions. Among non-Catholics, those who are religiously observant in every age cohort are significantly less likely to support Kennedy than those who are less religious, likely reflecting the anti-Catholic political messages emanating from many Protestant churches in the 1960 campaign. Among Catholics, conversely, religious commitment is consistently associated with much *stronger* levels of support for John Kennedy. In addition, age plays an interesting role. Of all groups identified in the table, the highest Democratic support comes from observant Catholics under forty (what might be termed the "future of the church")—an overwhelming six out

22. In 1960 frequent church attenders were defined as those who reported attending services "regularly" (about 70 percent of Catholics and 40 percent of non-Catholics); infrequent attenders are all others. Among Catholics, the limitation to whites is a trivial one, as very few Catholics in the National Election Study sample are black. It is an important qualifier among non-Catholics, however, as the inclusion of African Americans would significantly inflate the levels of Protestant support for Democratic candidates.

Table 9-1. Democratic Vote among White Catholics and Non-Catholics, by Age and Religious Attendance, 1960

	Infrequent attendance		Frequent attendance	
Religion and age	Percent	Number	Percent	Number
Non-Catholics				
21–39	50	255	19	144
40–59	40	277	29	179
60+	37	178	18	73
Catholics				
21–39	48	27	86	102
40–59	74	38	81	99
60+	36	11	72	36

Source: American National Election Study, 1960 survey.

of every seven of these individuals reported a preference for John Kennedy. Moreover, the contrast between these young, committed Catholics and their religiously observant Protestant counterparts could scarcely be more stark: fewer than one out of every five religiously observant non-Catholics under forty supported Kennedy. Clearly, these basic cross-tabular data provide strong support for the idea that an ethnocultural or Catholic liberalism voting model was operative in the 1960 election. White Catholics tended to support Kennedy, while white Protestants tended to oppose him, a divergence that was particularly pronounced among the more observant members of each religious tradition.

An examination of similar data from 2004, however, reveals dramatically different patterns. Table 9-2 reports the preferred candidate of white Americans prior to the 2004 election by age and frequency of church attendance.[23] Once again, church attendance is a consistent predictor of candidate preference for both Catholic and non-Catholic voters, but, unlike in 1960, it now works in the *same direction* for both groups. In every age cohort, for both religious groups, frequent church attenders were significantly less likely to support John Kerry than were their less religious counterparts, a finding consistent with a culture war model of politics. In addition, the effects of age are once again very suggestive. Age makes little difference among religiously observant non-Catholics; Kerry won the support of about one-third of these

23. In 2004 frequent church attenders are defined as those who reported attending services at least "once or twice a month" (about 55 percent of Catholics and 45 percent of non-Catholics); infrequent attenders are all others.

Table 9-2. Democratic Vote among White Catholics and Non-Catholics, by Age and Church Attendance, 2004

	Infrequent attendance		Frequent attendance	
Religion and age	Percent	Number	Percent	Number
Non-Catholics				
18–39	57	143	31	95
40–59	46	140	33	114
60+	46	83	34	92
Catholics				
18–39	62	47	26	35
40–59	59	51	45	56
60+	79	14	43	53

Source: American National Election Study, 2004 survey.

voters, regardless of age. Among Catholics, however, there are clearly discernible age cohort effects. While Kerry lost among all groups of religiously observant Catholics (a major departure from Kennedy's showing in 1960), his deficit in the older cohorts was not dramatic—about 10–15 percent vis-à-vis Bush. Among younger observant Catholics, however, his support dropped off precipitously. Only about one in four church-attending Catholics under forty (again, the "future of the church") supported the Catholic Democratic candidate for president in 2004—the same group that had given the Catholic Democrat more than 85 percent of its votes in 1960. Indeed, this reflects the lowest level of support for Kerry of any cell in table 9-2.[24] While a residuum of ethnocultural political socialization may remain among older observant Catholics, mitigating Democratic losses, that constraint on Republican gains is clearly not operative among the youngest cohort. Conversely, Kerry did quite well among young nominal Catholics, and indeed among nominal Catholics of all ages, winning more than 60 percent of their support. This serves to underline an overall pattern very much in line with the culture war thesis—for every age group, but especially among the young, the effects of religious observance are much greater than those of religious tradition. The old tribal loyalties and denominational divisions seem to have given way to interdenominational political coalitions based on shared values and issue positions. This change in the political landscape clearly worked to the detriment of a Catholic Democrat among religiously committed American Catholic voters.

24. This result is consistent with the findings of at least one other treatment; see Mockabee (2007).

From this initial look at the data, it would appear that the bonds of denominational group identity had weakened or changed by 2004 to the point that a respondent's Catholicism provided no discernible boost in his or her likelihood of supporting the Catholic candidate for president. Indeed, quite the reverse appeared to be the case: the more seriously one took one's Catholicism, the *less* likely one was to support the Catholic candidate against his Protestant rival. This was in stark contrast to 1960, when, as one would expect, those Catholics most committed to the church were the ones most likely to support the candidate who shared their religious faith. Of course, we should not be too quick to credit such a stunning reversal. Church attendance, after all, is only one rough indicator of the strength of a person's Catholic identity and religious commitment. To truly establish that the relationship between Catholic identity and vote choice has shifted in a fundamental way, we must explore the question more deeply.

Because of the importance of Catholicism in the 1960 campaign, that year's National Election Study included a variety of items tapping the nature and strength of respondents' connections to the Catholic Church. For example, it allows us to see the relationship between church attendance and the likelihood of supporting John Kennedy. Support for Kennedy, fairly strong (60 percent) even among infrequent attenders, was overwhelming (82 percent) among Catholics who attend church regularly. More important, this result is confirmed in other indicators as well. Catholics who "feel pretty close to Catholics in general" are 13 percentage points more likely to support Kennedy than Catholics who do not feel this way.[25] Those who call themselves "strong" Catholics are 19 percentage points more likely to support him than those whose Catholicism is "not very strong." Respondents who have a "good deal"

---

25. All differences reported here are significant at a 95 percent or higher confidence level. The exact wording for this and subsequently referenced questions is as follows: "Some Catholics feel that they have a lot in common with other Catholics, but others we talk to don't feel this way so much. How about you? Would you say that you feel pretty close to Catholics in general or that you don't feel much closer to them than you do to other people?" (NES Var 600259). "Would you call yourself a strong Catholic or a not very strong Catholic?" (NES Var 600258). "How much interest would you say you have in how Catholics as a whole are getting along in this country? Would you say you have a good deal of interest in it, some interest, or not much interest at all?" (NES Var 600260). "In election campaigns, different groups work for one candidate or another. Are there any groups on this list that you particularly trust— that is, would you be more likely to vote for candidates they recommend? Which ones? Are there any groups on the list that you don't trust—that is, would you be more likely to vote against candidates that they recommend? Which ones?" "Catholic groups" was offered as item on presented list (NES Var 600169).

of interest in how other Catholics in America are faring are 9 percentage points more likely to support Kennedy than those who have only "some" interest, and 22 percentage points more likely than those who have "not much" interest. Finally, those Catholic respondents who actively trust the political judgments of Catholic organizations are 19 percentage points more likely to support Kennedy than those who have no opinion, and 37 percentage points more likely than those few who actively *dis*trust Catholic organizations. Clearly, by every available measure, the strength of Catholic voters' religious identification in 1960 was positively associated with their likelihood of supporting the Catholic, Democratic candidate for president.

The 2004 National Election Study, unfortunately, contains many fewer items tapping specifically Catholic religious identity. Still, it is worth examining what is there to provide some comparison with the election of 1960. The most analogous measure of religious identity is church attendance and a feeling thermometer rating of "the Catholic Church."[26] Both of these measures show diametrically opposite patterns from those observed in 1960; stronger attachment to Catholicism in 2004 clearly pushed respondents *away from* the Catholic candidate for president. Those who attend church at least "once or twice a month" were 22 percentage points less likely to support Kerry than those nominal Catholics who attend seldom or never, and those Catholics who express positive affect for the institutional church (the 70 percent of them who rate it above 60 on the feeling thermometer) were 14 percentage points less likely to support him than the minority who express ambivalence or hostility toward the church. The conclusion is unmistakable: Kerry's Catholicism, unlike Kennedy's four decades earlier, did nothing to attract committed Catholics to his cause.

While the bivariate results mentioned so far are striking and illustrative, a full comparison of Catholic voters' decision calculi in 1960 and 2004 requires multivariate modeling. Such models can help to answer two key questions: Is the comparative lack of Catholic enthusiasm for John Kerry merely a product of increasing Catholic affluence and resulting Republican inclination? If not, what specific issues that were not influential in 1960 now seem to be driving Catholic vote choice? To address these questions, table 9-3 presents

---

26. This feeling thermometer item is less than ideal, both because of individual variation in use of the feeling thermometer scales (Wilcox, Sigelman, and Cook 1989) and because of the necessarily arbitrary task of creating a dividing line for purposes of comparing groups. Still, it does provide at least a general indicator of respondents' affective attachment to the institutional church.

Table 9-3. Probit Models of Presidential Vote Choice among Catholics, 1960 and 2004[a]

Variable	1960	2004
Constant	−1.28	−3.80**
	(0.76)	(1.12)
Female	0.09	−0.29
	(0.22)	(0.29)
Black	−0.47	n.a.
	(0.75)	
Hispanic	n.a.	0.33
		(0.46)
Irish	1.63**	0.12
	(0.37)	(0.34)
Age	−0.02*	0. 02*
	(0.01)	(0.01)
Education	−0.10	0.04
	(0.10)	(0.12)
Income	0.05	−0.02
	(0.06)	(0.03)
Union membership	−0.01	0.51
	(0.22)	(0.31)
South	0.62	0.14
	(0.43)	(0.53)
Midwest	0.56*	1.11**
	(0.25)	(0.34)
West	0.95*	0.82*
	(0.37)	(0.39)
Public housing	0.09	n.a.
	(0.07)	
Job guarantee	0.15*	0.09
	(0.08)	(0.09)
Education spending	0.12	n.a.
	(0.09)	
National health care	0.15	0.14
	(0.09)	(0.09)
Isolationism	0.09	−0.37
	(0.09)	(0.35)
Foreign aid	0.12	0.03
	(0.09)	(0.19)
Anticommunism	0.09	n.a.
	(0.08)	
Civil rights	0.08	0.15
	(0.09)	(0.11)
Integration	0.08	n.a.
	(0.07)	
Aid to blacks	n.a.	0.02
		(0.10)
Abortion	n.a.	0.11
		(0.15)
Women's role	n.a.	0.29*
		(0.14)
Gay marriage	n.a.	0.70*
		(0.30)

(*continued*)

Table 9-3. Probit Models of Presidential Vote Choice among Catholics, 1960 and 2004[a] (*continued*)

Variable	1960	2004
Pocketbook evaluation	−0.37*	−0.08
	(0.16)	(0.13)
Church attendance	0.47*	−1.04**
	(0.23)	(0.31)
Trust in Catholic organizations	0.73*	n.a.
	(0.31)	
Feeling thermometer Catholic Church	n.a.	0.01
		(0.01)
Number of observations	306	156
LR χ^2	95.8	75.5[b]

Source: American National Election Study, 1960 and 2004.
n.a. Not available.
a. Dependent variables coded such that 0 = Republican vote, 1 = Democratic vote. Numbers in parentheses are standard errors.
b. $p < 0.01$.
* $p < 0.05$, two-tailed test.
** $p < 0.01$, two-tailed test.

vote choice models, run among Catholics only, for the two years. For purposes of comparison, these models are as nearly identical as the data permit. Both model vote choice as a function of demographic items (gender, race, ethnicity, age, education, income, union membership, and region), a broad range of issue positions tapping economic redistribution, foreign policy predispositions, and racial attitudes, personal economic assessments (because a national retrospective assessment is unfortunately lacking in the 1960 study), and attachment to the church, measured in each year through mass attendance and one affective item. The only significant difference between the models is the inclusion in the 2004 model of the "culture war" issues of abortion, gay marriage, and the role of women in society—these items, of course, are absent in the 1960 study.

Party identification is absent from these models. The problem with including it is that, because it is so causally proximate to vote choice, it wipes out the effects of virtually every other variable. In 1960, for example, 98 percent of Catholic self-identified Democrats voted for Kennedy. Moreover, it is not especially interesting or insightful to say that Catholics supported John Kerry less than John Kennedy because they had become more Republican over time. This is no doubt true, but it obscures the underlying reason for that shift.

An examination of the first columns in table 9-3 reveals exactly the patterns that the bivariate analyses would lead us to expect. Catholic support for

John Kennedy is affected positively by Irish ethnicity (to a very large degree), some regional variables, attitudes toward the welfare state (captured in the "job guarantee" item), and, most significantly, attachments to the Catholic Church. It is affected negatively by age (as older Catholics in 1960 would have been politically socialized in the strongly Republican era of the 1920s) and by positive economic assessments (not surprising given that Republicans were the incumbent party). Only one of the bevy of issue items has any effect on Catholic vote choice. For Catholics, the 1960 election was not about issues, but about the affirmation of group ties, a reality reflected in the fact that ethnic and denominational attachments largely drive this model.

The other columns in table 9-3 present a similar vote choice model run in 2004 (though, regrettably, on a smaller total sample of Catholics). The results here confirm and extend the pattern that emerged from the bivariate data. Ethnicity clearly declined as a factor in vote choice among Catholics (with the exception of race for African Americans, which drops out of the model because all of the few black Catholics in the sample supported Kerry), perhaps in part because of the ambiguity surrounding Kerry's ethnic origins. Age now positively predicts Democratic support, not surprising given that older Catholics were socialized in an era of both greater Democratic strength and more ethno-cultural politics. The effects of religious attachments have reversed, with more frequent church attendance driving voters away from the Catholic Democrat (as reported previously in the tabular data). Most significant, none of the wide range of issues thought to embody the vaunted Catholic liberalism (welfare state, internationalism, racial justice) matter *at all* for Catholic vote choice in 2004. Instead, the two issues that do significantly distinguish Catholic Bush supporters from Catholic Kerry supporters are unambiguously "culture war" questions: gay marriage and women's social roles.[27] That the ethnic and welfare state variables have become insignificant, while moral issues have emerged and the effects of attachment to the Catholic Church have reversed, speaks very strongly to the emergence of culture war politics within the Catholic electorate.

A final, graphic demonstration illustrates the sharp reversal over time in the relationship between religious observance among Catholics and the like-lihood that they will support a Catholic Democratic presidential candidate. Figure 9-1 plots, by frequency of church attendance, the probability that a Catholic voter would have supported John Kennedy in 1960 and John Kerry

27. It is somewhat surprising that abortion attitudes, though properly signed, are not significant in this model. This is likely due in large part to the strong association between church attendance and abortion attitudes among Catholics. They are correlated in the NES at about 0.6.

Figure 9-1. Church Attendance and Democratic Voting among Catholics, 1960 and 2004

Probability of Democratic vote (percent)

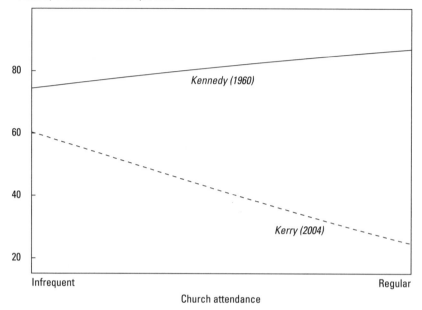

Church attendance

Source: Author's calculations derived from probit models in table 9-3. Based on shifting church attendance from minimum to maximum, while holding all other variables constant at their mean.

in 2004. These figures are based on predicted probabilities calculated from the probit models reported in table 9-3, where church attendance is varied from its minimum to its maximum and all other variables are held constant at their mean. The pattern is once again unmistakable. In 1960 Catholics of all stripes supported Kennedy, but the probability of voting for him increased from about 75 percent among the least observant to approaching 90 percent among the most devout. In 2004, however, this gentle upward slope was replaced with a downward plunge. Here, the average nominal Catholic had a greater than 60 percent probability of supporting Kerry, but the probability dropped precipitously with church attendance, such that the typical highly observant Catholic had only about a 25 percent chance of voting for the Democrat. Moreover, these figures, if anything, underestimate the total impact of religious commitment, because they capture the direct effects of church attendance only, net of clearly related variables such as attitudes toward the church and positions on social issues. In terms of the relationship between religious commitment and political choice among Catholics, 1960 and 2004 could scarcely be more different.

Conclusion

From the preceding analyses, it is clear that the factors shaping Catholic vote choice in America have changed dramatically over the last several decades. These changes, moreover, have had dramatic consequences for how Catholics, especially religiously committed ones, evaluate one of their own seeking the presidency. In an era of ethnocultural politics, simply "belonging" was enough for a Catholic candidate. That he simply was Catholic and not Protestant, that he was on this rather than the other side of that great tribal divide in white American society, was sufficient to motivate strong support from his co-religionists, in both the church hierarchy and the mass public. John Kerry, in an attempt to tap into those reflexive group loyalties, often mentioned to Catholic audiences that he had been an altar boy, even bringing it up during the second presidential debate.[28] "Vote for me," he seemed to say, "because we share this sociological bond, because we have familiarity with the same religious rituals of childhood." It was an appeal in the old style of group identity politics.

And, as has been documented here and elsewhere, it fell flat. Or, at least, it fell flat among the only group of Catholics who might really have cared—those who are religiously committed and remain meaningfully connected to the church. Bearing the trappings of Catholicism was, for most committed Catholic voters, simply no substitute for taking the "right" position on abortion, gay marriage, stem cell research, and so forth. They were willing to embrace an evangelical Protestant who shared their position on these issues before a fellow Catholic who did not. That they did so, and did so decisively, provides powerful support for the culture war thesis. The political divide between the faithful and the nominal, present now for some time among American Protestants but heretofore muted among Catholics, emerged strongly in the 2004 election. Ironically, it did so at a time when one might have expected the greatest solidarity among Catholic voters—when a Catholic candidate was on the ballot. The comparison of responses to John Kennedy and John Kerry makes it abundantly clear that, for American Catholics, "believing" has replaced "belonging" as the key political variable.

---

28. Bottum (2004).

George W. Bush and the Evangelicals

Religious Commitment and Partisan Change among Evangelical Protestants, 1960–2004

Geoffrey C. Layman and Laura S. Hussey

For more than two decades, students of American religion and politics have noted the political realignment of evangelical Protestants—those (mostly white) individuals holding, and belonging to churches espousing, traditionalist Protestant beliefs on matters such as the authority of Scripture, adult religious conversion, and the centrality of faith in Christ to salvation. Strongly Democratic throughout most of the post–New Deal period, since 1980 the most committed evangelicals have become the most loyal component of the Republican electoral coalition.[1]

Consistent with this transformation are the assessments, noted throughout this volume, that evangelicals were critical to George W. Bush's 2004 reelection bid. Less consistent with a pattern of long-term realignment is commentary highlighting President Bush's unique attraction to evangelicals and suggesting that the 2004 election was a watershed for the emergence of religious and moral conservatives in politics. The fact that a plurality of respondents to Election-Day exit polls chose "moral values" as the most important factor in their voting decision created quite a stir among journalists and political observers and led many

---

1. Miller and Wattenberg (1984); Rothenberg and Newport (1984); Green and others (1996); Oldfield (1996); Miller and Shanks (1996); Wilcox and Larson (2006); Kohut and others (2000); Layman (2001); Leege and others (2002).

to herald the arrival of the "values voter" as a new force in American politics.[2] One early election postmortem argued that "a powerful new political creature was born—or born again—on Tuesday: the values voter."[3]

Meanwhile, despite the prolonged growth in committed evangelical support for the Republican Party, press coverage has often emphasized the unique role of Bush's own evangelicalism in appealing to this constituency. Exhibiting the tendency to attribute Bush's evangelical support to shared religion and group identity, Dallas reporter Wayne Slater declared, "I don't think any political president ever in the history of this country was able to harness and assemble the kind of organized and consistent evangelical religious support from the political side as George Bush. . . . One of the reasons that George Bush has the support of the evangelical community is because he's a true believer. . . . He is one of them, and they see it."[4]

Thus there is something of a disjuncture between scholarship on evangelical political behavior and popular commentary on evangelicals' support for George W. Bush. From the perspective of the former, the support Bush has received from evangelicals is a natural extension of a partisan realignment that began at least two decades before Bush's national political career. Any additional backing Bush may have received compared to previous Republican presidential candidates was probably due to the continuing growth of evangelicals' GOP loyalties and Bush's staunch conservatism on the cultural and moral issues that underlay that growth. From the latter perspective, Bush's appeal to evangelicals is unique because it is based not just on shared policy positions and Republican affiliation but also on religious experience and group identification. Thus the support that Bush received from evangelical Protestants—and the degree to which this group became more loyal to the GOP during his presidency—should exceed what we would expect based on political trends and policy attitudes.

In this chapter we assess which of these viewpoints best represents the relationship between George W. Bush and evangelical Protestants by comparing evangelical political orientations during the Bush years and in the preceding four decades. Using the American National Election Study (NES) surveys for 1960 through 2004, we find that the answer depends on the level of religious commitment—specifically the frequency of church attendance—of evangelical adherents. While Bush's support among committed evangelicals largely

2. Meyer (2004b).
3. Gorski (2004).
4. Slater (2004).

represents a continuation of long-term developments, it does appear that Bush has been uniquely able to attract less committed evangelicals into the Republican fold. We argue that the discrepancy between the political behavior of more and less committed evangelicals is due to differences in the factors shaping their political orientation. Devout members of the tradition are motivated principally by their highly conservative views on moral and cultural matters, and their partisan orientations have closely followed the growing differences between the two parties on those matters. Less devout evangelicals are less conservative on moral and cultural issues and care less about these concerns. Thus their political behavior should be shaped more by factors such as personal evaluations of Bush, evangelical group identification, and attitudes toward other types of policy issues. Our analysis of evangelical partisanship and presidential candidate support in 2000 and 2004 shows that moral and cultural attitudes are more important for devout evangelicals, while attitudes toward social welfare and defense and foreign policy issues matter more to the less devout members of the tradition.

Explaining Evangelical Political Behavior

There has been considerable debate over whether a "culture war" engulfs the United States. Some scholars suggest that contemporary American society is beset by deep-seated divisions between those with "orthodox" and those with "progressive" religious and moral perspectives.[5] Others raise doubts about the relevance of such a conflict for American society as a whole and for many religious groups.[6]

Regardless of the overall accuracy of the culture war thesis, it appears to work rather well in explaining the political behavior of committed evangelical Protestants. Evangelical religious leaders have formed political organizations, such as the Moral Majority and the Christian Coalition, that focus on advancing conservative positions on the issues at the heart of the cultural conflict—issues such as abortion, women's rights, homosexual rights, embryonic stem cell research, and the place of religion in the public square—and on mobilizing ordinary evangelicals to support these positions and the political candidates who advocate them.[7] Committed evangelicals have more conservative attitudes on cultural issues and attach more importance to them than do

---

5. Wuthnow (1988, 1989); Hunter (1991); White (2003).
6. For example, Williams (1997); Baker (2005); Fiorina, Abrams, and Pope (2005).
7. For example, Oldfield (1996); Wilcox (1992).

members of any other religious group. They vote in overwhelming numbers for culturally conservative candidates, identify strongly with the party on the conservative side of cultural issues, and support culturally conservative measures on state and local ballots. In short, devout evangelical Protestants translate their traditionalist religious orientations and moral values into conservative attitudes on cultural policy issues and connect these attitudes to strong support for the Republican Party and its candidates.[8]

Thus political change among churchgoing evangelicals may be seen as a long-term policy-based realignment in response to the growing polarization of the two parties on cultural issues.[9] This implies that the traits and personalities of particular Republican candidates are relatively unimportant for the political loyalties and decisions of this group, so long as the candidates support the GOP's culturally conservative agenda. In other words, the presence of a fellow evangelical at the top of the Republican ticket in 2000 and 2004 may not have led them to be more attached to the Republican Party or more likely to vote Republican than usual.

In contrast, those evangelical Protestants who are relatively uninvolved in their church have not exhibited this pattern of steady Republican realignment based on cultural issues. That, we argue, is because of their very lack of religious commitment. Participating in worship services and other religious activities exposes individuals to cues from clergy on moral and political issues, to social interaction with fellow congregants that may shape and reinforce moral and political views, and to appeals by groups seeking to use religious groups and congregations as a basis for political mobilization.[10] Within evangelicalism, such involvement encourages congregants to give prominence to cultural and moral issues, to hold conservative views on those issues, and to link those views to support for culturally conservative candidates and the Republican Party.

Lacking exposure to these factors, less committed evangelicals should not connect their religious beliefs to politics as strongly as their committed brethren, they should be less conservative on moral and cultural issues, and those issues should not be as relevant for their political loyalties. If this group has significantly increased its level of Republican voting and attachment to the GOP during the George W. Bush era, then the explanation may lie somewhere besides Bush's moral conservatism.

8. Green and others (1996); Kohut and others (2000); Wilcox (1992); Layman (2001); Green, Rozell, and Wilcox (2003); Layman and Green (2006).

9. Layman (2001).

10. Wald, Owen, and Hill (1988); Wald, Kellstedt, and Leege (1993); Guth and others (1997).

One place it may lie is simply in the attitudes of less committed evangelicals on other policy issues. They may have been attracted by Bush's economic conservatism—exemplified by his efforts to privatize Social Security and his commitment to substantial tax cuts—or his aggressive use of the U.S. military in prosecuting the war on terror and the war in Iraq. Another possibility is that the party loyalties and political behavior of less committed evangelicals are based less on attitudes toward policy issues and more on candidate affect and group identification. Models of the voting decision have long highlighted the importance of these latter factors,[11] and the traditional view of party identification is that it is a psychological attachment based, in part, on social group membership and assessments of which groups are associated with which parties.[12] The social identity perspective on party identification characterizes the rare change that occurs as individuals gradually recognize that more and more members of their social group adhere to a particular party.[13]

Because evangelical Protestants consider George W. Bush to be "one of us," they should find him quite attractive personally and may be significantly more likely to vote for him than for other Republican candidates. Moreover, having an evangelical at the top of the Republican ticket may send a particularly strong signal that the GOP is the party of conservative Christians and that part of being evangelical is being a Republican. Those signals may be less consequential for committed evangelicals, who are consistently exposed to cues that the Republican Party is "their party" and who, in the aggregate, already have realigned their party ties accordingly, than for less committed evangelicals, who are less likely to have realigned to the GOP and to perceive their group identity and interests in terms of cultural issues.

In sum, less committed evangelical Protestants are less likely than their more devout counterparts to base their political behavior and party attachments on cultural and moral issues and to have undergone a long-term realignment toward Republican identification based on those issues. To the extent that there were substantial upturns in evangelical voting for and identification with the Republican Party during the last two presidential elections, the gains should have come mostly from less committed evangelicals and been based less on traditionalist religious beliefs and moral and cultural conservatism than on other types of political orientations.

11. For example, Miller and Shanks (1996).
12. Campbell and others (1960).
13. Green, Palmquist, and Schickler (2002).

The Partisanship and Presidential Voting of Evangelicals, 1960 to 2004

In order to compare the party ties and electoral behavior of evangelical Protestants in the two elections won by George W. Bush to those orientations over the last several decades, we turn to the American National Election Study surveys that were conducted from 1960 through 2004. Although the NES surveys included few religious items prior to 1990, since 1960 they have included indicators of religious affiliation that make it possible to distinguish evangelical Protestants from other Protestant groups. Thus they provide the best—and, in fact, the only—means with which to assess trends in evangelical political behavior over the long run. We classify evangelical Protestants using essentially the same criteria as John Green and his coauthors in chapter 2.[14]

To examine changes over time in the partisanship and presidential voting behavior of committed and less committed evangelical Protestants, we divide evangelicals into two groups: frequent church attenders and infrequent church attenders.[15] Figure 10-1 shows the percentage of these two groups identifying themselves as Democrats, independents, and Republicans in all election years from 1960 to 2004.[16] Figure 10-2 shows the percentages of frequently attending

14. See Layman and Green (2006) for more details on classifying evangelicals with NES data. The NES list of religious affiliations was not nearly as detailed before 1990 as it was thereafter. Thus, in order to make our coding of the evangelical tradition as comparable as possible over the two periods, we employ a different evangelical category in the NES surveys from 1990 to 2004 (excluding 2002) for over-time analysis. It includes all affiliations that would have been coded as evangelical based on the pre-1990 scheme and does not include any affiliations that would not have been coded as evangelical based on that scheme. Unfortunately, the 2002 NES did not provide the detailed listing of religious affiliations provided in all of the other NES surveys since 1990. We tried to make our definition of the evangelical tradition in 2002 as comparable as possible to those in the other years involved in over-time analyses.

15. Before 1970, frequent attenders are those respondents describing their worship attendance as "regular," while infrequent attenders are respondents who "never," "seldom," or "often" attend church. From 1970 to 2004, frequent attenders are respondents who attend church "almost every week" or more often, while infrequent attenders are respondents who attend "once or twice a month" or less often. The percentage of frequent attenders among evangelical Protestants was 40.3 in 1960 and 45.2 in 2004.

16. Democrats and Republicans are defined as strong and weak partisans on the NES's seven-point party identification scale. The independent category includes pure independents and independent "leaners." No data point for 1962 is included in these figures because the religious affiliation variable in 1962 did not distinguish between different types of Protestants.

Figure 10-1. Party Identification of Evangelical Protestants, by Church Attendance, 1960–2004

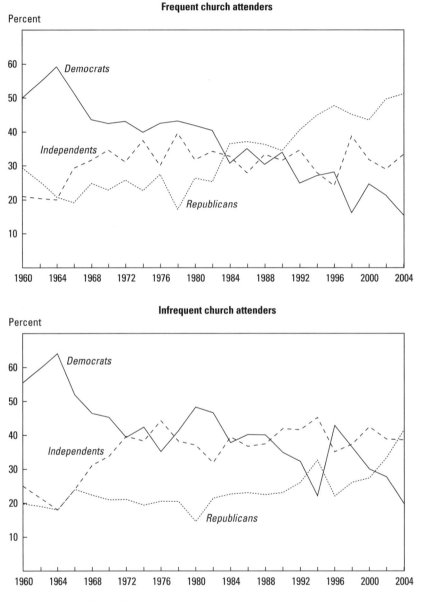

Source: American National Election Study, 1960–2004.

Figure 10-2. Voting for Republican Presidential Candidates among Evangelical Protestants and Non-Evangelical White Christians, 1960–2004

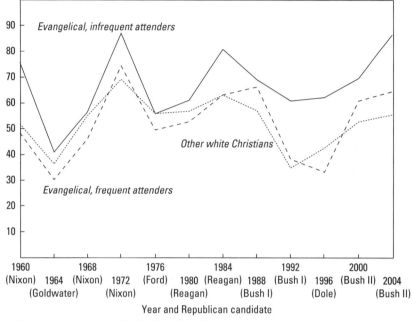

Percent voting Republican

Source: American National Election Study, 1960–2004.

and infrequently attending evangelical Protestants voting for the Republican presidential candidate from 1960 to 2004 and compares them to the percentage of all white Christians outside the evangelical tradition voting Republican.[17]

Party Identification

Among frequently attending evangelicals, there is clear evidence of a sharp and long-term partisan realignment. Between 1964 and the early-to-mid-1970s, there was a noticeable decline in the percentage of committed evangelicals

17. The large majority of non-evangelical white Christians are either Catholics or main-line Protestants, but we also include nontraditional Christian groups such as Mormons in this category. We use other white Christians rather than all non-evangelicals as the comparison group because the non-evangelical group consists disproportionately of African Americans and Jews, two overwhelmingly Democratic groups, and thus inflates the degree to which evangelical voters are distinct from the rest of the electorate.

identifying with the Democratic Party. Those Democratic losses, however, were not accompanied by Republican gains. Since it began after the 1964 election, when the national parties and their candidates first evinced distinct stands on civil rights for African Americans, and since evangelical Protestants were located disproportionately in the South, the first part of this partisan dealignment was likely part of the broader movement of southern whites out of the Democratic Party in response to its racial liberalism. In the 1970s, however, the cultural liberalism of George McGovern, the 1972 Democratic presidential nominee, and other Democratic notables likely became a force behind the continued growth of independence among committed evangelicals. With the Republicans not yet presenting a clear culturally conservative alternative, there may have been stronger incentives for conservative Christians to leave the Democratic fold than to identify with the GOP.[18]

After 1978, the pattern among regularly attending evangelicals changed from dealignment to realignment. The Democratic decline continued through the 1980s and 1990s. However, as the Republican Party staked out clearly conservative ground on cultural matters, it was accompanied by an enormous increase in Republican identification. By the mid-1990s, committed evangelicals were, as a group, closely tied to the GOP.

Those ties grew even closer over the course of George W. Bush's first presidential administration. However, the increases in Republican loyalty and further decreases in Democratic identification that occurred during the 2000s were not at all inconsistent with those that took shape during the 1980s and 1990s. Both the proportion of committed evangelicals identifying themselves as Republicans and their mean position on the party identification scale were significantly higher ($p < 0.05$) in the 2000s than in the 1990s (comparing averages across all elections in the two decades), but the proportion and mean in the 1990s were significantly higher than those in the 1980s, just as those in the 1980s were significantly higher than those in the 1970s. Over the last twenty-five years, committed evangelicals have become tied more closely to the GOP, as the party's candidates, leaders, and platforms have become more culturally conservative. It is clear, then, that President Bush

18. Lending support to the notion that the dealignment of the 1960s was based largely on race and region, while Democratic cultural liberalism may have played a role in the continued dealignment of the 1970s, Layman (2001) shows that the Democratic losses among regularly attending evangelicals were due almost entirely to losses among southerners between 1964 and 1972 but were due more to change among non-southerners than to further losses among southerners between 1972 and 1978.

alone is not responsible for drawing the most devout evangelical Protestants into identification with the Republican Party.

The over-time story is somewhat different for infrequently attending evangelicals. Through the 2000 election, the pattern for this group was largely one of dealignment from the Democratic Party. Like their more committed counterparts, infrequent attenders were overwhelmingly aligned with the Democrats in the early 1960s, but became much less Democratic and more independent over the course of the 1960s and 1970s. In keeping with the idea that the party ties of less committed evangelical Protestants may be shaped by group identification—seeing a presidential candidate as "one of us"— there were substantial rebounds in the group's Democratic attachment when Jimmy Carter and Bill Clinton, Democratic presidents from the South with ties to the Southern Baptist Convention, sought reelection in 1980 and 1996, respectively. Those upturns in Democratic loyalty, however, were followed immediately by noticeable declines.

Unlike frequent attenders, less committed evangelicals did not become noticeably more attached to the Republican Party over the course of the 1980s and 1990s. However, their GOP ties grew dramatically during the first administration of George W. Bush. Between 2000 and 2004, the number of infrequent attenders identifying themselves as Republicans grew from 27.4 to 41.6 percent. That represented the largest increase in GOP attachment over any four-year period to date, and it resulted for the first time in a plurality of infrequently attending evangelicals identifying with the party. The proportion of the group expressing a Republican loyalty was significantly higher in the 2000s than in any of the earlier decades.

Only time will tell whether these Republican gains will be sustained after Bush leaves the political scene. However, while Bush's presidency has simply maintained the already strong loyalties of committed evangelicals to the GOP, it appears to have drawn their less committed counterparts into the party fold in a much greater way than had prior Republican candidates and presidents.

Presidential Vote Choice

For the most part, the voting behavior of frequently attending evangelicals, infrequently attending evangelicals, and non-evangelical white Christians follows the same general pattern, based on the relative success of the Republican candidate in various years. In fact, outside of 1960 and 1972, when committed evangelicals were unusually supportive of the Republican standard-bearer—likely motivated by the Catholicism of the 1960 Democratic nominee and the association of the 1972 Democratic nominee with "acid, amnesty, and abortion"—the voting patterns of the three groups were virtually indistinguishable through 1980.[19]

That began to change in 1984. While neither low-attendance evangelicals nor non-evangelical white Christians were noticeably more likely to vote for Ronald Reagan in 1984 than in 1980, churchgoing evangelicals—presumably attracted to Reagan's cultural and moral conservatism—increased their support for the president by nearly 20 percentage points. Although the difference in the voting behavior of the three groups declined in 1988, the gap between devout evangelicals and the other two groups was clearly evident in the two elections of the 1990s. While both low-attendance evangelicals and non-evangelical white Christians gave a plurality of their votes to Bill Clinton in 1992 and 1996, more than 60 percent of committed evangelicals voted Republican in both elections. Republican voting increased among all three groups in the 2000s, but the support of evangelical churchgoers for Bush in 2004 was significantly higher than that of either of the other constituencies.[20]

Although devout evangelical Protestants were nearly unanimous in their support for Bush in the 2004 election, their loyalty to the Republican standard-bearer was not at all unprecedented. Churchgoing evangelicals have unquestionably become the backbone of the Republican electoral coalition, outpacing the Republican voting levels of non-evangelical white Christians in every presidential election since 1984. Moreover, the 87 percent of committed evangelicals reporting a vote for Bush in 2004 was on par with the 87 percent voting for Nixon in 1972, the 81 percent supporting Reagan in 1984, and the 76 percent backing Nixon in 1960. The proportion of this group voting Republican in the 2000s was significantly higher ($p < 0.01$) than it was in the 1960s, but not statistically greater than it was in the 1970s, 1980s, or 1990s.

19. In 1960 and 1972, there was a statistically significant ($p < 0.05$) difference in the proportion voting Republican between high-attendance evangelicals and each of the other two groups, but not between low-attendance evangelicals and other white Christians. There were no other statistically significant differences in the proportion voting Republican among any of the three groups in any of the other presidential elections between 1960 and 1980.

20. The proportion of high-attendance evangelicals voting Republican was significantly ($p < 0.05$) higher than that of non-evangelical white Christians in all of the presidential elections from 1984 to 2004. It was significantly higher than the proportion of low-attendance evangelicals voting Republican in all of those election years except 1988 and 2000. The difference in the proportion of low-attendance evangelicals and other white Christians voting Republican was not statistically significant in any of the elections.

While devout evangelicals were establishing themselves as the most loyal Republican constituency in the 1990s, the less committed members of the tradition delivered more than 60 percent of their votes to candidates other than the Republican nominee in both 1992 and 1996. However, they moved strongly into the Republican camp in 2000 and 2004, giving Bush more than 60 percent of their votes in both elections. As with their committed counterparts, this did not represent altogether new territory for infrequently attending evangelicals. They simply returned to the levels of support for Republican presidential candidates that they had demonstrated in the 1970s and 1980s. However, it did represent a sharp and statistically significant break with the 1990s ($p < 0.01$), when the group was significantly *less* likely to vote Republican than it had been in the two preceding decades.

Linking Evangelicals to the GOP: Religious Orientations, Policy Attitudes, and Partisan Support

Why have less committed evangelicals been less supportive of the GOP than their more committed counterparts, and why have they only recently shown any real growth in GOP attachment? One explanation is that their attitudes on cultural issues are less conservative than those of committed evangelicals and that they find these issues to be less salient than do their more devout brethren.[21]

That evangelicals' conservatism on moral and cultural issues varies with religious commitment is evident in a comparison of the policy attitudes and political orientations of the two groups of evangelicals and, for comparison's sake, of non-evangelical white Christians. Table 10-1 shows the means for these three groups on an index of moral and cultural attitudes—which combines attitudes on cultural issues such as abortion and gay rights with the degree to which respondents exhibit traditionalist moral values (based on the NES's "moral traditionalism" battery)—as well as a variety of other policy-relevant attitudes. These include attitudes toward social welfare issues such as whether the government should provide health insurance and the government's responsibility to help African Americans, as well as two sets of core political values—egalitarianism (coded here as anti-egalitarianism) and support for limited government—that are commonly associated with social welfare opinion.[22] They also include several types of defense and foreign policy

21. For example, Kohut and others (2000, pp. 36–41).
22. For example, Feldman (1988).

Table 10-1. Political Attitudes and Orientations of Evangelical Protestants and Other White Christians[a]

Attitude	Evangelicals		Other white Christians
	Frequent attenders	Infrequent attenders	
Moral and cultural attitudes	0.65*+	0.49	0.45
Support for war on terror	0.84+	0.81#	0.76
Support for strong military	0.73+	0.72#	0.66
Support for Iraq war	0.64*+	0.51#	0.44
Military feeling thermometer	0.88+	0.85	0.82
Israel feeling thermometer	0.66*+	0.58	0.59
Patriotism	0.83	0.81	0.80
Social welfare attitudes	0.52	0.46	0.47
Anti-egalitarianism	0.44	0.39	0.40
Support for limited government	0.53	0.42	0.46

Source: American National Election Study, 2004.

*Mean for high-attendance evangelicals significantly different from that for low-attendance evangelicals at $p < 0.05$ (two-tailed).

+Mean for high-attendance evangelicals significantly different from that for other white Christians at $p < 0.05$ (two-tailed).

#Mean for low-attendance evangelicals significantly different from that for other white Christians at $p < 0.05$ (two-tailed).

a. Entries are mean scores on variables ranging from 0 for the most liberal position to 1 for the most conservative position. All variables except the feeling thermometers are scores from factor analyses. Persons interested in the variables involved in each analysis and their factor loadings should contact the authors. The number of observations used in computing means ranges from 60 to 87 for high-attendance evangelicals, from 63 to 101 for low-attendance evangelicals, and from 364 to 493 for other white Christians.

attitudes (support for the Iraq war, support for the war on terror, and support for a strong military) as well as values and group evaluations (patriotism and affect toward Israel and the military) that should underlie these positions.[23]

It is on moral and cultural concerns that churchgoing and less religious evangelicals most clearly differ. Like non-evangelical white Christians, less committed evangelicals have fairly moderate moral and cultural orientations, while more highly committed evangelicals are noticeably and significantly more conservative than both groups.

In contrast, the differences in other political orientations between the two groups of evangelicals are generally quite muted. Frequent attenders

23. With the exception of the two feeling thermometers, all of these variables are factor scores from principal-components factor analyses of several indicators. In each factor analysis, all of the items loaded strongly on the first dimension. All of our factor scores are from the first unrotated factor. Details about the specific indicators and their factor loadings are available from the authors upon request.

are slightly more supportive than infrequent attenders of conservative positions on social welfare issues, anti-egalitarian values, and a limited role for government. However, none of these differences is statistically significant, and neither group differs from other white Christians on these variables. Meanwhile, it is on defense and foreign policy concerns that the evangelical groups are closest to each other and farthest from non-evangelicals. Both frequent and infrequent attenders display levels of support for the war on terror and for a strong military that are quite strong and significantly higher than those of other white Christians. Churchgoing evangelicals are more supportive than less pious evangelicals of the war in Iraq, but the latter also favor the war more than do non-evangelical white Christians. All three groups display very high levels of patriotism and very positive evaluations of the military.

These patterns suggest that committed and less committed evangelical Protestants may have supported Bush and the Republican Party over the past two elections for rather different reasons. Much like their realignment to the GOP, the continued attachment of devout evangelicals to the party and its candidates is likely based on their traditionalist religious beliefs and staunch conservatism on moral and cultural matters. However, because less committed evangelicals are clearly less culturally conservative than their churchgoing counterparts but are nearly as conservative in their orientation toward social welfare and defense and foreign policy, their greater Republicanism during the Bush era likely resulted from factors other than religious traditionalism and "moral values." They may have been attracted by Bush's conservative stands on social welfare and foreign policy concerns, by his identification with the evangelical community, or simply by their personal affection for him.

To assess these expectations, we pool data from the 2000 and 2004 NES surveys and estimate structural equation models of Republican Party support—the combination of party identification, presidential vote choice, and comparative evaluations of the two major-party candidates—separately for frequently attending and infrequently attending evangelicals.[24] Figure 10-3 displays the estimates of these models in an easily interpretable format. The model is a relatively simple one in which the orthodoxy of evangelicals' religious beliefs—measured by respondents' views on the authority of the Bible— may affect their support for Bush and the GOP both directly and indirectly

24. Comparative candidate evaluations are measured as the difference between the feeling thermometer rating of Bush and that of his Democratic opponent.

Figure 10-3. The Impact of Belief Orthodoxy, Fundamentalist Affect, and Policy Attitudes on Evangelicals' Assessments of Bush's Traits and Support for the Republican Party, 2000–04[a]

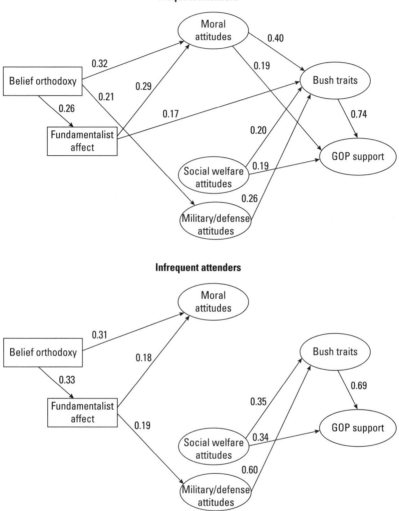

Source: American National Election Study (pooled), 2000 and 2004.

a. Only statistically significant (*p* < 0.05, one-tailed) paths are shown. Entries are standardized coefficients. Latent variables are represented by ovals, observed variables by rectangles.

through a number of other political orientations.[25] The first intervening variable is affect toward fundamentalist Christians, measured by respondents' ratings of them on a feeling thermometer. In lieu of more direct measures, we include this variable as an indicator of evangelicals' degree of group identification. Of course, not all evangelicals consider themselves to be fundamentalists, but those with stronger ties to the evangelical community should rate their fellow-tradition members more favorably. Stronger group identification may produce greater support for fellow evangelical George W. Bush and stronger Republican attachment.

The next two sets of intervening variables are, along with Republican support, "latent" variables, which combine multiple measures of a trait.[26] The first set of latent variables includes moral attitudes, social welfare attitudes, and military and defense attitudes, each measured separately. The observed indicators of moral attitudes are positions on four cultural issues (abortion, homosexual antidiscrimination laws, homosexuals in the military, and women's rights) and the four "moral traditionalism" items in the NES. The indicators of social welfare attitudes are positions on government guarantee of jobs, the trade-off between government services and spending, government responsibility to help improve the social and economic position of blacks, government provision of health insurance, and federal spending on social security and programs to help the poor. Opinions on defense spending and feeling thermometer ratings of the military combine to form our measure of military and defense attitudes. The final intervening variable is evaluation of Bush's personal traits, included to capture evangelicals' feelings for Bush himself. The observed indicators are assessments of how well five traits (moral, strong leader, cares about people like me, knowledgeable, and honest) describe Bush.[27]

25. The model also includes controls for a number of demographic factors—sex, age, southern residence, and rural residence—that may be related to both Republican Party support and religious traditionalism among evangelicals. Age is negatively related to positive assessments of Bush's personal traits and GOP support for both groups of evangelicals, and women rated Bush's traits more favorably than did men in the high-attendance group. Neither southern nor rural residence had statistically significant effects on either of these variables in either group. To account for the pooled nature of the data, we also allow a dummy variable for 2004 respondents to affect each endogenous variable in the model.

26. More technically, the latent variables are measured by confirmatory factor analyses of several observed indicators, each of which is treated as having measurement error.

27. To provide a scale for the latent variables, we constrain the factor loading for one observed indicator of each latent variable to be equal to 1. All of the observed indicators of religious beliefs, issue attitudes, and assessments of Bush's traits have been coded to range from −1 to 1, with higher scores representing more orthodox, conservative, or Republican orientations. The latent variables take on the same range of values.

In figure 10-3, an arrow connecting two variables indicates a statistically significant relationship between them, while the number on the arrow indicates the relative magnitude of that relationship.[28] The results provide considerable support for our expectations about the factors shaping Republican attachments for the two sets of evangelical Protestants. In the model for committed evangelicals, belief orthodoxy has strong effects on fundamentalist affect, moral values and attitudes (both directly and indirectly through fundamentalist affect), and military and defense attitudes; it also influences assessments of Bush and GOP support indirectly through those variables. Affect for Christian fundamentalists is also related to moral conservatism and is tied directly to positive assessments of Bush's personal traits. Such assessments, in turn, are linked tightly to Republican support. Military and defense attitudes affect GOP support through perceptions of Bush's traits, while social welfare attitudes exert both direct and, through trait assessments, indirect effects. Aside from evaluations of Bush, moral attitudes are the strongest predictors of committed evangelicals' GOP support, operating directly as well as indirectly through assessments of Bush's traits. They clearly have the strongest total impact on Republican attachments of any of the policy attitudes in the model.[29]

In contrast, moral values and attitudes have no effect at all on either the assessment of Bush's traits or Republican support among infrequently attending evangelicals. Thus while belief orthodoxy and feelings about fundamentalists are linked strongly to moral attitudes, their total impact on partisan orientations is much less for this group than for their churchgoing counterparts.

---

28. More exactly, the numbers on the arrows are standardized regression coefficients. There is no statistically significant direct relationship between variables not linked by an arrow. We do not exclude missing values from our analyses. We estimate our model using Amos 4.0, which computes full information maximum likelihood (FIML) estimates even in the presence of missing data (Andersen 1957). Wothke and Arbuckle (1996) describe this FIML procedure and show that the estimates produced by it are more consistent and efficient than those produced by pairwise or listwise deletion of missing observations. The full set of measurement and structural coefficients for the models is available from the authors upon request.

29. In a path analysis, the "total effect" of one variable on another is the sum of the former's direct and indirect effects on the latter. The total effect (0.49) of the moral attitudes variable on GOP support for frequent attenders is the sum of its direct effect (0.19) and its indirect effect through assessments of Bush's traits—the product of the direct effect of moral attitudes on trait assessments and the direct effect of trait assessments on GOP support ($0.40 \times 0.74 = 0.30$). The total effects of variables on GOP support for frequent attenders are 0.27 for belief orthodoxy, 0.27 for fundamentalist affect, 0.49 for moral attitudes, 0.34 for social welfare attitudes, and 0.19 for military and defense attitudes. For infrequent attenders, they are 0.02 for belief orthodoxy, 0.07 for fundamentalist affect, 0 for moral attitudes, 0.58 for social welfare attitudes, and 0.42 for military and defense attitudes.

It appears that the substantially greater Republicanism of less committed evangelicals during the 2000s is due neither to moral values nor to evangelical group identification, at least as measured here. Of course, their assessment of Bush's personal traits is linked very strongly to their partisan orientation. However, the Republican support of infrequent attenders is based no more on personal affect for Bush than is that of frequent attenders.

What is particularly important for the party attachments and candidate support of less devout evangelicals is their attitude on social welfare issues and on defense and military concerns. Both the direct effect of social welfare attitudes on GOP support and the indirect effect of these attitudes through evaluations of Bush's traits are much larger for this group than for committed evangelicals, and social welfare attitudes have the largest total effect on Republican loyalty of any variable in the model besides trait assessments. The impact of military and defense attitudes on GOP support is only indirect, but the indirect effect is very strong, as their influence on evaluations of Bush's traits is more than twice as large as that for churchgoing evangelicals. Military and defense attitudes also provide the only link between belief orthodoxy and fundamentalist affect and Republican Party support for this group.

Conclusion

George W. Bush received overwhelming support from committed evangelical Protestants in his two elections to the White House, and the group's already strong identification with the Republican Party has continued to grow during his administrations. However, because the attraction of committed evangelicals to Bush is based substantially on his highly conservative stands on moral and cultural issues and because the long-term realignment of this group to the GOP has been driven by party positions on these issues, the level of Republican voting and identification by devout members of the evangelical tradition has not been remarkably higher during the Bush years than in previous eras.

In contrast, Republican voting and identification among less committed evangelicals has reached substantially higher levels in the current decade than it did in earlier years. We argue that the sharp upturn in Republicanism among less committed evangelicals has occurred because this group was not a part of the evangelical realignment based on moral and cultural issues. Their party ties and political behavior are based more on social welfare attitudes, defense and foreign policy attitudes, and personal feelings for the political candidates. Bush successfully appealed to them on all of those fronts. In short,

Bush's election in 2000 and reelection in 2004 appear to have been assisted by the growth in Republican support from evangelical Protestants. However, the gains did not come mainly from the moral values voters in the evangelical tradition, but from those evangelicals who do not base their political orientations on moral values.

What role will evangelicals play in the 2008 presidential contest and beyond? Given that committed evangelicals have become strongly loyal to the GOP, not only in their voting behavior but also in their party attachments, the party should be able to rely on support from this group—as long as the GOP ticket leads with a culturally conservative, but not necessarily evangelical, candidate. At this writing, however, neither of the two frontrunners for the GOP presidential nomination would seem to generate much enthusiasm from this group. Former New York mayor Rudy Guiliani holds liberal positions on cultural issues—he is pro-choice on abortion and supportive of gay and lesbian rights—and that may threaten his support among committed evangelicals even if he does become the Republican standard bearer. Devout evangelicals are also wary of Senator John McCain due to his sharp critique of the Christian Right during his 2000 presidential bid and his often highly public battles with the GOP leadership and President Bush. However, committed evangelicals may be less likely to abandon a general election ticket headed by McCain than one headed by Guiliani, given that McCain's positions and voting record on abortion and other cultural matters have tended to fall in line with conservative orthodoxy.

In contrast, running with a cultural conservative is hardly a requirement for the support of less committed evangelicals. What appears more important for keeping this group in the Republican fold is the continued presentation of clearly conservative positions on social welfare and foreign policy issues. Both Guiliani and McCain have reputations as fiscal conservatives and foreign policy hawks, while the leading candidates for the Democratic presidential nomination are perceived as liberal in both areas. Thus, we suspect that a Republican ticket headed by either Guiliani or McCain would do relatively well within this less devout wing of evangelicalism.

Latinos and Religion

David L. Leal

Recent presidential elections have seen a number of unusual controversies. For 2000 the most important dispute involved the "hanging chads" in Florida. In 2004, while the election outcome itself was resolved without undue difficulty, one debated postelection issue was the level of Latino support for George W. Bush and John F. Kerry. Along with this controversy came arguments about whether Latinos were increasingly "up for grabs" politically. There was also discussion about the possible basis for the hypothesized growth in Republican support from this traditionally Democratic constituency. This chapter discusses one possible explanation for Latino support for Bush in 2004: religion.

Contemporary presidential elections feature a growing level of media speculation about the political importance of the Latino vote. Such news stories often note the growing number of Latinos, refer to Latinos as the "sleeping giant," and ask whether this is the year they will "awaken." As described by Louis DeSipio and Rodolfo de la Garza, however, "Each election is followed by a somewhat disappointing review in which the Latino promise is not met and in which ongoing problems (most notably low turnout) are advanced as easy explanations."[1]

1. DeSipio and de la Garza (2000, p. 398).

In 2004 there were once again many news reports about the potential importance of Latino voters to the campaigns. The main difference from the usual pattern was that data about the Latino electorate described a population growing in importance and moving in an unexpected direction. First, Latino turnout was estimated to have grown from 5.9 million in 2000 to 7.6 million in 2004.[2] Second, some exit polls suggested that 44 percent of Latinos voted for Bush. In previous work, I suggest that 39–40 percent is a more likely ballpark estimate, but either statistic would constitute a relatively high level of support for a Republican presidential candidate, and both suggest that a key constituency of the Democratic Party—and one the party is counting on to regain majority status—could instead fall under the GOP umbrella.[3]

Some evidence from 2004 suggests that religious affiliation might have been an important component of the Latino vote. Most important, preelection surveys uncovered few other clear sources of partisan differentials. In the October preelection survey conducted by the *Washington Post,* Univisión Television, and the Tomás Rivera Policy Institute (TRPI), Latino support for Kerry was strong across measures of socioeconomic status (SES). For example, levels of support did not vary substantially between those who earned less than $25,000 or more than $50,000. In short, "with regard to education, income, age, and immigrant status, every subsection of the Latino electorate stated a vote preference lower than 35 percent for President Bush."[4]

The one exception to this pattern is religious affiliation. The same survey found that Catholic Latino likely voters supported Kerry over Bush by 40 points, but Protestant Latinos were 13 points more likely to favor Bush over Kerry. Such statistics are consistent with previous research on religiously based political differences among Latinos.[5] By contrast, most research has found only modest evidence that Latinos are more likely to become Republicans as they become wealthier, and in any case the number of high-income Latinos is limited.[6]

Latinos: Demography and Religion

Perhaps the most important demographic trend in America today is the significant increase in the size and share of the Latino population. This growth,

2. Suro, Fry, and Passel (2005).
3. Leal and others (2005).
4. Leal and others (2005).
5. Kosmin and Keysar (1995).
6. Cain, Kiewiet, and Uhlaner (1991); Gimpel and Kaufmann (2001); Alvarez and Garcia-Bedolla (2003).

as well as the relative decline of the Anglo (non-Hispanic white) percentage of the American population, makes it increasingly difficult to understand many aspects of American politics without reference to Latinos. A key moment was the 2000 U.S. census, which found that Hispanics were becoming America's largest minority group. At that time, Latinos constituted 12.5 percent, African Americans constituted 12.1 percent, and Anglos constituted 69.1 percent of the overall U.S. population.

Given the substantial levels of immigration from Mexico, the Caribbean, and Latin America, as well as the relatively high birth rate of Latinos in the United States, this population will continue to grow. For instance, Latinos accounted for 49 percent of the nation's population growth from 2004 to 2005, and they were responsible for 70 percent of the growth in the population of children under the age of five.[7] As a result, the traditional black-white paradigm on racial questions will need to give way to a more complex multiethnic perspective. More recent data from the Census Bureau in 2005 indicate that the Latino population grew to 14.4 percent; Anglos now constitute 66.7 percent, and African Americans constitute 13.4 percent of the U.S. population. The Census Bureau estimates that by 2050 the Anglo population will have grown 7 percent and will constitute a bare majority (50.1 percent) of the population. By contrast, Latinos will have grown 188 percent and will constitute 24.4 percent, while African Americans will have grown 71 percent and will constitute 14.6 percent. This means that by mid-century one in every four Americans may be Latino.[8]

Such changes will be magnified in states where the minority populations are already large. Texas, California, New Mexico, and Hawaii already have majority-minority populations, and more states are likely to join them in the years to come. While minority populations are not yet the majority of the electorate in these states, as many Latinos are under the age of eighteen or not citizens, the Latino share of the electorate is growing steadily. Nevertheless, an understanding of Hispanics will be critical to politicians and policymakers as the U.S. transitions to a society in which no single ethnic or racial group is the majority.

In contrast to this rapid population growth, there is some stability within the Latino population in terms of religious affiliation. Approximately 70 percent of Latinos are Catholic, and about 20 percent are evangelicals.[9] While this

---

7. Cohn and Bahrampour (2006).
8. Census Bureau (2004).
9. Hunt (2000); Kosmin and Keysar (1995).

figure has been fairly stable for the last two decades, some Latinos are leaving the Catholic Church for evangelical and Pentecostal churches.[10] The stability of the Catholic percentage is due to immigration from Latin America. Acculturation is associated with a greater likelihood of non-Catholic affiliation, but this is balanced by the arrival of predominantly Catholic Latino immigrants, despite some success of Protestant proselytizing efforts in Latin America.[11]

Does this evangelical tendency among more acculturated Latinos have political implications? Previous research indicates that Anglo evangelicals are more conservative than are non-evangelicals across a number of moral issues and are a key component of GOP electoral coalitions. While Latino denominational choices do not necessarily imply a shift in political or moral opinions, some have noted that Latino evangelicals are more conservative than Latino Catholics on a number of social issues and were more supportive of George W. Bush in 2000.[12] In addition, given the lack of other substantial SES and demographic cleavages within the Latino population (aside from Cuban American partisanship), it appears that acculturation benefits Republicans and continuing immigration benefits Democrats.

While conservative Catholics and evangelicals sometimes have similar moral and policy positions, they are not necessarily willing to work together in the electoral arena. Speaking of the religious right generally, John Green, Mark Rozell, and Clyde Wilcox have noted, "Ethnic diversity presented both a challenge and a largely untapped opportunity for the movement: in most states, black Protestants and Hispanic Catholics shared many of the religious values of the movement's core supporters but rarely backed movement organizations."[13] They noted that ethnic religious communities were sometimes willing to support ballot propositions on morally related issues, but rarely Republican candidates.

Jongho Lee and Harry Pachon examined the overall level of Latino support for Bush and Kerry in 2004 using the *Washington Post*-Univisión-TRPI October preelection survey. They found that Latino evangelicals were more supportive of Bush and were more likely to identify as Republicans than were Latino Catholics. Nevertheless, this religious gap was not sufficient to transform Latinos into a swing constituency, as the share of Latino evangelicals was low (15 percent), and the strong majority of Latinos anticipated voting for Kerry

---

10. Greeley (1994, 1997).
11. Espinosa, Elizondo, and Miranda (2003).
12. Espinosa, Elizondo, and Miranda (2003).
13. Green, Rozell, and Wilcox (2003, p. 8).

(67 percent). In addition, according to Lee and Pachon, "Latino evangelicals have not yet been closely connected to the politics of their Anglo evangelical brothers and sisters."[14] For instance, more than half of Latino evangelicals consider themselves to be Democrats or independents. While this is smaller than the 81 percent of Catholics who identify as Democrats or independents, it is far larger than the comparative figures for Anglo evangelicals. In addition, Latino evangelicals were no more likely than Latino Catholics to report being certain about their vote choice, being politically mobilized, or following the presidential contest.

Do "Latinos" Exist?

This discussion of "Latino" religious affiliation and political behavior raises the question of whether a Latino community exists in the United States. Concepts like Latino or Hispanic are social constructions, and a number of researchers are interested in whether Latinos think of themselves in such panethnic terms, whether they prefer national-origin identifiers such as Mexican American or Cuban American, and what political consequences follow from such identities.[15]

Some scholars have studied the Latino category and found a number of important differences by national-origin group. As Enrique Trueba notes, "We cannot trivialize the ethnic, social, racial, and economic differences of Latino subgroups."[16] De la Garza and DeSipio argue that the study of the aggregate Latino population:

> confuses rather than clarifies our understanding because of the characteristics that distinguish the national-origin groups thus subsumed (Bean and Tienda 1987; de la Garza, Fraga, and Pachon 1988; Pachon and DeSipio 1988; Fuchs 1990). This approach fails to assess differences in political culture associated with the distinct socialization experiences within the United States and the countries of origin and neglects the link between those differences and political behavior.[17]

The advent of the Latino National Political Survey (LNPS), which was conducted in 1989–90, allowed researchers to compare the political and policy

---

14. Lee and Pachon (2005, p. 18).
15. De la Garza and others (1992); Jones-Correa and Leal (1996).
16. Trueba (1999, p. 33).
17. De la Garza and DeSipio (1994, p. 3).

attitudes of Latinos of Mexican, Puerto Rican, and Cuban descent. The investigators found a number of important differences among the groups on key issues and concluded, "There may be a Hispanic political community, but its parameters do not fit any existing presuppositions."[18] In his review of this research, Jorge Domínguez similarly points out the many unique orientations of Cuban Americans, although he also discusses several reasons why a panethnic Latino conception has some merit.[19]

In light of such research, scholars are increasingly cautious about using pan-ethnic terminology. Although this is not necessarily the case in the world of journalism and politics, researchers are more careful about making sweeping generalizations about the political behaviors and opinions of Latinos, and a growing literature on Latino politics examines the political orientations and engagements of specific national-origin groups. This is increasingly important as the Latino population diversifies. Although "Latino" is often conflated with "Mexican American," the United States over the last two decades has seen a significant increase in immigration from the Caribbean and Central America. For instance, the Puerto Rican population on the U.S. mainland is now smaller than the combined Central American populations in the United States.

It is also important to study the validity of the national-origin group categories. The fact of differences in public opinion and political participation between Latinos and Anglos does not prove that the Latino category is meaningful. For instance, while Latinos may be more likely than Anglos to favor government provision of health insurance, does this reflect a more liberal ideological orientation among Latinos or simply a lower level of health insurance?[20] In a similar way, it is not clear that Latino national-origin groups are coherent political entities. For example, the category of "Puerto Rican" may obscure geographic differences within this group. This chapter takes this possibility into account by examining the 2004 presidential vote according to both national-origin group and state of residence.

There is some scattered evidence in the literature that such ethnic and geographic differences may exist. According to *Los Angeles Times* journalist Frank del Olmo, "I have found that polls attempting to gauge Latino sentiment on issues or candidates seem to be more reliable when they focus on a specific national group like Cuban Americans or Puerto Ricans, or on a particular community like San Antonio or East Los Angeles, than when they deal with

---

18. De la Garza and others (1992, p. 13).
19. Domínguez (1994).
20. See Leal (forthcoming) for discussion.

Latinos as a national bloc."[21] Recent research has found that, among Cuban Americans, political opinions vary according to residence in Florida or elsewhere. By contrast, Mexican American opinion does not seem to differ significantly according to state of residence.[22] However, other factors do seem to affect political attitudes among Mexican Americans. According to Susan Keefe and Amado Padilla, "The significant differences within the Mexican American ethnic group demonstrate the importance of conducting subgroup analyses before making generalizations for the ethnic group as a whole."[23]

In sum, this chapter does not consider the Latino population as monolithic, but instead examines three important facets of it. The first is religious tradition (Catholic versus Protestant), the second is the different national-origin groups within the Latino community, and the third is the wide geographic variation.

Data and Models

Specifically, this chapter tests previous understandings of Latino evangelical political orientations by examining the anticipated vote for Bush and Kerry in the 2004 presidential election. It uses the 2004 *Washington Post*-Univisión-TRPI preelection survey. Conducted October 4–16, it polled via telephone 1,603 Latino registered voters in the eleven states with more than 100,000 Latino registered voters: California, Texas, Florida, New York, Arizona, Illinois, New Mexico, New Jersey, Colorado, Virginia, and Massachusetts. The survey is therefore representative of 88 percent of Latino registered voters nationwide. The samples were drawn from official lists of registered voters, and Latinos were identified through the U.S. census list of Spanish surnames. Interviewing Service of America (ISA) of Van Nuys, California, carried out the fieldwork.

While the trend in scholarship is often to aggregate to the largest level, this does not necessarily make sense for all projects. While single-state studies are less common in political science today than in earlier decades, they can be as useful as, or even more useful than, research based on a national sample, depending on the specific questions and the available data.[24] In this case, an investigation of presidential voting should take into account the Electoral College and examine opinion at the state level. In addition, there is some evidence that Latino opinion varies by state. There is also reason to think that

21. Del Olmo (1987, p. 25).
22. Leal (2006).
23. Keefe and Padilla (1987, p. 140).
24. For a more detailed discussion, see Nicholson-Crotty and Meier (2002).

the political role of the Christian Right varies by state, so the political implications of evangelical identification may not be the same from state to state.[25]

The next section begins by presenting aggregate data on anticipated vote
choice for evangelicals, Catholics, mainline Protestants, and the secular. It
then presents regression results for respondents specifically from five geographic groupings (California, Texas, Florida, New York, and a southwestern
group that includes New Mexico, Arizona, and Colorado) and two Latino
national-origin groups (Mexican Americans and Puerto Ricans). In all models,
the key independent variables are those measuring religious affiliation:
evangelical, mainline Protestant, and secular, with Roman Catholic being
the base case.

The religious affiliation variables are derived through two questions. The
survey asked, "Regardless of whether you now attend any religious services,
do you consider yourself closest to Catholic, Protestant, or something else?"
Responses to this question include Catholic, Protestant, just Christian, other
religious tradition or denomination, no religious preference, atheist, and
agnostic. The second question asked, "Would you consider yourself a born-
again or evangelical Christian or not?" Those who identified themselves as
both Protestant and as born-again or evangelical Christian were categorized
as evangelicals. Those who identified as non-evangelical Protestant or just
Christian were categorized as mainline Protestant. Those who responded no
religious preference, atheist, or agnostic were classified as secular.

This is a useful, but not ideal, classification scheme. While Catholic and
secular are clear categories, evangelical and, to a larger degree, mainline
Protestant are open to question. These variables were not created through
the respondents' identification with specific church affiliations but through
responses to two questions. The variable for mainline Protestant therefore
includes self-identified Protestants or other non-Catholic Christians who did
not report having had a born-again experience, which for Latinos may not be
the equivalent of traditional mainline Protestants in Anglo communities.
Unfortunately, none of the few political surveys of Latinos in the United States
includes detailed measures of religious affiliation; better measures of religious
affiliation clearly are needed to improve our understanding of the various
denominational affiliations of Latinos.

Table 11-1 shows the overall Latino anticipated vote for Bush and Kerry
by religious affiliation. The results are both similar to and different from the
more general understanding of how religion influences politics. Analysis of

25. Green, Rozell, and Wilcox (2003).

Table 11-1. Anticipated Latino Vote for Bush and Kerry,
by Religious Affiliation

Candidate	Catholic	Secular	Mainline	Evangelical
George W. Bush	26.5	36.5	43.8	63.6
John F. Kerry	73.5	63.5	56.2	36.4
Number of observations	1,024	104	96	198

Source: *Washington Post,* Univisión, and Tomás Rivera Policy Institute preelection survey,
October 2004.

recent presidential elections suggests that evangelicals are more likely to vote
for Republican presidential candidates, mainline Protestants are second but
moving toward the center, Catholics are very near the center, while the secular are the most likely to vote for Democrats. This table suggests that, among
Latinos, evangelicals are the most supportive of Bush, and Catholics are the
strongest Democrats. Mainline Protestants are less supportive of Bush than
evangelicals, which is not a surprise, but secular Latinos are 10 percentage
points more supportive of Bush than are Catholics.

Table 11-2 more systematically evaluates Latino support for Bush, using
a probit model of the presidential vote that includes many potentially confounding factors (a vote for Bush is coded as 1). The baseline model for anticipated vote therefore includes the following variables: evangelical, other
Christian, non-Christian, Bush approval, sincerity of Bush and Kerry outreach
to Latinos, assessment of national economic conditions, party identification,
education, generational status, gender, Puerto Rican, Cuban American, and
three variables for income: $25,000–$49,999, $50,000 and above, and miss-
ing. This model is similar to the model presented by Lee and Pachon, but it
omits several highly correlated variables.[26] For details on the coding of the
variables, see the appendix to this chapter.

The first point to note is that only one religious variable is statistically significant: evangelicals were the most likely religious group to support Bush.
The measures for mainline Protestants and the secular are statistically
insignificant, despite their apparent varying levels of support in table 11-1.

This suggests that, within Latino communities, only evangelical Protes-
tants are particularly distinct in their support for the presidential candidates.
It is important to note that the models already control for partisanship,
Bush approval, economic evaluations, a variety of demographic variables,

26. Lee and Pachon (2005).

Table 11-2. Probit Model of Overall Bush-Kerry Support among Latinos

Variable	Coefficient
Evangelical	0.625***
	(0.187)
Mainline Protestant	−0.721
	(0.261)
Secular	0.200
	(0.382)
Bush approval	1.054***
	(0.087)
Outreach to Latinos	0.651***
	(0.086)
Economic evaluations	0.310***
	(0.094)
Partisanship	0.372***
	(0.045)
Education	0.112**
	(0.054)
Born in the United States	0.067
	(0.145)
Puerto Rican	0.034
	(0.260)
Cuban American	1.247***
	(0.471)
Income ($25,000 to $50,000)	−0.193
	(0.191)
Income ($50,000 +)	−0.096
	(0.208)
Income (missing)	0.041
	(0.195)
Constant	−3.830***
	(0.252)
Pseudo R^2	0.74
Number of observations	1,360

Source: *Washington Post,* Univisión, and Tomás Rivera Policy Institute preelection survey, October 2004.
*** $p < 0.01$.
** $p < 0.05$.
* $p < 0.10$.
a. Numbers in parentheses are standard errors.

and the respondent's assessment of the candidate's sincerity in Latino outreach efforts.

Figure 11-1 displays the substantive effects of the religious denomination variables in this and all subsequent tables. In this model, the first-difference analysis indicates that Latino evangelicals were about 20 percentage points more likely to vote for Bush than were Latino Catholics—an effect approximately paralleled by the statistically significant religious variables in subsequent regressions.

Figure 11-1.   Change in Probability of Voting Republican among Latinos in the 2004 Presidential Election, by Religious Affiliation and State

Change in probability of Bush vote (percent)

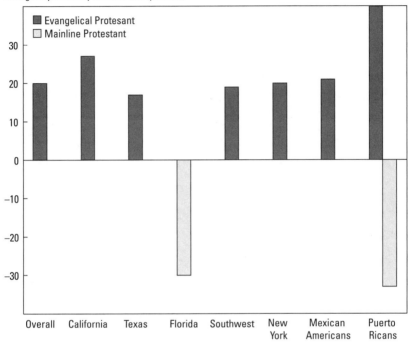

Source: Calculated using Clarify (Tomz, Wittenberg, and King 2001).
a. First-difference effects of a 0/1 change in selected religious denomination variables on the probability of voting for Bush. Other independent variables are set to their mean.

Using different data, Roberto Suro, Richard Fry, and Jeffrey Passel also find evidence of Latino evangelical support for Bush. Analyzing 2000 and 2004 National Election Pool (NEP) exit polls, they note, "Hispanic Protestants were both a growing and increasingly pro-Republican constituency between the two elections. Meanwhile, Bush's share of the Hispanic Catholic vote held steady at 33 percent in the state exit polls. The split between Latino Protestants and Catholics (23 percent) was larger than in the white vote in which 68 percent of Protestants and 56 percent of Catholics voted for Bush."[27] While the NEP did not distinguish between evangelical and mainline Protestants, Suro and his colleagues note that the large majority of Latino Protestants are evangelicals.

27. Suro, Fry, and Passel (2005, p. 14).

As discussed previously, it is not clear that an analysis of the aggregate Latino population is meaningful, even if several national-origin group variables are taken into account. Latino populations significantly differ in many important respects, and political dynamics may also vary at the state level. The following five models therefore examine Latino anticipated support for Bush and Kerry in four states: California, Texas, New York, and Florida. In addition, respondents from three states (Arizona, Colorado, and New Mexico) have been combined into a "southwest" category. In order to reduce the amount of missing data, some of the independent variables in table 11-2 were dropped from the state models.

The first pattern to note in table 11-3 is that evangelical support for Bush was strong in all but one state. With the exception of Florida, the evangelical variable is a statistically significant explanation of anticipated support for Bush. This also means that Roman Catholics, the base case in the regression,

Table 11-3. Probit Model of Bush-Kerry Support among Latinos, by State

Variables	California	Texas	Southwest[a]	Florida	New York
Evangelical	1.197***	0.491*	1.252*	0.867	1.695*
	(0.439)	(0.256)	(0.714)	(0.635)	(0.876)
Mainline Protestant	0.290	0.352	0.508	−1.162*	0.290
	(0.803)	(0.387)	(0.772)	(0.635)	(1.372)
Secular	−0.161	0.367	−0.941	−0.170	1.457
	(0.893)	(0.586)	(0.886)	(2.385)	(1.101)
Bush approval	1.437***	1.100***	1.946***	1.355***	0.711
	(0.188)	(0.136)	(0.425)	(0.315)	(0.620)
Economic evaluations	0.754***	0.030	0.774**	0.571*	1.256*
	(0.189)	(0.153)	(0.376)	(0.317)	(0.749)
Partisanship	0.477***	0.471***	0.107	0.424**	0.692***
	(0.097)	(0.073)	(0.171)	(0.174)	(0.224)
Mexican	−0.290	−0.152	−1.022	. . .	. . .
	(0.306)	(0.258)	(0.632)		
Cuban	. . .	. . .	. . .	0.535	. . .
				(0.606)	
Puerto Rican	. . .	. . .	. . .	. . .	0.318
					(0.698)
Constant	−3.892***	−2.774***	−3.471***	−2.815***	−5.362***
	(0.485)	(0.331)	(0.928)	(0.530)	(1.452)
Pseudo R^2	0.74	0.62	0.80	0.79	0.80
Number of observations	390	390	157	166	115

Source: *Washington Post,* Univisión, and Tomás Rivera Policy Institute preelection survey, October 2004.
. . . Not applicable.
*** $p < 0.01$.
** $p < 0.05$.
* $p < 0.10$.
a. Arizona, Colorado, New Mexico.

were more likely to support Kerry than were evangelicals. As displayed in figure 11-1, the boost in Bush support among evangelical Latinos is substantial, ranging from 27 points in California to 17 in Texas.

The other two independent variables for religion—mainline Protestants and the secular—are not generally significant. This indicates that the opinions of the latter do not differ from those of Roman Catholics once a variety of political and demographic variables are taken into account; recall that, in table 11-1, secular voters were 10 points more supportive of Bush than Catholics and mainline Protestants were almost 17 points more supportive of Bush.

The one exception is Florida, where the evangelical variable is insignificant, while the mainline Protestant variable is statistically significant but negatively associated with anticipated Bush support (dropping Bush support by 30 points). The measures of Bush approval, economic evaluations, and partisanship are also significant and in the usual directions. This could be the result of either low evangelical support for Bush or relatively high Catholic support in that state. An examination of the Florida data suggests that relatively strong Catholic support for Bush is the explanation, but additional analysis and data are needed. Perhaps a mitigating factor for Latino Catholics in Florida is that then Governor Jeb Bush, the brother of the president, is a convert to Roman Catholicism.

Last, I examine anticipated support for Bush and Kerry in the Mexican American and Puerto Rican communities. Unfortunately, there are too few Cuban American respondents to model their presidential vote reliably. As reported in the first column of table 11-4 and displayed in figure 11-1, evangelical Mexican Americans were more likely to anticipate voting for Bush, as were Latinos overall, while mainline Protestants and the secular exhibited no unique patterns. Mexican American support for Bush rose by roughly 21 points among evangelicals. There do not appear to be any regional differences, although one might expect that Tejanos would have been more supportive than other Mexican Americans, especially given Bush's relatively positive relationship with Latinos during his time as governor.

For Puerto Rican respondents, a slightly different pattern emerges. The second column of table 11-4 indicates that, while evangelicals were particularly likely to anticipate voting for Bush, the variable for mainline Protestants is statistically significant and negative (dropping Bush's support by a substantial 33 points). This indicates that these respondents were less likely to vote for Bush than were Catholics, who are the baseline group in these models. For now, the low level of support for Bush among Latino mainline Protestants is a subject for further study, as a full explanation would require additional research into the meaning of mainline Protestant within Latino communities.

Table 11-4. Probit Model of Bush-Kerry Support among Latinos, by National-Origin Group[a]

Variable	Mexican Americans	Puerto Ricans
Evangelical	0.764***	1.117*
	(0.215)	(0.644)
Mainline Protestant	0.106	−2.165*
	(0.321)	(1.239)
Secular	0.215	0.003
	(0.626)	(2.261)
Bush approval	1.165***	1.187***
	(0.104)	(0.371)
Economic evaluations	0.331***	0.427
	(0.108)	(0.457)
Partisanship	0.364**	0.726***
	(0.053)	(0.272)
California	0.028	...
	(0.233)	
Texas	0.082	...
	(0.219)	
New York	...	−1.202*
		(0.640)
Constant	−3.137***	−3.284***
	(0.261)	(0.771)
Pseudo R^2	0.65	0.79
Number of observations	764	166

Source: *Washington Post,* Univisión, and Tomás Rivera Policy Institute preelection survey, October 2004.
... Not applicable.
*** $p < 0.01$.
** $p < 0.05$.
* $p < 0.10$.
a. Numbers in parentheses are standard errors.

Conclusions

This chapter investigated the role of religion in the Latino 2004 presidential vote. It analyzed anticipated voting behavior using an October 2004 national preelection survey. The chapter also examined the vote according to state of residence and national-origin group, two features not common to most research on Latino political behavior and public opinion. It thereby contributes to a larger literature on Latino political participation and to our more general understanding of religion in American politics.

Regardless of how the Latino community is analyzed, several patterns emerge. The first is the particularly strong support for President Bush among Latino evangelicals. Such unique support was found for Latinos overall, for Mexican Americans, for Puerto Ricans, and for Latinos in four states and regions. The one exception to this rule was Florida, where the variable was statistically insignificant. While the data in this chapter cannot explain this result with any certainty, it seems that the answer is not weak evangelical support for Bush but relatively high Catholic support.

This high level of Latino evangelical support for Bush mirrors larger political trends in American politics over the last four decades. A number of scholars have noted that Anglo evangelical Protestants have moved away from the Democratic Party and now align with the GOP.[28] In their chapter in this volume, Geoffrey Layman and Laura Hussey suggest a possible explanation for this trend: "Committed evangelicals have more conservative attitudes on cultural issues and attach more importance to them than does any other religious group." One might ask whether this explanation also underlies Latino evangelical support for Bush in 2004. Some scholars have noted that Latino evangelicals are more conservative than Latino Catholics on a number of social issues, but more research on this question clearly is needed.

Analysts might also ask about the directionality of the evangelical-Bush relationship. For instance, is there a connection between evangelical identification and acculturation, and are politically conservative Latinos attracted to evangelical churches, or are political conservatism and GOP identification learned through association with evangelical communities? They might also ask whether Latino evangelicals are personally attracted to the candidacy of Bush or more generally to the GOP. Layman and Hussey caution against the personalistic accounts favored by many journalists to explain evangelical support for Bush. While the models in this chapter control for partisanship, and thereby suggest some personal dynamic whereby evangelical voters were favorably inclined toward an evangelical candidate, the literature on Latinos, religion, and partisanship is not sufficiently developed to draw any certain conclusions.

In addition, there is evidence that mainline Protestants are relatively less supportive of Bush even after controlling for multiple political and demographic factors. In the Florida and Puerto Rican models, the variable is statistically significant and negatively associated with anticipated support for Bush. In Florida, this is the only religious effect. Among Puerto Ricans, the mainline Protestant variable plays a role alongside evangelical support for Bush. For now, these results are more suggestive than conclusive, as they raise questions to guide in-depth research into the communities in question.

Taken together, these findings indicate that the role of religion in the 2004 presidential election exhibited both similarities and differences at the state and

28. Green and others (1996); Wilcox and Larson (2006); Kohut and others (2000, p. 3).

national-origin group levels, dynamics not captured by the overall model. While the results document the original expectation of evangelical support for Bush, some differences at the state and national-origin group levels are worthy of further investigation. This reflects the growing understanding that "Latinos" are diverse and may best be understood by research designs that acknowledge their divergent historical experiences and contemporary contexts.

Appendix. Coding of the Variables

The generational status, gender, and national-origin variables are dummy measures. A standard income question was not used. Instead, income was taken into account through three variables, including a dummy for missing data, in order to keep as many respondents as possible in the models (the base case is the lowest income category)

The anticipated vote question is based on several survey items. The first simply asked, "If the 2004 presidential election were being held today, would you vote for George W. Bush and Dick Cheney, the Republicans, John Kerry and John Edwards, the Democrats, or Ralph Nader and Peter Camejo, the independents?" For those who answered "other," "neither," "would not vote," or "don't know," a follow-up question asked, "Which candidates are you leaning towards?" A third question enables us to ascertain those who have already voted through absentee ballots or early voting. Because this is a dummy variable, logistic regression analysis is used.

The sincerity-of-outreach question was worded as follows: "Which candidate, George W. Bush or John Kerry, do you think has made more of a sincere effort to reach out to the Latino community?" The variable is a three-point scale: 2 for Bush, 1 for either "both candidates" or "neither candidate," and 0 for Kerry. Overall, 41.7 percent of Latinos said that Kerry was more sincere, 30.5 percent said Bush was more sincere, 10 percent said that neither candidate made a sincere effort, 4.1 percent said the sincerity was the same, while 13.6 percent did not know.

Approval of President Bush was assessed through the following question: "Do you approve or disapprove of the way George W. Bush is handling his job as president? [If respondent says, 'Don't know,' probe once: "There is no right or wrong answer here, we're just looking for your best guess. Do you approve or disapprove of the way George W. Bush is handling his job as president?]" Overall, 51.4 percent of Latinos disapproved, 34.8 percent of Latinos approved, and the remaining 13.8 percent neither approved nor disapproved or did not know.

The Black Church
Maintaining Old Coalitions

Eric L. McDaniel

Based on media reports during the 2004 election, one might have thought the African American church was on the verge of a great transformation. The emergence of a black clergyman as a presidential candidate, George W. Bush's continued courting of black clergy, and gay marriage presented a variety of opportunities for the black church to factor into the election. However, in retrospect, the activities of the black church and blacks in general appear to have been business as usual. While Al Sharpton's presidential campaign may have sparked interest, blacks did not view him as having a real chance of winning. George W. Bush's courting of black clergy did not trickle down to the masses; any gains that he made were slight, as blacks once again voted overwhelmingly for the Democratic candidate. Finally, the issue of gay marriage appeared to be a non-issue, as there were few signs of a culture war emerging in the black church.

This chapter reviews the leading issues surrounding the black church in the 2004 election and black attitudes toward them. Using multiple data sources, I examine the role of religion in shaping black policy preferences, candidate evaluations, and, most important, vote choice. While press reports presented a fractured black religious community, the data show a different picture. Bush was able to gain support from a section of the highly religious black community, but overall national and denominational survey data show that, among blacks, religion served primarily to maintain old coalitions rather than build new ones.

Al Sharpton's Presidential Campaign: 1984 All Over Again?

One of the most notable aspects of the black church's role in the 2004 presidential election was the Reverend Al Sharpton's bid for the presidency. Not since the 1980s had an African American—Jesse Jackson in 1984 and 1988—launched a presidential campaign. Sharpton, like Jackson, made a name for himself protesting what he saw as injustice toward the black community. The major difference was that, while Jackson was connected to Martin Luther King Jr. and the legacy of the civil rights movement, Sharpton owed his prominence to his work in the New York City area. Sharpton won fame—or infamy—as an antagonist of former New York City mayor Rudolph Giuliani. In 1987 he gained national attention for defending Tawana Brawley, who falsely claimed that she had been kidnapped and raped by a group of white men. The following year, Sharpton was ordered to pay $65,000 in damages as a result of a defamation suit filed by a man he had accused of attacking Brawley. His credibility was further damaged when the media reported that he was a former FBI informant.[1]

Despite these differences between the candidates, the two election seasons presented strong commonalities. First, African Americans seemed displeased with the incumbent Republican president. Second, much of the rhetoric that Jackson used in 1984 and 1988 reappeared in Sharpton's campaign. Finally, Sharpton, like Jackson, accessed the network of black churches in an attempt to gain support for his campaign.

Al Sharpton's 2004 campaign seemed imminent as he and Jesse Jackson launched a "shadow" inauguration during President Bush's swearing-in ceremony in 2001. During this demonstration, which protested the Florida recount and subsequent election of George W. Bush, Sharpton argued that the nation was in the middle of a battle between "the Christian Right and right Christians."[2] Because of the issues surrounding the 2000 election and the war in Iraq, there was potential for Sharpton to draw support from an agitated black community. However, he was unable to gain the support or generate the fanfare that Jackson had inspired twenty years earlier. Jackson's candidacy was seen as evidence that African American politics was moving from protest

1. Walton and Smith (2006).
2. Harris (2001).

to politics, and his campaign energized the black community to seek greater influence through mainstream political channels, such as the major parties and the pursuit of elected office.[3] Sharpton's campaign attempted to accomplish the same goal, but it was not as well received. One poll found that, although 75 percent of African Americans recognized Sharpton's name, only 37 percent had a favorable opinion of him.[4]

From the beginning, Sharpton's campaign seemed doomed to fail, at least partly because of his controversial past. Furthermore, many believed he was trying to push Jesse Jackson aside in order to become the national spokesman for black America.[5] This tension was exacerbated by Jackson's neutrality toward Sharpton and his support of Howard Dean. When Jesse Jackson did speak of the Sharpton campaign, he argued that the role of Al Sharpton and Carol Moseley-Braun, the other African American candidate seeking the Democratic Party nomination, was to keep the other candidates honest.[6]

Sharpton was hurt most severely by the belief among many African Americans that voting for him was not a good use of their vote. Many African Americans who voted in the Democratic Party primaries may have supported Sharpton's positions, but they did not believe that he could defeat President Bush. As Representative James E. Clyburn of South Carolina said, "Black people aren't crazy. They're looking for somebody they think can win in November."[7]

Throughout the campaign, there was ample evidence of Sharpton's inability to gain the support of the black community. For example, whereas Jesse Jackson raised $7 million for his 1988 campaign, Sharpton struggled to raise $500,000.[8] In New York City, where he had gained early recognition, Sharpton garnered less support in the primary than in his 1997 mayoral bid and performed significantly worse than Jackson in 1984. In 1984 Jesse Jackson received 40 percent of the black vote in New York State and 85 percent in New York City. In 2004 Sharpton received 40 percent of the black vote statewide and about half in New York City.[9] Similarly, an examination of delegates to the Democratic Party's national convention shows a significant difference between the level of support for the two campaigns. In 1984 Jackson gained 12 percent

3. Tate (1993).
4. Walton and Smith (2006).
5. Nagourney (2001).
6. Slackman (2003).
7. Balz (2004).
8. Walton and Smith (2006).
9. Slackman and Connelly (2004).

of the delegates, and in 1988 he increased his share to 29 percent. In contrast, Al Sharpton had less than 1 percent.[10]

Despite his poor showing, Sharpton gained status as a political insider. For example, he was given the opportunity to speak at the Democratic national convention, where he delivered a popular and fiery speech. Even then, however, he was overshadowed by the emergence of Barack Obama, an African American senatorial candidate from Illinois.

Republican Inroads into the Black Vote: A Realignment?

The confusion surrounding the 2000 election left many in the African American community angry with the new administration and the Republican Party. Recognizing this, President Bush quickly reached out to the black community. His appointment of Condoleezza Rice and Colin Powell to high-level posts was seen as a sign of support for African Americans. In addition, the Bush administration used its proposal for faith-based initiatives—a plan to direct government money to religious charities—as an avenue for dialogue with the African American community. President Bush was very active in involving black clergy in the discussion of this program, and initially the effort seemed to pay off.[11] Several black clergy came out in support of President Bush and many of the issues on his agenda.[12] Such support was particularly likely among theologically conservative clergy, such as members of the Church of God in Christ.[13] However, the NAACP spoke out against many of the policies of the Bush administration, including the faith-based initiatives, suggesting the possibility of a clash within the black community.[14]

During the 2004 campaign, George W. Bush became even more aggressive in courting the black vote by arguing that the Democratic Party did not truly support the interests of blacks.[15] This effort was undercut to some extent by Bush's absence from the 2004 NAACP meeting, following his attendance in 2000. But Republican efforts were aided by the fact that John Kerry's campaign did little to court the black vote.[16] While many African Americans held a strong animus toward the current administration, Kerry

10. Walton and Smith (2006).
11. Oppel and Niebuhr (2000).
12. Kirkpatrick (2004a).
13. McDaniel (2003).
14. Miller (2001).
15. Stevenson (2004).
16. Dwyer and Wilgoren (2004).

did not offer an exciting alternative, and he did not make the connection to blacks that Bill Clinton had. Many leading African Americans criticized Kerry for not actively mobilizing the black community.[17] Not until late in the campaign did he make significant attempts to appeal to black voters and energize them for the upcoming election. In late October, Kerry started to make more frequent appearances at black churches and, when he did campaign, was able to garner a great deal of support from congregants and clergy alike. For example, one clergyman stated to his congregation, "I cannot tell you who to vote for, but I can tell you what my mama always told me, 'Stay out of the bushes.' "[18]

Along with faith-based initiatives, Bush's opposition to gay marriage provided fodder for his efforts to court African American voters. Many religious African Americans strongly opposed gay marriage, and some seemed willing to support any candidate who opposed it, regardless of party. One clergywoman even said, "If the KKK opposes gay marriage, I would ride with them."[19] However, most analysts believed that, despite their opposition to same-sex marriage, blacks would vote overwhelmingly for Kerry, as proved to be the case. Blacks and George W. Bush may have seen eye-to-eye on gay marriage, but that issue was not enough to sway the black vote in 2004.

2004 and 2005 Religion and Society Surveys

How did those within the black church respond to the 2004 election? To answer this question, I use the Religion and Society Surveys for 2004 and 2005. The 2004 survey was conducted in July during the General Conference of the African Methodist Episcopal Church (AME), which was held in Indianapolis. This survey yielded 315 respondents. The 2005 survey was conducted in June during the Congress of Christian Education of the National Baptist Convention (NBC) USA, which was held in Houston. The 2005 survey yielded 347 respondents. The AME respondents were surveyed in the middle of the 2004 campaign season, while the NBC respondents were surveyed seven months after the 2004 election. Both surveys targeted clergy and highly active church members. In 2004, 26 percent of the respondents reported being members of the clergy, and 89 percent of those who were not members of the clergy reported holding some form of position in their church. In 2005, 25 percent of

17. Fears (2004).
18. Farhi and Williams (2004).
19. Clemetson (2004).

the respondents reported being members of the clergy, and 85 percent of the rest reported holding some position in their church.

These surveys sought to shed light on the relationship between the black church and politics. The results presented in this essay focus on the reported activities of churches, voters' evaluation of groups and candidates, and vote choice. The format of the survey allowed the respondents to choose from a list of activities they and their churches participated in during the 2004 election.

Church Activities

The examination of activities begins with one of the least costly forms of participation: political discussion. In discussions with pastors and fellow congregants, the presidential election and the war in Iraq were the most popular topics of discussion; gay rights received significantly less attention. As table 12-1 shows, nearly half (45.6 percent) of the AME respondents reported

Table 12-1. Topics of Conversation with Pastors and Members

Percent

Topic	AME survey			NBC survey		
	Total	Clergy	Members	Total	Clergy	Members
Conversations with pastor						
Presidential election	n.a.	n.a.	44.9	n.a.	n.a.	33.9
War in Iraq	n.a.	n.a.	45.6	n.a.	n.a.	37.1
Gay marriage	n.a.	n.a.	17.9	n.a.	n.a.	14.3
Gay rights	n.a.	n.a.	10.3	n.a.	n.a.	7.6
Conversations with members						
Presidential election	85.5	82.3	86.6	71.9	77.0	70.1
War in Iraq	83.6	82.3	84.0	72.2	79.7	69.2
Gay marriage	51.5	53.2	50.7	45.1	51.4	42.9
Gay rights	31.2	27.9	32.0	28.8	36.5	26.3
Holds a conversation about this topic with pastor as least once a month						
Political issues	n.a.	n.a.	26.0	n.a.	n.a.	20.6
Social issues	n.a.	n.a.	n.a.	n.a.	n.a.	39.4
Community issues	n.a.	n.a.	n.a.	n.a.	n.a.	47.5
Holds a conversation about this topic with members as least once a month						
Political issues	42.5	51.9	39.0	30.4	33.8	29.6
Social issues	n.a.	n.a.	n.a.	56.3	56.3	56.6
Community issues	n.a.	n.a.	n.a.	67.7	68.1	67.3

Source: Religion and Society Surveys, 2004 and 2005.
n.a. Not available.

discussing the war in Iraq with their pastor, compared with 37.1 percent of the NBC respondents. The presidential election was mentioned by almost as many people (44.9 percent of the AME and 33.9 percent of the NBC respondents). Gay rights significantly trailed these two topics of conversation: less than one-fifth of the respondents reported talking to their pastor about gay marriage or gay rights. More respondents talked to other members of the congregation about each of these issues, but the pattern across issues was the same.

More broadly, 26 percent of the AME and 20.6 percent of the NBC respondents reported talking to their pastor about political issues at least once a month. Among the NBC respondents, who were asked about other topics of discussion, 39.4 percent reported talking to their pastor about social issues at least once a month and 47.5 percent reported discussing community issues with their pastor at least once a month. Similarly, community and social issues outranked political issues as topics of conversation with other members of the congregation. Two-thirds of both NBC clergy and members reported having conversations concerning community issues with their fellow congregants, while less than one-third of both groups reported discussing political issues.

Moving from topics of conversation to actual activities, the surveys show that churches provided an atmosphere for political engagement but were less likely to take a more active part in politics. Table 12-2 highlights the various activities that respondents reported having occurred in their church. The most popular activity was allowing public officials to speak at a service: nearly 50 percent of the respondents in both surveys reported that this took place in their church. The activities representing greater engagement, such as serving as a polling place or holding a forum, were less common, but AME churches were more likely to take part in these activities than their NBC counterparts.

Transitioning from the organizational level to the elite level, the analysis of clerical activities shows that clergy predominantly used the power of the pulpit as a channel for their political activity. Encouraging people to vote was the most widespread activity: 72.9 percent of the AME and 65.6 percent of the NBC respondents reported that their pastor took part in this type of activity. Clergy actively used their position to take a stand on moral and political issues both inside and outside the church. However, more direct forms of political involvement, such as running for office or creating a political action committee, were relatively rare. In addition, most clergy did not tell their congregation for whom to vote: only 9.7 percent of the AME and 12.1 percent of the NBC respondents indicated that their pastor told them to vote for a particular candidate.

Table 12-2. Reported Political Activities Occurring in Churches and by Pastors

Percent

Activity	AME	NBC
Church		
Allowed a public official to speak during worship service	50.2	49.8
Invited public officials to meetings	36.3	27.5
Allowed a political organization to meet in the church	26.7	12.5
Served as a polling place	14.2	13.8
Held a political forum	20.6	7.9
Pastor		
Criticized public officials	24.2	19.7
Spoke out on a moral issue	65.5	62.3
Spoke out on a political issue	55.5	46.6
Took part in a protest	16.1	9.2
Worked with a political party	12.9	10.8
Told the congregation for whom to vote	9.7	12.1
Formed a political action committee	11.6	5.9
Handed out voter guides	21.3	18.4
Commented on a moral issue during the sermon	54.8	42.6
Commented on a political issue during the sermon	40.0	29.8
Ran for office	8.4	6.2
Contacted a public official	28.8	21.0
Encouraged the congregation to vote	72.9	65.6

Source: Religion and Society Surveys, 2004 and 2005.

Evaluation of Candidates

How did members of the black church respond to the major-party presidential candidates? The surveys addressed this question by asking respondents to rate the parties and their presidential candidates using a "feeling thermometer," where a higher number indicates that the respondent feels greater "warmth" toward the subject. The results, which reflect traditional partisan ties, can be seen in table 12-3. Both the AME and NBC respondents gave John Kerry significantly higher ratings than George W. Bush. Likewise, both sets of respondents felt much greater warmth toward the Democratic Party than the Republican Party. A more in-depth examination shows that both groups overwhelmingly viewed the Democratic Party as better representing black interests. Finally, the NBC survey targeted attitudes toward religiously active politicians. First, the respondents were asked about support for politicians who have expressed a strong commitment to Christianity. The results show that the majority of the respondents (53.9 percent) felt that the black church should support these politicians. The next question asked whether or not the respondents believed that President George W. Bush's expression of faith made him

Table 12-3. Affect toward Public Figures, Political Parties, and Groups

	AME			NBC		
Issue	*Total*	*Clergy*	*Members*	*Total*	*Clergy*	*Members*
Feeling thermometer[a]						
George W. Bush	18.1	21.7	16.8	25.5	32.5	23.0
John F. Kerry	64.1	60.7	65.2	56.8	56.2	57.0
Republican Party	21.8	24.1	20.9	25.4	29.8	23.5
Democratic Party	75.3	71.8	76.4	72.6	67.8	73.9
Which party best represents blacks?[b]						
Republicans	0.3	0.0	0.5	2.9	2.5	3.1
Democrats	78.6	75.0	79.8	69.4	62.3	71.8
Neither	17.6	19.5	20.0	19.7	24.7	17.5
Both	3.4	5.3	2.8	8.1	9.9	7.6
Politicians who have shown a strong commitment to Christianity should receive more support from the black church[b]	n.a.	n.a.	n.a.	53.9	59.5	51.7
President Bush's expression of faith shows that he is a good ally for the black church[b]	n.a.	n.a.	n.a.	12.4	16.1	10.6

Source: Religion and Society Surveys, 2004 and 2005.
n.a. Not available.
a. Scores range from 0 to 100.
b. Percentage of individuals who agree.

a good ally for the black church. Slightly over one-tenth of the respondents agreed with this statement. These results suggest that the belief that President Bush's much discussed religious commitment would allow him to make inroads into the black religious community was unfounded.

Partisanship and Vote Choice

The final part of this analysis focuses on partisanship and vote choice. These results can be found in table 12-4. It is perhaps not surprising that the majority of the AME respondents (56.6 percent) and close to half of the NBC respondents (47.1 percent) identified themselves as strong Democrats. What is more interesting is that a number of respondents identified themselves as Republicans. While the numbers are small in both groups, it is clear that there are more Republican identifiers among the NBC respondents (18.5 percent) than within the AME group (5.8 percent).

When it comes to vote choice, the surveys reveal overwhelming support for the Democratic candidate in the 2000 and 2004 elections. However, the clergy appear to have been more attracted to Bush than the laity. In both 2000 and 2004 NBC clergy (13.8 and 15.2 percent, respectively) were significantly

Table 12-4. Partisanship and Presidential Vote Choice, 2000 and 2004

Percent

Indicator	AME survey			NBC survey		
	Total	Clergy	Members	Total	Clergy	Members
Party identification scale						
Strong Democrat	56.6	53.3	57.5	47.1	51.3	45.8
Democrat	16.2	21.3	15.5	13.8	10.3	15.1
Weak Democrat	12.8	10.7	13.6	10.1	9.0	10.4
Independent	8.6	9.3	8.4	10.4	6.4	12.3
Weak Republican	3.1	2.7	3.3	8.4	12.8	7.1
Republican	1.0	1.3	0.1	5.7	6.4	5.7
Strong Republican	1.7	1.3	1.9	4.4	3.9	3.8
Mean partisanship score	Democrat	Democrat	Democrat	Democrat	Democrat	Democrat
2000 election vote choice						
Bush	n.a.	n.a.	n.a.	8.0	13.8	5.5
Gore	n.a.	n.a.	n.a.	87.2	85.0	88.1
Others	n.a.	n.a.	n.a.	4.8	1.3	6.4
2004 presidential election vote choice						
Bush	1.7	4.8	0.6	9.6	15.2	7.5
Kerry	97.1	91.9	98.9	85.1	83.5	86.0
Others	1.2	3.3	0.6	5.3	1.3	6.5

Source: Religion and Society Surveys, 2004 and 2005.
n.a. Not available.

more likely to report voting for Bush than church members (5.5 and 7.5 percent, respectively). This was also the case for AME clergy in 2004. In addition, NBC respondents in general were more likely to report voting for Bush than their AME counterparts. Only 1.7 percent of the AME respondents reported that they intended to vote for Bush in 2004, while 9.6 percent of the NBC respondents reported having done so. Bush's attempts to win support within the black church were apparently more successful within the NBC. (This difference may be due to the fact that the NBC survey was conducted seven months after the heat of the election.) More broadly, however, the black church continued to show a relatively united front. Despite press reports of a growing cleavage within the black religious community, there is little evidence of such a split in these two denominations.

The Role of Religion in Shaping Black and White Attitudes

The preceding analysis provided a glimpse of how African American religious elites viewed the candidates and issues surrounding the election. What role did religion play in shaping these views? In this section, I analyze the impact of religiosity on both black and white political attitudes, using the 2004 National Election Study (NES), which yields a national sample of 1,212 observations. This survey includes a wealth of questions about religious views. It also has a significant number of African American respondents (180), which allows for a satisfactory comparison with whites.

The main concern of this analysis is vote choice in the 2004 election. The dependent variable is a dichotomous measure, with 1 indicating a vote for Bush and 0 indicating a vote for another candidate. The independent variables include race, religiosity, an interaction variable, and various controls.

Race

The NES asks respondents to report their race. In this essay, I focus on African Americans, using whites as a comparison group. Because the number of Latinos, Asians, and other racial categories in the NES is so small, they are excluded from the analysis.

Religiosity

The religiosity measure is a seventeen-point measure, coded so that the minimum value is 0 and the maximum is 1 ($\alpha = 0.826$). It is an additive measure composed of biblical literalism, church attendance, frequency of prayer, and importance of religion in daily life. The mean score on this measure is 0.647. A quick comparison of the racial groups shows blacks (0.756) ranking significantly higher than whites (0.620) on this scale.

Interaction of Race and Religiosity

To account for racial differences in the effects of religiosity, an interaction term (race * religiosity) was created. This term makes it possible to measure any difference in the impact of religiosity on blacks, as compared to whites.

Control Variables

All of the models control for other factors influencing vote choice, including age, sex, socioeconomic status, location, occupational and religious affiliation, ideology, and partisanship. The measures of socioeconomic status are income and education. Location captures whether or not the respondent lives in the South and the size of the town or city in which he or she lives. Religious affiliation primarily reflects whether the respondent is Protestant or Catholic. Occupational affiliation indicates whether or not someone in the household is a member of a union. (Since union membership is strongly correlated with partisanship, policy preferences, and vote choice, it is important to control for its effects.) Ideology is measured on a seven-point scale, with higher numbers reflecting more conservative beliefs. Finally, partisanship is measured on a seven-point scale ranging from strong Democrat to strong Republican. To facilitate interpretation of the results, all of the measures are scaled from 0 to 1.[20]

Religiosity and Vote Choice

Although religiosity significantly pushes both blacks and whites to vote for Bush, the large shift of blacks predicted by some in the media did not occur. The complete results are reported in the appendix (table 12A-1), while figure 12-1 displays the data to answer the critical question: Did Bush make significant gains among religious blacks? Answering this question is a matter of interpretation. On the one hand, blacks at the high end of the religiosity scale are much more likely to have voted for Bush than African Americans who have a lower level of religiosity. On the other hand, those at the high end of the scale still only have a 25 percent chance of voting for Bush, compared to 68 percent for their white counterparts. In addition, blacks at the high end of the scale make up slightly more than 25 percent of the total black population in the sample. Essentially, Bush gained support from a quarter of a quarter of the black population, or 6 percent of the black vote. While 6 percent is not a lot, in a close election such as the 2004 election, it could be pivotal. However, it is also important to note that blacks

20. Because of the interaction term, the interpretation of these results is slightly different from other regression models. Because of the interaction term, the effects of race and religiosity are now contingent on each other. Analyzing the lower-order terms, race and religiosity, being independent of each other, would lead to a faulty understanding of the results (Braumoeller 2004; Freidrich 1982). The coefficients for the variables for religiosity and race are not their direct effect on the dependent variable, but their effect on the dependent variable when one or the other is set at 0. In this case, the religiosity term represents the effect of religiosity on whites. For this chapter, the coefficients for orthodoxy's effect on blacks is calculated using the linear combinations command in STATA version 8, which calculates the coefficients as well as the standard errors and confidence intervals. To further interpret how race and religion interact, the chapter uses predicted probabilities and predicted values. These are calculated using the spost command in STATA (Long and Freese 2001).

Figure 12-1. Predicted Probability of Voting for George W. Bush in 2004, by Race and Level of Religiosity

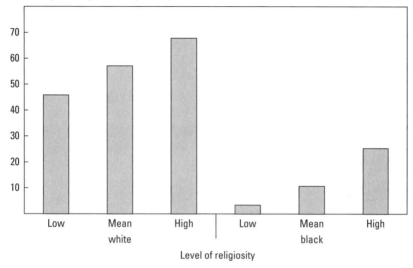

Probability of voting for Bush (percent)

Level of religiosity

Source: National Election Study, 2004.

make up a small proportion of the voting public. So, in the end, it may have had no real effect on the outcome of the election. It will be important to see if this connection between highly religious African Americans and Republican candidates remains in future elections.

Gay Marriage and the 2004 Election

Moving from presidential vote choice, the final part of the analysis examines one of the major issues in the 2004 election: gay marriage. In chapter 7, David Campbell and Quin Monson show that the issue of gay marriage mobilized white evangelicals. Did it do the same for African Americans?

Sentiment within much of the black community ran against gay marriage. Many of the historically black denominations, such as the African Methodist Episcopal Church, National Baptist Convention USA, and the Church of God in Christ passed resolutions or made statements that prohibited their clergy from officiating over a same-sex marriage ceremony. This opposition reflected a broader discomfort with homosexuality within the black church. Some scholars, such as Cathy Cohen, have argued that

Table 12-5. Attitudes toward Homosexuals and Issues Related to Homosexuals

Indicator	AME survey			NBC survey		
	Total	Clergy	Members	Total	Clergy	Members
Homosexual feeling thermometer[a]	29.3	26.3	30.2	22.8	22.8	22.9
Gay union preference[b]						
Gay marriage	1.6	0.0	2.1	1.6	0.0	2.2
Civil unions	14.1	9.1	15.9	4.0	3.2	4.37
Both	2.0	3.0	1.6	2.8	3.2	2.7
Neither	82.4	87.9	80.4	91.67	93.6	90.7
Churches should oppose any legislation that provides homosexuals with the same rights as others[b]	48.2	65.3	42.2	n.a.	n.a.	n.a.
Homosexuals' quest for equal rights is similar to that of blacks[b]	15.3	17.9	14.4	16.0	11.0	17.6

Source: 2004 and 2005 Religion and Society Surveys.
n.a. Not available.
a. Scores range from 0 to 100.
b. Percentage of respondents who agree.

this attitude is partly responsible for the growth of the AIDS/HIV epidemic.[21] They argue that the black church's reluctance to address the issue of homosexuality has allowed the disease to spread throughout the black community.

In addition, many church leaders were put off by the fact that advocates of gay rights framed the gay marriage issue in terms of civil rights. Jesse Jackson, for example, referred to the comparison between the campaign for gay marriage and the African American civil rights movement as a "stretch."[22] The data presented here show that most members of the black church shared these attitudes. As illustrated by the feeling thermometer data shown in table 12-5, feelings toward homosexuals in general were relatively cool. Both the AME and NBC respondents overwhelmingly opposed gay marriage and civil unions, although the AME respondents were somewhat more open to civil unions. Both groups were also highly opposed to viewing homosexuals' quest for equal rights as similar to that of blacks. However, this opposition was stronger among the clergy than among congregation members. Among the AME respondents, 65.3 percent of clergy favored using the church to oppose gay rights compared with 42.2 percent of members.

21. Cohen (1999).
22. Clemetson (2004).

Figure 12-2. Predicted Probability of Supporting Laws That Protect
Homosexuals from Job Discrimination, by Race and Level of Religiosity

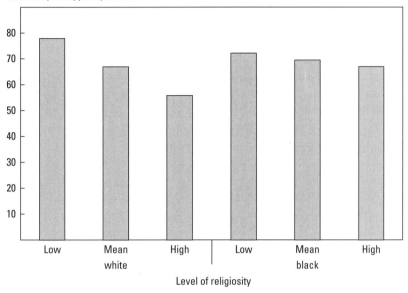

Probability of support (percent)

Source: National Election Study, 2004.

Data from the National Election Study point to a similar conclusion.[23]
Religiosity had a negative impact on support for same-sex marriage among
both blacks and whites. Religiosity was also negatively related to support for
strengthening gay rights laws. However, there is an intriguing racial difference. Religiosity had significantly less impact on blacks than whites. As shown
in figure 12-2, blacks at the low end of the religiosity scale were more opposed
to strengthening gay rights laws than whites with the same level of religiosity.
But at the high end of the religiosity scale, whites were more opposed than
blacks. In other words, among African Americans there appears to have been
some level of support for ensuring that the rights of homosexuals are not
being unduly limited.

23. The gay marriage variable is a dichotomous measure based on the response to the following question, "Should same-sex couples be allowed to marry, or do you think that they
should not be allowed to marry?" The legal protection variable is a four-point measure based
on the strength to which respondents favored or opposed laws to protect homosexuals from
job discrimination. The measure is scaled from 0 (oppose strongly) to 1 (favor strongly).

This support may be reflected in the fact that not all black clergy opposed gay marriage. A small but significant number argued that making it impossible for homosexuals to marry amounted to discrimination, which the black church should not support. As one black clergy member stated, "Oppression is oppression is oppression."[24] Yet this dissension within the ranks of the black religious community was far from taking the shape of a culture war. Few analysts believed that the debate over gay marriage would lead to major changes in black political alignments. Many believed that blacks would oppose any measures supporting same-sex marriage but nonetheless would vote overwhelmingly for Kerry.

Conclusion

With the Sharpton presidential campaign, George W. Bush's push for black votes, and the same-sex marriage debate, many speculated that the black church was on the verge of a significant political shift. However, this does not appear to have occurred. Sharpton was not able to mobilize the black church, Bush did not make major gains in the black vote, and the gay marriage issue did not inspire much debate in the black church. However, there are some interesting points to take from this analysis of the 2004 election. First, religiosity's effect on political attitudes is contingent on race. Second, among blacks, religion serves to maintain old coalitions, not build new ones. If the Republican Party hopes to make gains in upcoming years, it has a hard path to tread. George W. Bush was able to gain some support from black clergy, but it does not appear that the members of their congregations followed suit. Blacks—even religious blacks—continue to ally with Democrats. Race supersedes the effects of religion.

24. Banerjee (2005).

Appendix Table 12A-1. Multivariate Models of Vote Choice and Attitudes on Homosexual Issues

Variable	Voted for Bush in 2004	Strengthen gay rights laws[a]	Allow same-sex marriage[b]
Black * religiosity	1.789	0.297*	0.135
	(1.549)	(0.173)	(0.714)
Black	−2.926*	−0.141	−0.335
	(1.322)	(0.134)	(0.522)
Religiosity	1.090***	−0.425***	−1.977***
	(0.390)	(0.064)	(0.281)
Age	−0.306	−0.001	−1.229***
	(0.429)	(0.065)	(0.286)
Female	0.121	0.057*	0.107
	(0.181)	(0.029)	(0.125)
Education	−0.647*	0.181***	1.119***
	(0.388)	(0.060)	(0.267)
Income	0.717*	−0.021	−0.748***
	(0.404)	(0.065)	(0.277)
South	0.815***	0.011	0.058
	(0.215)	(0.032)	(0.141)
Urbanicity	0.103	0.063	−0.007
	(0.336)	(0.053)	(0.227)
Union	−0.273	0.021	0.053
	(0.218)	(0.038)	(0.158)
Ideology	0.696***	−0.075**	−0.639***
	(0.224)	(0.036)	(0.142)
Partisan	3.332***	−0.122**	−0.683***
	(0.332)	(0.050)	(0.211)
Catholic	−0.119	0.093***	0.309**
	(0.197)	(0.034)	(0.139)
	−2.889***		
Constant	(0.494)	0.872***	1.516***
		(0.074)	(0.316)
Adjusted R^2	−136.009	0.166	
Log likelihood	88.46		−285.093
Correctly predicted			79.37
Number of observations	494	590	664

Source: 2004 National Election Study.
a. A four-point measure.
b. A dichotomous measure.
* $p < 0.10$.
** $p < 0.05$.
*** $p < 0.01$.

A Gentle Stream or a "River Glorious"?

The Religious Left in the 2004 Election

Lyman A. Kellstedt, Corwin E. Smidt, John C. Green, and James L. Guth

A religious left is not just vital—it's possible. There are millions of people of faith wanting their better halves appealed to, willing to act, waiting for a vehicle to do so.

—Amy Waldman, "Why We Need a Religious Left," *Washington Monthly*, December 1995

In recent years, the "religious right" has often seemed like a raging torrent, moving voters to the polls. Not so the "religious left." Certainly no credible observer would characterize the latter as a "raging torrent" in terms of its impact on voters. But is it at least a gentle stream? And could it grow into a "river glorious"?[1] This chapter attempts to answer these questions.

When the religious right appeared in the late 1970s, it surprised many observers and, despite fluctuating assessments of its vitality, has become a fixture of national politics.[2] As a consequence, scholars know a great deal about the religious right, including its potential constituencies among

---

1. Havergal (1974).
2. Wilcox (1992); Smidt and Penning (1997, p. ix); Green, Rozell, and Wilcox (2003).

voters.[3] In contrast, the contemporary religious left has received much less scholarly attention. This lacuna is ironic: for much of the twentieth century various kinds of liberals dominated the religious contribution to American public life, playing a significant role in the civil rights, women's, peace, and environmental movements. But at the turn of the twenty-first century, such voices were much less audible in the public square. As a consequence, scholars know little about the potential following of the religious left in the American mass public.[4]

This chapter investigates the potential constituencies of the religious left in the American electorate. First, we put the religious left in historical context. We then turn to the question of how to define it conceptually and operationally. With these definitions in mind, we examine the relative size of several potential constituencies of the religious left and describe their social-demographic, religious, and political characteristics. In each case, we compare the constituency to secular liberals and traditionalist conservatives, defined in an analogous fashion. We conclude by assessing the role of these constituencies in the 2004 presidential campaign and their potential impact in the future.

Historical Background

Historically the religious left has had both political and religious components. On the political side, it has been characterized by a variety of liberal social movements. In religious terms, it often has reflected "liberal" or "modernist" theology, especially among white Christians. This combination is not accidental: the early twentieth-century agitation for social reform encouraged departures from traditional religious thinking, especially among religious elites, while at the same time theological innovations encouraged the drive for social reform.[5] Indeed, the connection between "liberal" politics and "liberal" theology was a theme of the famed fundamentalist-modernist dispute within American Protestantism in the early 1920s. Many—but not all—Social

3. Guth and Green (1988); Guth and others (1995); Green and others (1997); Appleby (1997); Calhoun-Brown (1997); Wald and Sigelman (1997). Throughout the chapter, we use the term "religious right" to refer to the public constituencies made up of religious conservatives, most of whom are Christians, but with some from other religious traditions. The term "Christian Right" is reserved for a specific social movement led by conservative Christians, mostly evangelical Protestants. We use the term "religious left" in an analogous fashion.

4. See Olson (2007).

5. Cherry (1995).

Gospel advocates embodied that political and theological combination, while most opponents remained wedded to an "individual gospel" that preserved historic doctrines and favored a more passive conservatism.[6]

This basic religious divide seemed a permanent feature of American politics throughout the twentieth century, more or less visible at various times. From the progressive era through the 1950s, liberal activists from many traditions, but especially mainline Protestantism, worked for economic reform and social justice, while also attending to issues of war and peace. In the 1960s and 1970s, such activists were critical to the struggle for civil rights and against the Vietnam War.[7] By the 1980s, these activists added new causes to the older ones, including women's rights, the plight of illegal immigrants, environmentalism, and gay rights.

This brief sketch of liberal social movements implies more organizational continuity than actually existed. While specific movements frequently had "contagion" effects on later movements, most were freestanding efforts and short-lived, leaving little in the way of an institutionalized religious left over the decades. A partial exception was the mainline Protestant elite, speaking through denominational social agencies and the National Council of Churches and providing a continuing "prophetic witness" on these matters. Indeed, the religious left's most striking achievements, as on civil rights in the 1960s, derived from the combination of institutional leadership with effective short-term mobilization of local clergy and grassroots laity.[8] However, such efforts regularly suffered from minimal funding, ineffective communication with constituents, and resistance from some clergy and many laity. Neither these institutional elites nor the episodic movement organizations combined effective lobbying with skillful electoral mobilization, an important factor in the political success of groups and movements.[9]

Despite the limitations of specific liberal social movements, religious involvement in politics was dominated by liberals until at least the 1970s.[10] Some scholars were puzzled by the absence of an organized religious right, but others thought that "otherworldly" theology could never be conducive to political engagement.[11] To be sure, religious conservatives resisted many of these liberal movements and were especially critical of the "new breed" of

6. See Guth and others (1997).
7. Marsh (1997); Quinley (1974).
8. Findlay (1993).
9. Hertzke (1988); Hofrenning (1995); Hansen (1991).
10. Waldman (1995).
11. Quinley (1974, p. 29).

activist liberal clergy, but such responses were usually scattered and sporadic, with occasional successes derived more from political inertia than from effective counter-organization.

The left's monopoly in religious politics ended dramatically in the 1970s with the rise of the Moral Majority and similar groups. Since then, religious conservatives have taken the initiative in politics, deploying a series of organizations over the past thirty years. Like the earlier liberal social movements, these pro-life, pro-family, and traditional values movements at first had an ad hoc quality about them, but a broader religious right eventually emerged, drawing on traditionalists from across the religious landscape, creating an array of movement organizations and influencing the Republican Party.

These developments would seem to have set the stage for explicit "two-party" competition in American religious politics, with an organized religious left opposing the newly mobilized religious right. Indeed, developments within American religion seemed to point toward just such heightened competition, as theological divisions between modernists and traditionalists spread and deepened across the religious landscape. At the same time, the unaffiliated and secular populations continued to grow, as did the ranks of religious and ethnic minorities. As internal denominational conflicts flared, traditionalists from different religious backgrounds "found" each other, discovering that they had more in common than they did with modernist members of their own churches, while the modernists built a similar alliance. Both alliances found some support among secular conservatives and liberals, and both sought aid from ethnic religious minorities. Taken together, these developments were dramatic enough to be labeled a "restructuring" of American religion.[12]

This religious restructuring both encouraged and was aided by changes in the political agenda. The rise of social issues was of particular importance: as religious modernists embraced social innovations, from women's rights to gay marriage, religious traditionalists mounted counterattacks. But once these cultural disputes were under way, other issue domains were gradually subsumed. By the end of the twentieth century, there was much more issue constraint among religious traditionalists and modernists than in the past, with the two alliances lining up on opposite sides of social welfare policy, economic issues, and foreign policy as well as social issues. This contributed to the growing polarization of national politics in the 2000 and 2004 presidential elections (see chapter 2 of this volume). The increasing ease of organizing

12. Wuthnow (1988); Hunter (1991).

citizen groups of all kinds seemed to suggest that both the religious right and religious left would be well represented in the interest group universe.[13]

Despite these auspicious circumstances, the religious left was not an imposing political force at the beginning of the twenty-first century. True, there have been recent efforts to form national organizations of liberal religious activists, often directed at countering the lobbying and electoral efforts of the religious right.[14] Probably the best known are the Interfaith Alliance and the Call to Renewal, both founded just prior to the 1996 election. In 2005 the Interfaith Alliance website claimed 150,000 members, representing a diverse set of religious communities. And other organizations have appeared, some local, some statewide, and others seeking a broader national constituency. To this point, none has exerted a major influence over legislative or electoral politics—much less both. Still, many religious left leaders sense a growing opportunity for mobilizing like-minded voters.

Are there, in fact, constituencies within the American public that might be mobilized by such efforts? Where are they located, and what are their numbers? How do they compare to the constituencies of the religious right and to their potential allies in the secular left? And what role did these constituencies play in the 2004 election?

Data and Definitions

Our analysis is based on the Fourth National Survey of Religion and Politics, which was conducted in 2004 and contained an especially rich set of religious and political measures useful for addressing these questions (see chapter 2 for a full description of the survey). Any effort to assess the mass constituency for the religious left must define the term, a difficult task.[15] Two simple strategies

---

13. Walker (1991).

14. A religious left political action committee—JustLife—was formed in 1986 to promote a "seamless garment of life" perspective (Smidt and others 1994, p. 139), but it had disbanded by the mid-1990s (Guth and others 1995, pp. 60–61). There are other "left" interest groups with a religious base, such as Bread for the World, Habitat for Humanity, and the Religious Coalition for Reproductive Choice, but they focus primarily on issues and not on contesting elections (Hall 1997). In addition to the Interfaith Alliance (see www.interfaithalliance.org), other religious left organizations include Progressive Christians Uniting, CrossLeft, the Center for Progressive Christianity, Protestants for the Common Good, Spiritual Progressives, and the Catholic organization Call to Action. We acknowledge the help of Calvin College students Deborah Kwak and Christine Holst in a newspaper and website search for information on religious left organizations.

15. Olson (2007, p. 3).

Table 13-1. Alternative Approaches to Determining a Religious Left

Percent

Approach	Sample
Political approach: Ideological self-classification	
Political Left (liberals)	28.2
Political Center (moderates)	27.5
Political Right (conservatives)	44.2
Theological approach	
Secularists	21.2
Religious Left (theological modernists)	29.9
Religious Center (theological centrists)	25.6
Religious Right (theological traditionalists)	23.3
Combined approach[a]	
Secularist	
Liberals	9.3
Moderates	6.2
Conservatives	5.6
Modernist	
Liberals (core religious Left)	9.4
Moderates (religious Left periphery)	8.4
Conservatives	8.9
Centrist	
Liberals (religious Left periphery)	6.2
Moderates	5.8
Conservatives	11.1
Traditionalist	
Liberals (religious Left periphery)	3.3
Moderates	3.8
Conservatives (core religious Right)	14.4

Source: Fourth National Survey of Religion and Politics, University of Akron, 2004.

a. Percentages do not add up to 100 percent in the combined approach, as some respondents did not answer the ideology question or did not use the terms "liberal," "moderate," or "conservative" in their answer.

suggest themselves. First, the religious left could be defined in strictly political terms, focusing on self-identified ideological "liberals," rather than "moderates" or "conservatives," expecting the movement to be liberal politically. In the Fourth National Survey of Religion and Politics, almost 30 percent of Americans saw themselves as liberal to some degree (from very to slightly), while about the same percentage chose moderate (see table 13-1). A solid plurality, however, classified themselves as conservative (just over 44 percent).

An alternative strategy is to use religious liberalism as the defining source of the religious left. Although some would argue that the terms "conservative" and "liberal" are inappropriate for identifying theological perspectives, in fact they are used regularly for that purpose.[16] Typically, religious conservatives

16. Olson (2007).

favor traditional theology and religious practice, while religious liberals prefer nontraditional or modernist theology and practice. Unlike other scholars who must depend on this sort of religious self-identification, we can use many direct measures of belief and behavior for this purpose. Accordingly, we divided the sample of the Fourth National Survey of Religion and Politics into five groups: traditionalists, centrists, modernists, nominals, and seculars (see the appendix to chapter 2 for details). One advantage of this terminology is that it reduces confusion by using different labels for politics and theology.

These religious categories cut across religious traditions, as both the contemporary religious left and right are transdenominational phenomena. For present purposes, we combined the nominally religious, given their marginal religious interests, with the seculars, producing four theological categories (see table 13-1). Modernists are the largest group, just shy of 30 percent of the public, while centrists make up about one-quarter of the population, followed by traditionalists, with just under one-quarter. Finally, seculars (and the nominals) constitute a bit more than one-fifth of the sample.

Our review of the historical antecedents of the contemporary religious left suggests that both political and religious liberalisms are important for locating the mass base of this movement. Combining the three ideological and four theological categories creates twelve groups (see table 13-1).[17] We consider in depth the four groups that are likely constituencies of the religious left. Naturally, the best prospects are individuals who are "left" in both a political and religious sense: the modernist liberals (9.4 percent of the sample). Three other groups qualify less clearly: centrist liberals (6.2 percent) and traditionalist liberals (3.3 percent), based on ideology, and modernist moderates (8.4 percent), based on religion. Although modernist conservatives are a religious fit, their political identity pushes them beyond the religious left.

The vital question is whether the three peripheral groups exhibit attitudes and behaviors similar to the "core" constituency of modernist liberals. If they all do, the mass constituencies of the religious left are much larger (27.3 percent of the public) than the core constituency itself and could constitute a sizable force in politics. In the tables that follow, therefore, we consider both the "core left" and three "peripheral" groups. For comparison, we also report data for secular liberals, potential allies of the core left, and the traditionalist conservatives, their natural opponents (the "core right," being the core constituency of the religious right). We are especially interested in points at which the attitudes and attributes of these potential constituencies of the religious

17. For an alternative approach, see Olson (2007).

left converge, facilitating cooperation, and where they diverge, rendering joint activity problematic.

The Religious Bases of the Religious Left

Do religious factors provide a basis for unity among the potential con-stituencies of the religious left? As table 13-2 reveals, there is considerable diversity in the religious beliefs and practices of the four categories of the religious left. The core left and two of the peripheral groups (the modernist moderates and centrist liberals) hold similar religious beliefs, but centrist liberals are more active, attending church and praying more frequently and giving more to religious causes. The really distinctive group, however, is the tradi-

Table 13-2. The Religious Left and Religious Beliefs and Practice

Percent unless otherwise noted

	Core left	Peripheral religious left groups			Core right
Belief and practice	Secular liberals	Modernist liberals	Modernist moderates	Centrist liberals	Traditionalist liberals	Traditionalist conservatives
Religious beliefs						
Inerrant or literal Bible	3	33	34	51	85	92
A personal God	0	21	28	41	82	86
Jesus only salvation[a]	n.a.	45	51	51	89	91
Religion must modernize	n.a.	71	63	68	44	33
Favor women's ordination	92	81	72	79	69	49
Favor gay ordination	74	43	28	40	21	2
All religions equally true	64	54	42	44	18	13
Absolute moral standards exist	57	63	66	67	81	88
Religious practice						
Daily prayer	11	58	57	77	96	96
Weekly attendance	2	26	28	46	89	93
Tithe	2	17	18	22	67	64
Number of observations	372	377	335	246	132	578
Percent of sample	9.3	9.4	8.4	6.2	3.3	14.4

Source: Fourth National Survey of Religion and Politics, University of Akron, 2004.
n.a. Not available (no data).
a. Asked of Christians only.

tionalist liberals, who are much more conservative in theology and more religiously active than the other three.

Such religious diversity is clearly an obstacle to the formation of coalitions on the religious left. Traditionalist liberals are well represented in the religious left "elite," both by prominent evangelicals such as Jim Wallis, Ron Sider, and Tony Campolo and by many traditionalist Catholics, such as Robert Casey Jr., the newly elected U.S. senator from Pennsylvania. However, they may find the theological heterodoxy of their potential allies a barrier to close cooperation. Such differences may not drive traditionalist liberals into the arms of the religious right or the Republican Party, but they may sideline them politically. The greater religious activism of centrist liberals, who resemble modernist liberals on theology, is likely less problematic in terms of forging an alliance.

But perhaps the greatest problem for unity appears when comparing all four religious left constituencies with the secular liberals: any such broader alliance must ignore religious beliefs, as the latter are naturally quite distinct on religious measures. Indeed, they are likely to resist the religious left argument that Democrats cannot afford to be identified as the "anti-" or "non-religious" party in a society as devout as the United States.[18] In fact, their frequently hostile reaction to devout Democrats has created controversy within the party.

In sum, potential religious left constituencies do not hold a homogeneous set of religious beliefs. And although their religious involvement varies, together it is less than that of traditionalist conservatives. These differences give the religious right a real edge in conducting lobbying and electoral campaigns: their mass base agrees on "fundamental" theological issues, allowing religious arguments to bolster political appeals. Greater religious involvement also facilitates religious right political activation through church and parachurch organizations, whether from the Southern Baptist Convention or Focus on the Family. In contrast, religious left organizations, given their mass constituency, find it hard to use religious arguments effectively for political purposes, although they seek mightily to find common theological ground in God's concern for the poor, the global environment, or world peace. And the religious left's modest religious involvement makes activists more difficult to locate—at least in the pews.

The striking differences in religious belief and behavior are complicated further by diversity of religious affiliation. As table 13-3 shows, the core left is especially diverse, drawing similar percentages from five distinct traditions:

18. Wallis (2005).

Table 13-3. The Religious Left and Religious Affiliations

Percent unless otherwise noted

Religious tradition	Secular liberals	Core left — Modernist liberals	Peripheral religious left groups — Modernist moderates	Centrist liberals	Traditionalist liberals	Core right — Traditionalist conservatives
Evangelical Protestant	4	8	9	29	32	54
Mainline Protestant	11	16	15	27	26	17
Black Protestant	0[a]	18	20	3	14	7
Latino Protestant	0[a]	5	5	2	2	2
White Catholic	11	13	15	36	20	17
Latino Catholic	2	14	10	1	3	1
Other Christian	0[a]	2	6	2	3	2
Liberal faiths	3	5	2	0	0	0
Jewish	8	3	2	0	0	0
Other Non-Christian	2	4	2	0	0	0[a]
Unaffiliated	58	13	14	2	0	0[a]
Number of observations	372	377	335	246	132	578
Percent of sample	9.3	9.4	8.4	6.2	3.3	14.4

Source: Fourth National Survey of Religion and Politics, University of Akron, 2004.
a. Less than half of 1 percent.

mainline and black Protestants, white and Latino Catholics, and the unaffiliated.[19] And over one-quarter come from a broad scattering of other groups, from evangelical Protestants to Jews. Modernist moderates closely resemble the core left in affiliation, while the two other peripheral categories are less diverse. Among centrist and traditionalist liberals, the three large white traditions (evangelical, mainline, and Catholic) predominate, as representation from religious minorities drops dramatically. And while centrist liberals resemble the core left in religious beliefs (table 13-2), their affiliations are quite different, making communication and cooperation more difficult.

Naturally, there is also a dramatic contrast between the core left and core right. Only one in ten of the core left is an evangelical, while the core right draws more than half its base from that tradition. The evangelical predominance among traditionalist conservatives should come as no surprise to observers of American religion, although the substantial contributions of mainliners and Catholics might. No doubt these folks represent the

19. The unaffiliated for the core left and peripheral groups come from respondents who said they have no religious preference but exhibited significant levels of religiosity.

Table 13-4. The Religious Left and Social-Demographic Characteristics

Percent unless otherwise noted

Characteristic	Core left	Peripheral religious left groups				Core right
	Secular liberals	Modernist liberals	Modernist moderates	Centrist liberals	Traditionalist liberals	Traditionalist conservatives
Socioeconomic status						
College graduate	46	20	20	25	19	24
Income > $75,000	38	20	15	27	18	22
Demographics						
Female	44	52	53	57	66	57
Under 40 years of age	47	56	44	40	38	32
Over 55 years of age	17	17	30	24	29	32
Marital status						
Single, never married	40	42	30	24	21	11
Married, never divorced	29	23	35	34	35	57
Spouse same religion	53	72	75	74	81	93
Region						
Northeast	29	25	28	22	18	16
West	28	24	20	18	14	16
Midwest	24	20	19	24	30	29
South	19	31	33	36	38	39
White	84	56	54	89	74	88
Number of observations	372	377	335	246	132	578
Percent of sample	9.3	9.4	8.4	6.2	3.3	14.4

Source: Fourth National Survey of Religion and Politics, University of Akron, 2004.

"orthodox" side of the "culture war" struggles within both the mainline Protestant denominations and the American Catholic Church.[20] Still, the heterogeneity of the religious left and the homogeneity of the religious right are the key to their political potential: just as the religious left is divided by religious belief and practice, it is also scattered across a wide range of religious institutions—especially in comparison with the religious right—hindering political recruitment, communication, and mobilization.

Social-Demographic Characteristics of the Religious Left

Perhaps demographic factors such as common educational backgrounds, similar social traits, or regional concentration might facilitate cooperation within the religious left and between core left and secular liberals. As table 13-4 shows, however, differences between religious left constituencies and secular liberals are dramatic. The latter are the best educated, have the highest

20. Hunter (1991).

incomes, and have the highest proportion of males of any group (by large margins). In addition, secular liberals have the lowest percentage of spouses with the same religious preference and tend to reside in the Northeast and West, the least religious regions in the country. All these differences are likely to complicate cooperation between secular liberals and the religious left groups.

The religious left groups also differ somewhat among themselves. Centrist liberals tend to have higher socioeconomic status, while traditionalist liberals include a preponderance of women. The modernist liberals include the most respondents who have never married and the lowest proportion of those who are married and have never divorced. They are also the youngest group and, along with the modernist moderates, have the highest percentage of nonwhites. These differences are not as wide as the religious divisions noted earlier but may be significant nonetheless. For example, the fact that the core left is made up of large numbers of young, single, and never married individuals suggests that the group has not yet settled into "normal adult patterns," making political recruitment and mobilization difficult.

These religious left groups are also quite different socially from the core right. The latter has the highest percentage of individuals who are over fifty-five years of age, married and have never divorced, have a spouse with the same religion, and reside in the South of any of the groups in the table. They also are mostly white, as are the centrist and secular liberals. In sum, religious diversity on the religious left is accompanied by social diversity, while religious homogeneity on the religious right is accompanied by social homogeneity. Perhaps the religious left has exciting political potential as a "rainbow religious coalition," but the religious and social complexity of that constituency presents real obstacles to recruitment and mobilization.[21]

Political Issues and the Religious Left

If religious and social factors divide the potential constituencies for a broad religious left and, perhaps, for an even more powerful alliance of the religious left and the secular left, do political attitudes provide a solid basis for mobilization? As Laura Olson has argued, historically religious left leaders have achieved some degree of consensus around several issues, with the greatest unity around "socioeconomic justice," the fight for equal rights among disadvantaged groups, opposition to militaristic American foreign policy and support for international institutions, and, more recently, concern for the

21. For a more optimistic assessment of this diversity, see Hart (2001, p. 235).

global environment.[22] "Moral" issues, the unifying catalyst for the religious right, have created fissures within the religious left. Fortunately, we have items allowing us to evaluate how the potential constituencies of the religious left view these questions.

Social welfare issues have united the religious left since the Social Gospel days of the early twentieth century. Indeed, from that time until now, religious left leaders have consistently argued that "economic justice" is a "moral" issue and has a firm theological basis.[23] These concerns expanded greatly in the 1960s to include civil rights and concern for disadvantaged racial minorities. Such questions have received sustained attention from institutional leaders of the religious left, from mainline Protestant denominations and the National Council of Churches to the American Catholic bishops. Thus we might expect considerable unity here.

Table 13-5 provides some support for that expectation. Although there are modest variations, the four religious left groups have very similar attitudes on "economic justice" issues. There is massive support across the groups for increasing taxes on the wealthy to raise funds to fight poverty, solid agreement that large tax cuts have been bad and that government should do more to assist the disadvantaged, and even that the middle class should be taxed more to eliminate poverty. Note, however, the equivocal backing for special assistance for minorities and also the fairly even split on whether government should increase public services and spending. Still, on all these issues the religious left groups, especially the traditionalist liberals, match up very nicely with the secular left, the most liberal group. Moreover, all the liberal groups differ significantly from the traditional conservatives, the anchor of the religious right.

To summarize these findings, we constructed a social welfare index combining the items.[24] As the middle section of table 13-5 shows, substantial numbers in all the religious left categories fall into the two most liberal quintiles of the index, led by the secular liberals but followed closely by the modernist and traditionalist liberals, respectively. Thus social welfare issues do serve to unify the religious left and may constitute a fruitful basis for organization.

Some "newer" issues that are often added to the social justice agenda may also provide the basis for greater unity, but others may not. For example,

---

22. Olson (2007).

23. Rauschenbusch (1964); Wallis (2005).

24. The index resulted from a factor analysis of the six items in table 13-5. For presentation, the factor scores were recoded into the five equal categories reported in the table.

Table 13-5. The Religious Left and Social-Welfare Issues

Percent unless otherwise noted

| Issue | Core left | Peripheral religious left groups | | | Core right |
	Secular liberals	Modernist liberals	Modernist moderates	Centrist liberals	Traditionalist liberals	Traditionalist conservatives
Social welfare issue						
Tax wealthy to help poor	89	86	55	87	86	40
Large tax cuts bad	75	53	62	60	57	26
Public aid to "disadvantaged"	72	63	52	63	64	54
Tax middle class to help poor	70	56	46	57	58	43
Minorities need special help	52	47	40	38	46	37
More government services	48	46	39	47	44	21
Social welfare index						
Very liberal	42	27	17	26	36	10
Liberal	18	28	25	22	16	16
Moderate	17	20	24	23	19	18
Conservative	12	16	24	17	16	19
Very conservative	11	9	10	12	13	37
Standard deviation	1.39	1.28	1.24	1.35	1.44	1.38
New issues						
Protect environment	71	48	41	54	54	57
Oppose death penalty	44	36	32	33	42	32
Number of observations	372	377	335	246	132	578
Percent of sample	9.3	9.4	8.4	6.2	3.3	14.4

Source: Fourth National Survey of Religion and Politics, University of Akron, 2004.

many religious left leaders have joined the growing international concern over the environment, which has also attracted the attention of Catholics and even the National Association of Evangelicals. In a different vein, the American Catholic bishops and liberal Catholic activists have renewed a campaign against the death penalty and have been joined by other religious and secular groups. As the bottom of table 13-5 shows, however, the environmental initiative seems to have more potential than the campaign against the death penalty, claiming substantial support from across the spectrum (but with massive backing only from the secular liberals). Although some prominent religious left activists have argued for a "consistent life ethic" that would oppose the death penalty,[25] this position does not yet resonate with the mass public. Opposition to the death penalty is greatest among secular liberals and

25. Wallis (2005).

Table 13-6. The Religious Left and Foreign Policy Issues

Percent unless otherwise noted

Issue	Secular liberals	Core left Modernist liberals	Peripheral religious left groups Modernist moderates	Centrist liberals	Traditionalist liberals	Core right Traditionalist conservatives
Foreign policy issue						
Use international organizations	92	83	80	87	83	51
Iraq war unjustified	76	59	49	58	47	15
Not favor Israel in Middle East	68	57	40	56	54	18
No special role for U.S.	52	46	55	50	49	25
Oppose preemptive force	45	26	19	30	23	11
Foreign policy index						
Very liberal	42	27	19	32	21	5
Liberal	25	21	32	24	22	8
Moderate	16	23	23	16	16	17
Conservative	13	19	17	18	27	23
Very conservative	4	10	9	10	14	47
Standard deviation	1.20	1.39	1.21	1.36	1.37	1.20
Number of observations	372	377	335	246	132	578
Percent of sample	9.3	9.4	8.4	6.2	3.3	14.4

Source: Fourth National Survey of Religion and Politics, University of Akron, 2004.

traditionalist liberals but does not include much more than one-third of any other religious group. On both issues there are only modest differences between the religious left and religious right.

Foreign policy has also been a continuing focus of the religious left. Some elements are drawn from the historic "peace" churches, such as Quakers and Anabaptists. From the end of World War I to the present, many mainline Protestant churches have periodically flirted with pacifism or demanded strict application of "just war" theories to international conflicts and been strong proponents of multilateral cooperation through institutions such as the United Nations.[26] One of the most massive religious mobilizations of modern times occurred during the Vietnam War, and since the early 1980s the Catholic bishops have frequently criticized American defense policies and military initiatives, including the recent Iraq War. Do international issues provide the raw material for a religious left in the twenty-first century? Table 13-6 looks at this question.

26. Wilson (1988).

A clear point of unity among religious left groups is agreement that the United States should try to cooperate more with international organizations. Reactions to the Iraq war, however, are more complicated. The war clearly separates the secular liberals, very much opposed to the war, from the core right, convinced that it is justified. More important, perhaps, solid majorities or pluralities of the religious left groups hold that the Iraq war is not justified, with the core left and centrist liberals most critical. Still, divided opinion among religious left groups created a dilemma for the Democrats in 2004, as presidential candidate John Kerry did not wish to appear "unpatriotic" and directly attack American intervention. Instead, he argued that the United States had failed to cooperate with other nations and with the United Nations, a stance that resonated with all the liberal groups and even had a modicum of support in the core right.

On other foreign policy issues, there is even more division among religious voters and, especially, among the religious left groups. While the core right strongly favors American support for Israel over the Palestinians, secular liberals want an even-handed or even pro-Palestinian policy, a position favored by majorities in three of the four religious left groups. Similarly, while the core right echoes President Bush's belief that the United States has a special role to play in world affairs, an idea going back as far as the nation's founders, all the left groups are split down the middle. And although the secular liberals are closely divided on whether preemptive war can be justified in the contemporary world, given terrorist threats, large majorities of all "religious" groups are willing to entertain that possibility, led by traditionalist conservatives.

To summarize our findings, we constructed a foreign policy index from the items in table 13-6.[27] On this measure, the secular left is clearly the most "liberal," followed by the centrist liberals, modernist moderates, modernist liberals, and traditionalist liberals, in that order. Although both secular and religious left groups are far less conservative than the religious right, there are considerable differences among them, differences that would seem to make organizing the religious left on the basis of foreign policy instead of social welfare more daunting, especially given the transitory nature of some foreign policy issues.

What about the so-called "moral issues" that received so much attention from observers in the wake of the 2004 election? For the religious right, such issues have always been at the center of attention. Abortion has been at the

27. The foreign policy score was produced by the same procedures used for the social welfare index.

forefront, but in 2004 gay rights, same-sex marriage, and stem cell research were not far behind. Other controversial issues raised recently include public posting of the Ten Commandments, charitable choice programs, and vouchers for private and parochial schools. How do such issues affect prospects for the religious left?

To provide a general answer: in 2004 hot-button social issues divided the secular from the religious left and also created fissures among religious left groups. Consider the data on abortion in table 13-7. A pro-choice stance is almost universal among secular liberals, but almost nonexistent among traditional conservatives. The religious left groups fall in between, but with a wide range between the number of traditionalist liberals supporting choice (41 percent) and that in the other three groups (60 to 62 percent). Almost identical patterns appear on gay rights and civil unions for homosexuals. Secular liberals also oppose posting the Ten Commandments in public places

Table 13-7. The Religious Left and "Moral" Issues

Percent unless otherwise noted

	Core left		Peripheral religious left groups			Core right
Issue	*Secular liberals*	*Modernist liberals*	*Modernist moderates*	*Centrist liberals*	*Traditionalist liberals*	*Traditionalist conservatives*
Moral policy issue						
Favor choice on abortion	92	62	60	60	41	12
Favor gay rights	88	61	55	62	43	36
Favor civil unions	88	63	48	59	38	10
Favor stem cell research	88	67	48	64	52	30
Oppose school vouchers	78	58	41	61	55	31
Oppose charitable choice	68	37	28	41	34	23
Oppose posting the Ten Commandments	64	34	16	26	11	3
Moral issue index						
Very liberal	73	33	21	24	12	1
Liberal	20	28	23	28	14	4
Moderate	4	19	24	19	26	10
Conservative	2	11	20	20	21	29
Very conservative	1	9	12	9	27	56
Standard deviation	0.77	1.29	1.31	1.29	1.33	0.86
Number of observations	372	377	335	246	132	578
Percent of sample	9.3	9.4	8.4	6.2	3.3	14.4

Source: Fourth National Survey of Religion and Politics, University of Akron, 2004.

and financing charitable choice programs by two-to-one margins, but all four religious left groups, including traditionalist liberals, approve of these programs (though not as strongly as the core right does). School vouchers, however, are opposed by the religious left groups, except for the modernist moderates, with their high percentage of minorities. Again, the secular liberals are most opposed, and the core right are most in favor, a pattern evident as well on the stem cell research ban.

A moral issue index naturally shows the stark differences between secular liberals and traditionalist conservatives but also reveals the gaps between the former and the religious left groups.[28] There is a considerable range of positions across the religious left, and large standard deviations on the moral issue index for those groups, compared to the greater unity of both secular liberals and traditionalist conservatives. The religious left groups are also divided, with the core left most liberal on this issue package. Modernist moderates and centrist liberals hold similar, left-leaning, positions, while traditionalist liberals come down on the conservative side. In sum, "moral" issues cannot possibly serve as a rallying cry for the religious left as they have for the religious right; rather they are a source of conflict.

What can we conclude about the issue basis for a broad religious left? Not surprising, in 2004 most issues divided the religious left from the traditionalist conservatives, but, with the partial exception of social welfare, they also complicated formation of a solid alliance with the secular left. In particular, "moral" issues created divisions within both the religious left and the broader liberal alliance. As a result, religious left activist groups were limited to recruiting and mobilizing on the basis of "economic justice" issues. Here, at least, there is a large—though not overwhelming—mass constituency that, as Amy Waldman suggested over a decade ago, are "wanting their better halves appealed to, willing to act, waiting for a vehicle to do so."[29]

The Religious Left in the 2004 Campaign

Much of the speculation about the religious left's potential sees the movement providing the Democratic Party with the sort of religious infrastructure that the religious right gives the GOP. In any event, whatever the divisions among the religious left groups, their generally liberal or moderate

28. The moral issues index resulted from a factor analysis of the seven items in table 13-7. Loadings on charitable choice and school vouchers are lower than those for the other items, no doubt reflecting some confusion in the mass public.

29. Waldman (1995, p. 39).

Table 13-8. The Religious Left and Political Behavior in the 2004 Election

Percent unless otherwise noted

Behavior	Secular liberals	Core left Modernist liberals	Peripheral religious left groups Modernist moderates	Centrist liberals	Traditionalist liberals	Core right Traditionalist conservatives
Party identification						
Democratic	81	68	50	63	58	12
Republican	5	16	19	21	32	81
Voted for Kerry	93	88	71	76	62	10
Turnout in 2004	73	55	41	67	57	80
Most important issue						
Economic	26	46	54	44	36	14
Foreign policy	45	35	26	36	38	25
Social or moral	24	12	15	15	18	53
Number of observations	266	247	237	154	74	418
Percent of sample	9.8	9.0	8.7	5.6	2.7	15.3

Source: Fourth National Survey of Religion and Politics, University of Akron, 2004, postelection survey.

stances should at least make the Democrats more appealing to them than the Republicans.

How did the groups align themselves in 2004? Table 13-8 provides some answers using data from the postelection survey (N = 2,730). Democratic Party identification is clearly strongest among secular liberals, followed at some distance by the core left—the modernist liberals. Still, Democrats easily outnumber Republicans in all three peripheral left groups, with a comfortable margin even among traditionalist liberals, drawn to the Democrats by their ideology but to the Republicans by their traditionalism. The core right, naturally, is overwhelmingly Republican. Actual choices in the 2004 presidential race reflect this party identification. Kerry's high vote of 93 percent came from secular liberals.[30] Among religious left voters, support for Kerry ranged from 88 percent of modernist liberals to only 62 percent of traditionalist liberals. Meanwhile, the core right gave Bush 90 percent of their votes.[31]

30. The Kerry vote rose to 95 percent among core left respondents who identified themselves as "strongly liberal," a group that made up fully 7 percent of the sample (data not shown).

31. We have not discussed secular conservatives, but they are much less conservative than the core right in issue positions, party identification, and vote choice, although they lean in a conservative direction in each instance (data not shown). In contrast, secular liberals, as we have seen, are much more liberal than religious left groups across-the-board, with the possible exception of social welfare issues.

What reasons did voters give for their presidential choice? For secular liberals, foreign policy issues overshadowed all others, but for the religious left economics dominated, with foreign policy following, except among traditionalist liberals where the two were closely matched. No religious left group listed "moral" issues as particularly important, in stark contrast to the core right, where over half chose these as most vital. The secular left gave moral issues a little higher priority, perhaps reflecting frustration with the conservative emphasis on such issues during the campaign and with the activity of Christian Right organizations.[32]

Of course, the impact of various groups depended not only on vote choice but also on willingness to go to the polls. Traditionalist conservatives and secular liberals had extremely high turnout, 80 and 73 percent, respectively. For most religious left groups, however, turnout rates lagged behind the national average of 61 percent; only the centrist liberals were an exception. These low levels of voting were sometimes accompanied by low levels of other political activities. Secular liberals were the most politically active group in the sample—far outpacing the religious left groups and even the core right. In contrast, the modernist liberals, the core of the religious left, and centrist liberals fell a bit short of the traditionalist conservatives in how closely they followed the campaign and how frequently they talked about politics, made financial contributions, and attempted to persuade others how to vote (data not shown). Obviously, religious left forces will have to step up their involvement if they are to challenge secular liberals and have an impact on the Democratic Party.

The analysis up to this point reveals a religious left divided on matters of religion, but exhibiting some unity on social welfare concerns (and, to a lesser extent, on foreign policy). In addition, religious left groups were fairly cohesive in their identification with the Democratic Party and support for Kerry in 2004. But the religious left also posted low turnout rates and limited activism in 2004 compared to the core right and secular liberals. Thus the relatively small numbers of the religious left, at least when compared to the religious right, were rendered even less effective by low turnout and modest activism. What accounts for this lack of involvement?

There are several possible answers. First, religious left groups lack some resources that traditionally encourage political involvement, especially in comparison with secular liberals: they are not as highly educated, have lower

---

32. Fully 94 percent of the secular liberals felt "far from" the Christian Right in response to a question asked about groups active in the 2004 campaign (data not shown).

incomes, include more racial minorities, and are located disproportionately in the electorally noncompetitive South (table 13-4). Although on many such traits they resemble the politically active traditionalist conservatives, the latter have the advantage of greater age and "settledness," as evidenced by the high proportion of married couples.

Second, the 2004 campaign's focus on moral and foreign policy issues may have energized secular liberals and traditionalist conservatives, but left potential religious left voters cold. Had economic justice issues dominated the campaign, such voters may well have responded with both higher turnout and even greater support for Kerry. Part of the explanation may also lie with a fundamental orientation of many religious left members: their discomfort with religion in public debate—or even in private political decisions. We asked a series of questions about the role of religion in the 2004 presidential campaign (see table 13-9). Not surprising, most secular liberals perceived that religion played too large a role, while virtually all traditionalist conservatives disagreed. Almost half of the core left agreed with the secular liberals, compared to only one-fifth of the traditionalist liberals. A similar pattern appears regarding whether there was too much political discussion in churches. In each of the religious left groups, fewer perceived too much effort by religious groups to get out the vote. More important, perhaps, many religious left voters held that faith either was "not important at all" or was "less important than other factors" in their electoral decision. Only among traditionalist liberals did a majority say that faith was "as important" as or "more important" than other factors. Among the "core" modernist liberals, fully 65 percent reported that religion was *less important* than other factors in their choice. Compare this to the three-fifths of traditionalist conservatives who said that religious considerations were *more important.*

To summarize, we constructed an index from these items.[33] The results clearly show that the core left—the modernist liberals—see only a small role for religion in politics, something that would be hard to imagine among the religious civil rights or antiwar activists of a generation past. These negative attitudes may reflect, in part, lower levels of religiosity in these groups (table 13-2) as well as a negative reaction to the religious right's version of "faith-based politics." Still, as shown in the standard deviations, there is considerable disagreement within the four religious left groups.

---

33. The role for religion index resulted from a factor analysis of the four previous items in table 13-9, with the factor score divided into five equal categories.

Table 13-9. The Religious Left and the Role of Religion in the 2004 Campaign

Percent unless otherwise noted

Role	Core left	Peripheral religious left groups			Core right
	Secular liberals	Modernist liberals	Modernist moderates	Centrist liberals	Traditionalist liberals	Traditionalist conservatives
Churches in 2004 campaign						
Too much religious discussion	71	40	29	33	20	6
Too much issue discussion	64	34	27	41	25	7
Too much voter mobilization	41	30	20	26	16	3
Importance of faith to vote						
Not at all important	70	40	51	37	24	4
Less important than other factors	18	25	17	19	10	3
About as important as other factors	10	23	16	34	39	34
More important than other factors	3	13	16	9	27	59
Index: Role for religion in politics						
Very small	70	43	40	37	24	3
Small	14	16	13	17	8	9
Some	8	12	19	14	12	12
Large	3	15	16	13	21	22
Very large	6	15	13	18	35	54
Standard deviation	1.13	1.51	1.46	1.54	1.59	1.13
Number of observations	266	247	237	154	74	418
Percent of sample	9.8	9.0	8.7	5.6	2.7	15.3

Source: Fourth National Survey of Religion and Politics, University of Akron, 2004, postelection survey.

Finally, it is possible that the religious left's limited involvement in the election was a function of poor mobilization by religious groups, by other liberal organizations such as labor unions and environmental groups, and even by the Democratic Party. Our postelection survey contained fourteen questions about campaign contacts by both secular and religious entities.[34] Despite all

34. The contact items include those by candidates, political parties, liberal issue groups, conservative issue groups, labor unions, business groups, environmental groups, gun owners' groups, moral or religious groups, gay rights groups, and conservative Christian groups. Mobilization efforts at churches by pastors and friends are also included, along with information on the parties and candidates provided at church.

the media talk about massive mobilization by both parties and their interest group allies, many potential voters did not recall being contacted. Nevertheless, table 13-10 shows that traditionalist conservatives were far more likely to report contacts than any other group. They received far more contacts from religious sources, matched secular liberals in secular contacts, and easily outpaced religious left groups in *both* categories. In contrast, the core left group experienced fewer contacts overall than either centrist or traditionalist liberals.

For contacts with "partisan" content, the secular liberals and traditionalist conservatives are almost mirror images, with a rough two to one advantage for their favored party, but the Republicans closely matched Democratic contacts in all the religious left groups—supposedly a "natural" Democratic constituency. Thus ineffective mobilization by the Democrats and their allies may help to explain the low turnout on the religious left—and perhaps even the loss of a few potential Kerry converts. Although it would be too much to say that the Democrats simply ceded religious turf to the Republicans (except for black churches and Jewish synagogues), they clearly failed to reach many potential religious left constituents in 2004.

Conclusions

Using a combination of political ideology and religious traditionalism, we have identified four possible constituencies for the religious left in the American public. The core left—that is, modernist liberals—accounted for roughly one-tenth of the adult population in 2004. This group has the requisite religious

Table 13-10. The Religious Left and Mobilization in the 2004 Campaign

	Core left	Peripheral religious left groups			Core right
Contact	Secular liberals	Modernist liberals	Modernist moderates	Centrist liberals	Traditionalist liberals	Traditionalist conservatives
All contacts (mean)	2.02	2.30	1.74	2.44	2.54	3.42
Percent receiving						
Secular contacts	69	49	45	62	59	69
Religious contacts	15	28	22	27	35	39
Percent receiving						
Democratic contacts	51	37	29	34	35	26
Republican contacts	29	29	37	39	38	54
Number of observations	266	247	237	154	74	418
Percent of sample	9.8	9.0	8.7	5.6	2.7	15.3

Source: Fourth National Survey of Religion and Politics, University of Akron, 2004, postelection survey.

and political perspectives that make them prime targets for recruitment by activist groups and for mobilization by both the Democratic Party and other interest group allies. The addition of three peripheral left groups—centrist liberals, traditionalist liberals, and modernist moderates—would bring the constituency for the religious left to more than one-quarter of the potential electorate.

However, our analysis paints a rather pessimistic picture for such an alliance. In this respect, it is instructive to compare the potential of the core left and the core right. First, the core right is larger and much more homogeneous in religious beliefs, practices, and affiliation.[35] This ideological and spatial concentration of voters aids political operatives seeking to mobilize through religious appeals. Those hoping to activate the religious left confront a much more difficult challenge, whether in distributing literature, getting voters to the polls, or creating political networks. Moreover, the greater religiosity of traditionalist conservatives makes them more receptive to religious appeals than is true of the core religious left. Indeed, the core religious left, as well as most of its potential allies, sees only a small role for religion in American politics and attaches little importance to faith in making political choices. Even well-crafted appeals using religious symbols by activists will fall mostly on deaf ears.

These findings do shed some light on the "culture war" interpretation of contemporary American politics. There are potential mass constituencies for both religious left and right. But there are far more people in the middle on both political and religious grounds, and these centrists hold the balance of power in elections. Indeed, attracting them is critical to the success of either side, and the religious right appears to have had more success at this task in 2004.

Can the religious left broaden its base? One option is to appeal for support in the secular community. During the past decade, some religious left leaders have simply echoed the mantra of candidates who oppose the religious right (preserve "separation of church and state" or "religion is a private matter, not for the public square"). Although such appeals have much resonance among religious left constituencies, it is hard to see how these themes can facilitate *religious* mobilization. Ironically, such arguments actually counter current efforts by many Democrats to develop a religious voice, one more reflective

---

35. While not the focus of this chapter, the peripheral groups on the religious right are also larger and closer to the positions of the core right than is the case on the religious left. In addition, many religious right activist groups have been engaged in electoral activity for decades, giving the religious right a sizable advantage over the left.

of the historic Social Gospel and social justice traditions. Were the religious left to adopt positions articulated by secularists, it would risk not only losing its religious flavor *but* also being labeled "anti-religious"—hardly an advantage in a religious society.

A second alternative is to strengthen the organizational base of the movement in a manner similar to that of the Christian Coalition in the years following the 1988 presidential election. Press conferences by religious left leaders and pronouncements from denominational social agencies are not bad ideas, but they are no substitute for effective grassroots organizations in local communities and local churches. Still, our analysis shows some impediments to such organizing, especially in the religious, social, and ideological heterogeneity of the potential activist pool. As a resource mobilization approach would suggest, social movements such as the Christian Right have drawn on preexisting religious, social, and organizational networks—the very kinds of networks missing on the religious left. Perhaps the growing networks of local religious activists described by Hart and others might provide such a base, but that is by no means a sure thing, as many of these seem to have an aversion to electoral politics.[36]

In sum, at this point we see the religious left as a "gentle stream." There is a significant grassroots constituency that can be mobilized more successfully than has been done in the past. But can the movement become a "river glorious?" Can it seriously challenge the religious right? Our findings do not answer these questions conclusively, but they do suggest the obstacles confronting such a possibility.

36. Hart (2001).

Conclusion

From Event to Theory
A Summary Analysis

David C. Leege

American elections are grand-scale rituals of legitimation. Historically, all political systems have had to settle the question: Who has the right to rule over others? In the past, many monarchs were believed to rule by divine right. But by the later eighteenth century, the ideology of equality demanded a different rationale. When leadership status was no longer conferred by ancestry but by ballot, the people had to have a basis for determining trust. In the fledgling United States, as de Tocqueville pointed out, that became the function of religious discourse. Politicians quickly grasped that policy promises were insufficient without the invocation of divine sanction. Thus God-talk became and has remained a staple of American political campaigns. It is one part, perhaps an inevitable part, of the way we legitimate choice.

George W. Bush absorbed this lesson during his father's 1988 campaign. Observing the Reverend Pat Robertson in Iowa and South Carolina, the younger Bush allegedly said, "I can do that; I can talk that language." And he could. He had recently been born again and was a regular in Bible study. Religious discourse came readily to his lips. A few years later, these qualities helped to make him an irresistible candidate for governor of Texas in the eyes of Karl Rove.

Bill Clinton shared Bush's affinity for religious language, despite the many differences in their backgrounds. Early in life, Clinton found solace in his Sunday school and Baptist church choir, escaping an oppressive alcoholic stepfather. His religious side became almost an alter ego for a youth who learned early to compartmentalize. As a result, he too could address the voters freely with religious language that suggested he was one of us—worthy of our trust.

Whether facility with religious language on the stump is sincere or strategic is in some respects irrelevant. It is part of the script and biography we have come to expect of our candidates and an increasingly important part of many campaigns.[1] In the 2004 election, which is the focus of this book, religious language proliferated. Religious denominations divided in their partisan loyalties. Cultural conflict was sharp over certain issues. But these facts alone do not mean that electoral choice in 2004 was "a matter of faith." Rather, as Sunshine Hillygus (chapter 4), Scott Keeter (chapter 5), and Barbara and Jan Norrander (chapter 8) elaborate, for many, choice reflected other dominant issues—terrorism, the war in Iraq, the economy, and Social Security. Nevertheless, faith may have been compounded within issues of foreign, defense, or economic policy. Choice may have been influenced by religious reference groups or affinity rather than a creedal dimension of faith. Finally, mobilization and turnout of religious groups may have been more important to the understanding of 2004 than vote choice itself. The essays in this book suggest a complex research agenda.

In this chapter, I sketch the contours of this research agenda by formulating and applying broader theories to the findings and puzzles embedded in the book. In the manner common to voting behavior specialists, I first address the importance of understanding turnout and then discuss the importance of understanding choice. This discussion highlights a number of useful theories and concepts, such as issue publics, social categorization, relative deprivation, reference groups, social networks, contextual effects, the two-step flow of influence, attitude constraint, political marginalization and social displacement, anticipatory socialization, and dual reference groups. In addition, I examine measurement issues, particularly the evangelical bias in devotional measures, proto-theory about religions of fear and religions of hope, and suggestive findings from cognitive science.

---

1. Like the first decade of the twenty-first century, the early nineteenth and late nineteenth century were expansive times for religious discourse and religious impact in presidential campaigns, according to ethnohistorians. Kleppner (1970); Swierenga (1990).

The Importance of Understanding Turnout

Several chapters refer to Karl Rove's 2001 speech to the American Enterprise Institute, in which he bemoaned the fact that only 15 million evangelicals voted in the tight 2000 election, compared to the 19 million the Bush camp had expected. In preparation for 2004, he promised to devote special efforts to mobilizing evangelical Christians. According to Scott Keeter (chapter 5) and David Campbell and Quin Monson (chapter 7), these efforts succeeded. As Keeter says, "The proportion of evangelicals voting for president did rise— from 68 percent in 2000 to 78 percent in 2004." These numbers represent a striking change for a religious tradition that only a generation or two before eschewed politics as corrupt and the work of the devil. The evangelical transformation, as Geoffrey Layman and Laura Hussey (chapter 10) and John Green and associates (chapter 2) map for us, is one of the unfolding events that has changed the American party system, the mode of discourse in presidential and other campaigns, the issue agenda, and the circulation of political elites.

But mobilization is not all that matters. Dismantling and demobilizing the opposition party's coalition are equally important. Majorities can be achieved by mobilizing more supporters than the opposition party, but they can also be achieved by demobilizing segments of the opposition. Years ago, Walter Dean Burnham changed the focus of participation and turnout studies to partisan efforts to control the *size* and *composition* of the electorate.[2] Brian Kruger, Paul Mueller, Kenneth Wald, and I build on that work by arguing that, in the second half of the twentieth century, Democrats held such a sizable majority in party identifiers that Republicans acted strategically to reduce the size of the electorate by dampening turnout among vulnerable Democratic groups.[3] Republican campaigns created disillusionment among groups such as southern white Democrats or Roman Catholics or white working-class ethnics by promoting the belief that the national Democratic Party gave unfair advantage to African Americans or women or was owned by pro-choice feminists or communist coddlers. Republicans created potent symbols, such as "tax and spend liberal," to bundle together feelings about race, gender norms, anti-elitism, and distrust of government. The decline in target group turnout resulting from such disillusionment was often more effective

---

2. Burnham (1970).
3. Leege and others (2002).

than partisan defection resulting from anxiety, to use the language of George Marcus and his collaborators.[4]

The Republican strategy proved particularly effective among evangelicals. Only once in the last half century—Lyndon Johnson's election in 1964—did the proportion of Democratic evangelicals who turned out to vote for the Democrats' presidential candidate outweigh the proportion of loyal Republicans and Democratic crossovers who turned out and voted Republican. Failure to vote among evangelical Democrats was best predicted by negative feelings toward Democrats on racial matters and on issues of American strength and patriotism. Attitudes toward race, patriotism, and by the 1980s social conservatism also largely explained partisan defection.

This illustration shows that mobilization is only part of the story. Demobilization not only shrinks the active electorate but also builds resentment that pays dividends, first in disillusionment, then in defection, and then in realignment. In 2004 both parties sought to exploit this dynamic by targeting groups in the opposition coalition that disagreed with their leaders on important issues. As Hillygus points out, these groups were fairly large: "Among Republicans (excluding leaners), 31 percent disagreed with the party's [leaders'] stance on abortion, 40 percent on stem cell research, 14 percent on gay marriage. Among rank-and-file Democrats, 14 percent disagreed with the party's stance on abortion, 15 percent on stem cell research, and 40 percent on gay marriage." Such dissent was particularly likely among devout Democrats and less religious Republicans.

Internal divisions were not limited to the parties. In chapter 2, John Green, Lyman Kellstedt, Corwin Smidt, and James Guth show that each religious group contained a substantial residual of members whose behavior and attitudes were at odds with those of the group majority. When these minorities also constituted *issue publics*—groups whose perception of an election is shaped largely by a specific issue or theme—they were particularly vulnerable to disillusioning or anxiety-creating appeals.

In chapter 6, Quin Monson and Baxter Oliphant invoke *social categorization* theory to analyze the nature of these appeals. Social categorization is a psychological process through which a party or group asserts common identity and claims privileged status among its adherents. This process nurtures a *reference group*. A political group can promote this process by sending its

---

4. See Marcus and others (1996) for the application of this psychological theory to voting.

adherents communications replete with mobilizing symbols. If it can isolate individuals within its coalition who form an issue public, the messages can be tailored to their special concern. But the process does not stop with the mobilization of loyalists. A political party will seek to attract vulnerable groups within the opposition coalition by claiming that its leadership no longer respects group norms. It delivers the following message: You will not be leaving the party; rather the party has left you and can no longer lay legitimate claim to your loyalty.

Advances in the use of demographic and psychographic information facilitate both within-group reinforcement and outside-group dismantling. Not only do campaigners know where different racial, ethnic, socioeconomic, religious, or age cohorts and groups live (from census-type data), but now they can merge this information with vote records (from past precinct data) and consumer taste records (from credit card purchases and website hits). Such microtargeting reached new levels of sophistication in 2004, particularly as practiced by Republicans in battleground states.

Monson and Oliphant analyze *microtargeting* efforts based on oversamples of Florida and Ohio, the most contested of the battleground prizes. They identify the campaign organizations that sent nonbroadcast communications, classify the appeals, and, most valuable, display the Republicans' twenty-four microtargeting segments, which included both Republicans and vulnerable Democrats. Some of the resulting microtargeted appeals were obviously intended to outrage party loyalists and thus encourage them to vote. Others were intended to create a situation of dissonance and confusion among the opposition's vulnerable groups so that they would sit out the election. Still other appeals played on the theme of *relative deprivation:* these messages suggested that by making promises to groups with different values, the opposition party had abandoned the values cherished by the targeted groups. In cultural politics, outsiders are often treated as morally wrong, un-American, or godless. Many of the Republican National Committee appeals aimed at vulnerable Democrats carried such content.

Microtargeting can be highly effective because, as David Campbell and Quin Monson remind us in chapter 7, presidential elections are won in the Electoral College. As a result, generating small majorities in battleground states becomes a critical goal. Campbell and Monson argue that the Bush campaign helped to build such majorities by taking advantage of intense press coverage of gay marriage in early 2004 as well as the apparently independent efforts of Republicans in the evangelical base to place referenda banning same-sex marriage on the ballots of eleven states. Their analysis shows that evangelical turnout increased along with the Bush vote in ten of the eleven states with referenda, notably hard-fought Ohio and Arkansas.[5]

In understanding the dynamics of turnout in 2004, besides social categorization and its companion, relative deprivation, we find evidence of other theoretically rich behavior, such as social network activities and contextual effects. In efforts quietly encouraged by Republican operatives, leaders of Catholic dioceses warned their flocks that only Catholics with an "erroneous conscience" would support a pro-abortion candidate, and several said they would withhold communion from Kerry. Evangelical organizations, such as Focus on the Family and the Christian Coalition, often engaged with Catholic leaders in coordinated appeals in key states. The Bush campaign sought church membership lists, and, according to Monson and Oliphant, when this tactic was widely criticized, recruited religious conservatives as "faith and values team leaders" in local churches. The tasks of these leaders included information dissemination, recruitment, and mobilization. This approach created a climate in which congregants felt that they were expected to vote and to vote for Bush. Scholars see in these mobilization strategies data points for theories of *contextual effects* (that is, the climate of the group reinforces conformity to norms), *social networks* (that is, viewpoints of discussion partners are respected and reinforcing),[6] and *two-step flow of influence* from communications theory (that is, a mass appeal from a distant source is personalized and reinforced by a close communication partner).[7]

Another theme that emerges from the chapters is the nuanced role that reference groups played in 2004. In some cases, the impact of reference groups has clearly declined. For example, in chapter 9, Matthew Wilson's comparison of Catholics in 1960 and 2004 suggests that, over time, the basis for voting shifted from identity politics to value-norm politics (voting on the

---

5. Neither this chapter nor Matthew Wilson's chapter on Catholics nor David Leal's chapter on Latinos addresses the way in which the selection and framing of the gay marriage issue either disillusioned *Catholic* Democrats, reducing their turnout, or angered Catholic Democrats about their party, leading to crossover voting. Certainly that was part of the Bush-Rove design of the ongoing "Catholic Project." Remember that President Bush's first reference to the issue was not in the 2004 State of the Union address, but in the midst of a Rose Garden press conference in August 2003, days before the papal statement against gay marriage. Just as he had in public ways adopted the Catholic position against stem cell research, he now occupied the same issue space on gay marriage, just before its papal promulgation. Thus a companion study to Campbell and Monson's might address Catholic Democratic turnout and party loyalty in contested states as a function of the gay marriage issue.

6. Huckfeldt and others (1995); Wald, Owen, and Hill (1988, 1990).

7. Katz and Lazarsfeld (1964).

basis of religious ideology rather than religious communalism). In other cases, reference groups remained a dominant influence, as shown by Eric McDaniel's discussion of Democratic solidarity among African Americans in chapter 12. And in still others, reference groups never formed. In chapter 11, David Leal argues that Latino identity is almost nonexistent for historical and geographic reasons, and in chapter 13, Lyman Kellstedt, Corwin Smidt, John Green, and James Guth observe that the religious left lacks a base either in the parish or in the denominational tradition, at least when contrasted with the religious right's base in fundamentalist, evangelical, and Pentecostal churches.

The study by Kellstedt and his colleagues is especially revealing. The authors analyze levels of religious involvement, ideology and issue consensus, political interest, and mobilization efforts within the core religious right and the core and peripheral religious left. For the religious right, nearly all indicators suggest common purpose and mobilization. For the religious left, nearly all indicators suggest ideological fragmentation (except on social justice issues), lack of common purpose, and ineffective mobilization. In fact, most of the religious left regards the admixture of religion with politics as illegitimate in the American setting, just the opposite of the religious right at this point in history.

One explanation may be that past successes in promoting racial equality and economic security have taken the motivating force out of the religious left. By contrast, the same developments appear to have stimulated political engagement on the religious right. The first mobilization of the religious right in the 1960s and 1970s followed massive resistance to racial integration in the 1950s as well as opposition to the civil rights acts of the 1960s. Then the rough edges of race-based conflict were smoothed by President Reagan's doctrine of egalitarian individualism and other code words in the 1980s. Finally, family values themes resonated with an already politically attentive base throughout the 1980s and 1990s.

Highly devout evangelicals were at the forefront of this movement. Lower levels of public religiosity, in contrast, have traditionally been associated with a preference for the Democratic Party. Yet according to Green and his coauthors, nominal evangelicals nearly tripled their vote for the Republican presidential candidate from 1992 to 2004. In addition, they had the highest increase in turnout—up 29 percentage points from 1992 to 2004—of any religious group. This suggests not only that there was substantial affinity between George W. Bush and all types of evangelicals but also that group identity is forming for evangelicals with much the same force it had for

Catholics in the early 1960s. In other words, as the chapter by Layman and Hussey suggests, for evangelicals, being Republican is becoming part of their cultural identity. This development reminds us of Talcott Parsons's early dictum: "The individual seems to vote, other things being equal, with the people he feels to be his own kind. . . . [The] question is not so much *for what* he is voting as it is *with whom* he is associating himself in voting."[8]

Based on the evidence provided by John Green and John Jackson (chapter 3), this dictum applies with particular force to Republicans. Green and Jackson show that Republican convention delegates are far more likely than Democratic delegates to come from similar religious origins, to practice their religiosity in conventional public ways, and to share a common ideology and issue position on social issues.[9] They use the concept of *attitude constraint* to describe the Republican delegates, although in this case both attitudes and behavior reinforce each other. They also document the extent to which a unified view of a moral order permeates Republican elites. Ideology among Republicans has come to be connected more strongly to traditional religious values than to economic interests. This trend was apparent as early as 1976, when Pamela Conover and Stanley Feldman showed that, at the rank-and-file level, "conservative" and "liberal" were decreasingly economic referents and increasingly referents to a moral order.[10]

The Importance of Vote Choice

This election was the setting in which 22 percent of the respondents to the 2004 National Election Pool's exit poll chose "moral values" from a seven-item list as the "*one* issue [that] mattered most in deciding how you voted for president." A flurry of analysis followed, with journalists and Democrats flagellating themselves for underestimating the "values voters," academics and some pollsters questioning the ambiguity of the item or showing that other items were really more dominant, and evangelical Christian leaders calling for payback in policies and court nominees. The reception of this raw datum from a survey device that has evident unreliability and uncalculated generalizability shows how quickly "knowledge" becomes politicized.

Several chapters unpack this datum. Through analysis of multiple indicators, meaning inference, and cross-validating samples, Scott Keeter (chap-

8. Parsons (1959, p. 96).
9. For parallel findings, see Layman (2001).
10. Conover and Feldman (1981).

ter 5) shows convincingly that, although more voters listed terrorism and Iraq as most central to their choice, at least a quarter of the electorate voted on the basis of Bush's stance on social issues. Kerry's voters came disproportionately from those concerned about economic issues and the president's conduct of the war in Iraq.

Hillygus (chapter 4) does not deny that social issues were on conservative voters' minds. But she does question whether they drove vote choice and the election outcome. In a series of issue-by-issue comparisons, she shows that Social Security was listed as important to a voter's choice by 52 percent, education by 45 percent, and the economy and jobs by 40 percent, *followed* by abortion (32 percent), the environment (30 percent), and gay marriage (26 percent). Ultimately she concludes, "Of the nine different political issues, Iraq, terrorism, and the economy—rather than abortion and gay marriage— were more closely related to support for Bush." Perhaps such findings help us to understand why, according to the NEP exit polls, between 2000 and 2004, support for Bush increased by 23 percentage points among gays and lesbians, 36 percentage points among those who never go to church, 25 percentage points among those who feel abortion should always be legal, and 6 percentage points among Jews—all segments of the electorate notably liberal on social issues. Campbell and Monson (chapter 7) reaffirm that social issues were indeed an important part of vote choice, especially among groups targeted for mobilization or demobilization, but they were hardly dominant in the electorate as a whole.

Or were they? None of the authors has conducted path analyses to find out what moral or religious values are confounded within voters' positions on the Iraq war and terrorism, in particular. Anecdotally, we know that many of President Bush's supporters in the war on terror and the war in Iraq have negative feelings about Muslims, think Islam is a bloody infidel religion, and welcome the opportunity to open Iraq to Christian proselytism (forgetting, of course, that only a few decades ago, about 20 percent of Iraqis were Chaldean Christians and that the Ba'athist party was founded to protect Christians and later secular Sunnis from fundamentalist Shia). Anecdotally, we also know that many of the president's supporters view him as a man of God chosen by God at this point in U.S. history to protect Christian civilization from both Muslim terrorists and secular imperialism in American culture. Thus vote choices that appear to be driven by the war in Iraq may at a deeper level be shaped largely by religious beliefs.

A similar argument for the other side can be made about Catholics who seek to follow church teaching on war and peace. The pope and many Catholics did not consider "preemptive doctrine" consistent with "just war" theory. Polls leading up to the war in Iraq found Catholics far less supportive of President Bush's actions than evangelicals; as the war has lingered, erosion in Catholic support has outpaced support in other groups. None of the chapters in this book models the religious roots of the antiwar position.

Layman and Hussey (chapter 10) show us how fruitfully path analysis can capture attitude constraint (that is, an integrated worldview) among religiously active evangelicals and distinguish it from the group-related factors that led less religious evangelicals to support Bush. A similar path analysis including surrogates for religious positions—for example, a feeling thermometer addressed to Islam or the religious right, a biblical literalism scale, or a feeling thermometer toward Catholic leadership—in interaction with a measure of attitudes toward Iraq war policy—could isolate the latent factors driving positions on terrorism and Iraq. Unfortunately, in 2004 most surveys did not tap into these fundamentalist or apocalyptic viewpoints or into Catholic "just war" theory. We will not fully comprehend the extent of religiously grounded values in 2004 vote choice until some method of identifying the role of such beliefs is found. Until then, the arguments of those who scoff at moral or religious value determinants of vote choice and confine their models to traditional determinants will likely carry the day.[11]

Similarly, full path models focusing on economic policy positions will substantially enrich our understanding of 2004. Once politically mobilized, evangelicals quickly embraced conservative economic positions for a variety of reasons, including their rapid upward mobility (a traditional SES explanation), their disdain for the dependent poor (grounded in a Calvinist ethic of righteousness found deep in American culture), and their fear of big government (rooted in traditional southern apprehension about any initiative of the federal government—recall the lore of the "war of northern aggression" and the occupation of the South by carpetbaggers). Analysis of the 2000 election shows that those Democrats who crossed over and voted Republican held negative feelings not only about blacks but about anyone who they felt depends on government to bail them out of the consequences of their lifestyle.[12] Martin Gilens and Tali Mendelberg have helped to uncover the deep religious and cultural roots of such positions through survey-based modeling of the roots of anti-welfare and anti-black positions, and Jennifer

---

11. See Fiorina, with Abrams and Pope (2005); Bartels (2005).
12. Leege, Mueller, and Wald (2001).

Hochschild has used in-depth interviews to shed light on why many Americans place limits on equality.[13]

In addition, there is strong reason to believe that Catholic theology leads to distinctive positions on the economy and social justice. In the post–Vatican II era, few religious bodies have been as consistently clear as the Catholic Church on the fundamental dignity of all human beings and the range of government policies needed to shape a just economy. Thus many Catholics (as well as many mainline Protestants) have religious reasons for fostering a just economy through public policy. In 2004 many felt that President Bush was taking the wrong direction, and they held him accountable for policies that seemed to lead toward greater discrepancies in life chances. This "moral" path to vote choice based on economic policy appears to be influential within parts of the religious left, but we lack models that capture this dynamic.[14]

Vote Choice among Particular Groups

Vote choice may also reflect the extent to which a group feels it has become politically and culturally marginalized. Several chapters point to an emerging political coalition that is reacting to the advance of evangelical Republicans. The coalition contains both religious groups and seculars; it includes many mainline Protestants, many Catholics, unaffiliated believers, seculars, Jews, and African American Christians. Previous research has found that, as the Republican Party shifted its historic stance on the role of government, on race, on women, and on cultural freedom, many mainline Protestant and Catholic Republicans defected from the party. Similarly, seculars first sat out elections and then defected to the Democrats and began to vote more regularly. In the 2004 election, both trends were reflected in higher turnout in sectors of this new opposition coalition.

One source of growing opposition to Republicans among mainline Protestants may be a sense of *social displacement.* Mainline Protestants—the social and political elites of much of American history—founded the Republican Party. But as a result of Kevin Phillips's "southern strategy," the party's traditional leaders have been displaced. They may be able to adjust to the southern accents of the converted Democrats in the Republican leadership, but they resist the "culture wars" rhetoric and efforts to use government to limit

13. Gilens (1999); Mendelberg (2001); Hochschild (1981).
14. Kellstedt and others (chapter 13).

personal freedom.[15] Party leaders like former Senator John Danforth, an Episcopal priest, have called for religious moderates to organize around their own program and counterbalance the religious right.[16] But the right continues to pursue its agenda aggressively. Despite these differences, moderate leaders are reluctant to bolt the party (more than 30 percent of the Republican delegates surveyed by Green and Jackson are mainline Protestants), but the rank and file have not been so constrained. This is an emerging trend that specialists on American voting behavior need to map and interpret.

Evangelical Latinos also present a rich research opportunity, particularly for the application of *anticipatory socialization* theory and *dual reference group* theory. Roman Catholicism is the dominant religion in both Mexico and Puerto Rico. Many immigrants, however, have become evangelicals, either back home or once in the United States. How is this group likely to vote? Cultural theory provides at least two answers to this question. Anticipatory socialization theory, as pioneered in George C. Homans's 1950 classic *The Human Group*, suggests that a group's newer members are more likely than its older members to take on the group's central values.[17] Thus Latino evangelicals may be particularly likely to merge conservative theology and social values with political action. (This theory gains some support from Leal's finding that Latino evangelicals are both more likely to vote and more likely to vote Republican than Latino Catholics.) In contrast, dual reference group theory suggests that individuals with dual identities—for example, being Puerto Rican and being evangelical—pick and choose when to act "Puerto Rican" and when to act "evangelical." If neither identity is that strong, cross-pressure is less likely to be felt, and reference group theory does not help to untangle vote choice.[18]

In principle, African Americans could have been in a similar position in 2004. McDaniel points out that they belonged mostly to evangelical churches, embraced conservative social values, and were subject to efforts by ministers to mobilize voters on behalf of President Bush. However, these factors were outweighed by the judgment that the Bush administration had not done anything to diminish the cultural and political oppression affecting the African American community. Thus what could have been an interesting dual reference group situation never materialized.

15. Phillips (1969).

16. Slevin (2006).

17. Homans (1950).

18. For a discussion of dual reference group theory, see Bock, Beeghley, and Mixon (1983).

Other Research Considerations

In the founding days of the religion and politics field, scholars were forced to compete for scarce space on the American National Election Studies and the General Social Surveys, commercial polls like Gallup, and exit polls. The resources available for research have changed considerably over the last quarter century. The chapters in this book attest to the availability of a much wider range of data sets: the Pew studies, the Akron Studies, state polls, the Knowledge Networks Internet panel, specialized studies of African Americans and Latinos, and a wide range of findings from specialized projects. Scholars can no longer argue that they are sunk because the American National Election Study (NES) board of overseers does not appreciate the significance of their problems and variables. Yet difficulties in access to adequate data abound.

A major breakthrough came after the 1989 pilot study, when the NES adopted a sequence of questions that better classified denominational affiliation and, with it, a defensible conceptualization of religious traditions. The question sequence also permitted more accurate estimates of secularism and the extent of religious participation. The problem remains, however, that other surveys and polls have often lacked the richness in denominational affiliation and the details of religious participation needed for scholars to replicate their NES-based models.

Equally important, analytic progress has been hindered by the indiscriminate application of concepts and measures derived from particular traditions. The field's early scholars created something of a conceptual monster by using terms like "orthodoxy," "faithfulness," and "devotion" to describe those who believed and behaved in certain ways. Out of this research, both journalists and scholars, uninitiated in the differences among religious denominations and traditions, have appropriated the maxim: the higher the level of religious faithfulness (orthodoxy, devotion), the higher the probability of voting Republican. But this conclusion is based on analysis of the evangelical tradition and, for the most part, fails to capture the relationship between devotion and political preferences in other traditions. The result is a dangerous simplification of the role that faith plays in politics today.

In fact, even the use of the word "orthodoxy" in this context represents a misleading simplification. Historically, "orthodoxy" refers to the canon of the Christian faith and practice over two millennia. At its center is the notion that Christ comes to us in Word and Sacraments, that in the Eucharist Christ is present in the body and blood, that weekly or daily communion is normative, that infant baptism has the same efficacy as baptism following an adult's born-again conversion, that the turning point in salvation is not *my* acceptance of Christ into my heart but the recognition that *God* has claimed my life, that the Church and not the individual is the measure of doctrinal truth, and that it is the duty of the church to shape collectively the personal and social consciences of its adherents. Today, however, adherents of church bodies who have historically heterodox beliefs and practices are mislabeled "orthodox."

A quick review of the field reveals other conceptual errors and lacunae. With Jews we have no measure of keeping the law, and we work, again limitedly, with temple observance. We have no measure that incorporates the five pillars of Muslim faithfulness. For the Abrahamic faiths as a whole, we have no measure of the extent of sanctification—that is, doing the works of charity and social justice by which Christians claim adherents will be judged on the Last Day (Matthew 25).

Attention to a theologically charged content domain is absolutely essential in our field. There is no avoiding it in favor of a common universal measure. Green and his colleagues' creative effort to solve this conceptual problem by introducing measures of traditionalism is promising. This allows the respondent to use his or her own denominational framework. The problem is that we do not know the meaning of the questions for the respondent, and such difficult questions usually require prompts. On validation, for example, we have the born-again and biblical literalism question for evangelicals, but for Catholics we have nothing about the Eucharist or the Church.

An important theoretical advance came with the publication of Peter Benson and Dorothy Williams's *Religion on Capitol Hill.*[19] Instead of relying on the customary Likert or Guttman-scaled items to measure the content of religious beliefs, Benson and Williams analyzed the content of open-ended responses. Four bipolar dimensions emerged from this process: agentic (individualistic) versus communal (communitarian), vertical versus horizontal, comforting versus challenging, and restricting versus releasing. Several scholars have tried to measure the political consequences of individualistic and communitarian elements of beliefs. There may, however, be a larger payoff in understanding the restricting-releasing dimension of faith. Just as there is a *theology of fear* and a *theology of hope*, there is a *politics of fear* and a *politics of hope*. For some, religion is all about law, social control, and punishment. Many Christian evangelism programs start with the question, Where will you spend eternity? Most

---

19. Benson and Williams (1982).

end with hope, the good news of the Gospel; yet the origin of religiosity still remains anchored in fear. If not hellfire and damnation for eternity, then it is the fear of personal or cultural chaos, anomie, helpless addiction to alcohol, other drugs, sex, or, more generally, sin, and the power of Satan that impels people toward religion. Recent research measuring *imagery of God* finds bipolar images: God as judge, focusing on religious norms that restrict behavior, and God as lover, focusing on God's grace, the release from sin's dominion, and the freedom to respond to others' needs.[20] The latter affirms that God's creatures have never totally lost the divine spark of love, empathy, and unity with all creation. People who envision God as judge are conservatives, see the primary function of government as being to maintain order and legislate restrictions on our own worst impulses, and rely on military might to subdue evil enemies. People who think of God as lover are political progressives or liberals who see government's proper role as furthering opportunities for those shut out by economic, social, or political hierarchies at home and abroad and who advocate primarily for diplomatic negotiations to settle conflict and maintain peace. In short, in their respective ways, they put a *theology* of fear and a theology of hope into a *politics* of fear and a politics of hope.

On the one hand, cold war, terrorists, preemptive doctrine, and giving military might priority over addressing domestic or foreign needs probably respond to a theology of fear in which, when our nation is beset by enemies, both domestic and foreign, all vigilance must be practiced and little dissent will be tolerated. In the end, you are either with us or against us. A theology of hope, on the other hand, while not denying the dangers of terrorism or cultural anomie, relies on nuanced responses that never lose sight of human development, freedom, and civil liberties. Both the discourse and the group targets are different. Neither side may be able to achieve its objectives without appealing to the other's discourse. For example, the rationale for invading Iraq floundered so long as it was couched in terrorism and weapons of mass destruction, but it gained acceptance when it spoke of establishing a democratic beachhead in an Islamic culture in the Middle East. Because policymakers and culture framers now speak of the long war as they once spoke of the cold war, scholars in the field of voting behavior are likely to have several elections in which to measure discourse couched in a theology of fear and a theology of hope.

Advances in neuroscience may amplify these studies by showing us directly how voters respond to campaign discourse—whether with joy and positive

20. See Welch and Leege (1988); Greeley (1981).

reinforcement or with fearful arousal.[21] For the first time we are able to tap into sectors of the brain to see what happens neurologically when politicians use religious discourse to justify their policies and promises. As a result, we may be entering a brave new world where surveys, polls, and focus groups are replaced by the portable MRI. We know how Frank Luntz's research in 1994 shaped the fourteen points of the Contract with America and helped political handlers to select language that would generate the desired response in target groups. In the future, advanced technologies in the same spirit may cause an even larger share of American politics to be sanctified through religious discourse, unless its practitioners are exposed as religious frauds.

21. See Vedantam (2005) for a summary.

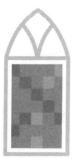

References

Abramowitz, Alan. 1995. "It's Abortion, Stupid: Policy Voting in the 1992 Presidential Election." *Journal of Politics* 57, no. 1: 176–86.

———. 2004. "Terrorism, Gay Marriage, and Incumbency: Explaining the Republican Victory in the 2004 Presidential Election." *Forum* 2, no. 4: article 3.

Abramowitz, Alan I., John McGlennon, and Ronald B. Rapoport, eds. 1986. *The Life of the Parties: Activists in Presidential Politics.* University of Kentucky Press.

Abramowitz, Alan, and Kyle L. Saunders. 1998. "Ideological Realignment in the U.S. Electorate." *Journal of Politics* 60, no. 3: 634–52.

———. 2005. "Why Can't We All Just Get Along? The Reality of a Polarized America." *Forum* 3, no. 2: 1–22.

Adams, Greg D. 1997. "Abortion: Evidence of Issue Evolution." *American Journal of Political Science* 41, no. 3: 718–39.

Aikman, David. 2004. *A Man of Faith: The Spiritual Journey of George W. Bush.* Nashville, Tenn.: W Publishing Group.

Alter, Jonathan. 2005. "The 'Pro-Cure' Movement." *Newsweek,* June 6, p. 27.

Alvarez, R. Michael, and Lisa Garcia Bedolla. 2003. "The Foundations of Latino Voter Partisanship: Evidence from the 2000 Election." *Journal of Politics* 65, no. 1: 31–49.

American Enterprise Institute. 2001. "The Bush Presidency: Transition and Transformation" [transcript prepared from a tape recording] (www.aei.org/events/eventID.14/event_detail.asp).

Andersen, T. W. 1957. "Maximum Likelihood Estimates for a Multivariate Normal Distribution When Some Observations Are Missing." *Journal of the American Statistical Association* 52, no. 278 (June): 200–03.

Appleby, Scott. 1997. "Catholics and the Christian Right: An Uneasy Alliance." In *Sojourners in the Wilderness: The Christian Right in Comparative Perspective,* edited by Corwin Smidt and James Penning, pp. 93–114. Lanham, Md.: Rowman and Littlefield.

Associated Press. 2004. "Kerry Signed Letter Backing Gay Marriage." *USA Today,* February 11.

———. 2005. "Conn. All but OKs 10-Year $100 Million Stem-Cell Plan." *Arizona Daily Star,* June 1.

Baker, Wayne. 2005. *America's Crisis of Values: Reality and Perception.* Princeton University Press.

Balz, Dan. 2004. "Black Voters in S.C. Look to Electability; Sharpton's Message Has Played Better on the Stump than in the Polls." *Washington Post,* February 3.

Banerjee, Neela. 2005. "Black Churches Struggle over Their Role in Politics." *New York Times,* March 6.

Bartels, Larry. 2000. "Partisanship and Voting Behavior, 1952–1996." *American Journal of Political Science* 44, no. 1 (January): 35–50.

———. 2005. "What's the Matter with 'What's the Matter with Kansas'?" Paper presented at the annual meeting of the American Political Science Association, Washington, D.C., September 1–4.

Bean, Frank, and Marta Tienda. 1987. *The Hispanic Population of the United States.* New York: Russell Sage Foundation.

Benson, Peter L., and Dorothy L Williams. 1982. *Religion on Capitol Hill: Myths and Realities.* New York: Harper and Row.

Blendon, Robert J., Mollyann Brodle, Drew E. Altman, John M. Benson, and Elizabeth C. Hamel. 2005. "Voters and Health Care in the 2004 Election." *Health Affairs* 11 (web exclusive supplement, March).

Bluth, Alexa H., and Laura Mecoy. 2004. "Boxer, Jones Split on Stem Cell Issue." *Sacramento Bee,* August 11.

Bock, E. Wilbur, Leonard Beeghley, and Anthony J. Mixon. 1983. "Religion, Socioeconomic Status, and Sexual Morality: An Application of Reference Group Theory." *Sociological Quarterly* 24 (Fall): 545–59.

Bottum, Joseph. 2004. "The Myth of the Catholic Voter." *Weekly Standard* 10 (November 1–8): 1–9.

Bowler, Shaun, and Todd Donovan. 1998. *Demanding Choices: Opinion, Voting, and Direct Democracy.* University of Michigan Press.

Bowler, Shaun, Todd Donovan, and Trudi Happ. 1992. "Ballot Propositions and Information Costs: Direct Democracy and the Fatigued Voter." *Western Political Quarterly* 45 (June): 557–68.

Branton, Regina P. 2003. "Examining Individual-Level Voting Behavior on State Ballot Propositions." *Political Research Quarterly* 56 (September): 367–77.

Braumoeller, Bear. 2004. "Hypothesis Testing and Multiplicative Interaction Terms." *International Organizations* 58 (Fall): 807–20.

Buell, Emmett H., and John S. Jackson. 1991. "The National Conventions: Diminished but Still Important in a Primary Dominated Process." In *Nominating the President,* edited by Emmett H. Buell and Lee Sigelman. University of Tennessee Press.

Burden, Barry C. 2004. "An Alternative Account of the 2004 Presidential Election." *Forum* 2, no. 4: article 2.

Burnham, Walter Dean. 1970. *Critical Elections and the Mainsprings of American Politics.* New York: Norton.

Byrnes, Timothy A. 1991. *Catholic Bishops in American Politics.* Princeton University Press.

Cain, Bruce, D. Roderick Kiewiet, and Carole Uhlaner. 1991. "The Acquisition of Partisanship by Latinos and Asian Americans." *American Journal of Political Science* 35, no. 2 (May): 390–422.

Calhoun-Brown, Allison. 1997. "Still Seeing in Black and White: Racial Challenges for the Christian Right." In *Sojourners in the Wilderness: The Christian Right in Comparative Perspective,* edited by Corwin Smidt and James Penning, pp. 115–37. Lanham, Md.: Rowman and Littlefield.

Campbell, Angus, Philip Converse, Warren Miller, and Donald Stokes. 1960. *The American Voter.* New York: John Wiley.

Campbell, David E., and J. Quin Monson. 2005. "The Religion Card: Evangelicals, Catholics, and Gay Marriage in the 2004 Presidential Election." Paper presented at the annual meeting of the American Political Science Association, Washington, D.C., September 1–4.

———. 2007 (forthcoming). "Dry Kindling: A Political Profile of American Mormons." In *From Pews to Polling Places: Faith and Politics in the American Religious Mosaic,* edited by J. Matthew Wilson. Georgetown University Press.

Carmines, Edward G., and Geoffrey C. Layman. 1997. "Issue Evolution in Postwar American Politics: Old Certainties and Fresh Tensions." In *Present Discontents: American Politics in the Very Late Twentieth Century,* edited by Byron E Shafer. Chatham, N.J.: Chatham House.

Chaves, Mark. 2004. *Congregations in America.* Harvard University Press.

Cherry, Conrad. 1995. *Hurrying toward Zion: Universities, Divinity Schools, and American Protestantism.* Indiana University Press.

Citrin, Jack, Beth Reingold, Evelyn Walters, and Donald Green. 1990. "The 'Official English' Movement and the Symbolic Politics of Language in the United States." *Western Political Quarterly* 43, no. 3 (September): 535–60.

Clemetson, Lynette. 2004. "Both Sides Court Black Churches in the Debate over Gay Marriage." *New York Times,* March 1.

Cohen, Cathy J. 1999. *The Boundaries of Blackness: AIDS and the Breakdown of Black Politics.* University of Chicago Press.

Cohn, D'Vera, and Tara Bahrampour. 2006. "Of U.S. Children under 5, Nearly Half Are Minorities," *Washington Post,* May 10, p. A10

Committee on Political Parties, American Political Science Association. 1950. *Toward a More Responsible Two-Party System.* New York: Rinehart.

Conover, Pamela Johnston, and Stanley Feldman. 1981. "The Origins and Meaning of Liberal/Conservative Self-Identifications." *American Journal of Political Science* 25, no. 4: 617–45.

Cook, Charlie. 2005. "Growing Pains." *National Journal,* May 10.

Cook, Elizabeth Adell, Ted G. Jelen, and Clyde Wilcox. *Between Two Absolutes: Public Opinion and the Politics of Abortion.* Boulder, Colo.: Westview Press.

Cooperman, Alan. 2004a. "Bush Tells Catholic Group He Will Tackle Its Issues." *Washington Post,* August 4, p. A4.

———. 2004b. "Churchgoers Get Direction from Bush Campaign." *Washington Post,* July 1, p. A1.

Cooperman, Alan, and Thomas B. Edsall. 2004. "Evangelicals Say They Led Charge for the GOP." *Washington Post,* November 8, p. A1.

Craig, Barbara H., and David M. O'Brien. 1993. *Abortion and American Politics.* Chatham, N.J.: Chatham House.

Dao, James. 2005. "A Democrat of Faith Turns Tables." *New York Times,* November 10.

David, Paul T., Ralph M. Goldman, and Richard C. Bain. 1960. *The Politics of National Party Conventions.* Brookings.

De la Garza, Rodolfo, and Louis DeSipio. 1994. "Overview: The Link between Individuals and Electoral Institutions in Five Latino Neighborhoods." In *Barrio Ballots: Latino Politics in the 1990 Elections,* edited by Rodolfo O. de la Garza, Martha Menchaca, and Louis DeSipio. Boulder, Colo.: Westview Press.

De la Garza, Rodolfo, Louis DeSipio, F. Chris García, John García, and Angelo Falcón. 1992. *Latino Voices: Mexican, Puerto Rican, and Cuban Perspectives on American Politics.* Boulder, Colo.: Westview Press.

De la Garza, Rodolfo, Luis Fraga, and Harry Pachon. 1988. "Toward a Shared Agenda." *Journal of State Government* 61, no. 2: 77–80.

Del Olmo, Frank. 1987. "A Journalist's View of Latino Public Opinion Polls." In *Ignored Voices: Public Opinion Polls and the Latino Community,* edited by Rodolfo de la Garza. Austin, Tex.: Center for Mexican-American Studies.

DeSipio, Louis, and Rodolfo O. de la Garza. 2000. "Forever Seen as New: Latino Participation in American Elections." In *Latinos: Remaking America,* edited by Marcelo M. Suarez-Orozco and Mariela M. Paez. University of California Press.

Dillman, Don A. 2000. *Mail and Internet Surveys: The Tailored Design Method,* 2nd ed. New York: John Wiley.

Domínguez, Jorge I. 1994. "Do 'Latinos' Exist?" *Contemporary Sociology* 23, no. 3: 354–56.

Donovan, Todd, and Joseph Snipp. 1994. "Support for Legislative Term Limitations in California." *Journal of Politics* 56, no. 2: 492–501.

Donovan, Todd, Caroline Tolbert, Daniel A. Smith, and Janine Perry. 2005. "Did Gay Marriage Elect George W. Bush?" Paper read at the annual meeting of the Western Political Science Association, Oakland, Calif., March 17–20.

Duin, Julia. 2003. "Bishops to Pressure Catholic Politicians, Urge Them to Follow Their Faith." *Washington Times,* December 4.

———. 2004a. "Kerry Advisers Tell Hopeful to 'Keep Cool' on Religion." *Washington Times,* June 18.

———. 2004b. "Kerry Cited in Catholic Heresy Case." *Washington Times,* June 30.

Dwyer, Jim, and Jodi Wilgoren. 2004. "Gore and Kerry Unite in Search for Black Votes." *New York Times,* October 25, p. 1.

Eckstrom, Kevin. 2005. "In 2004, Christians Stood at Front Lines." *Washington Post,* January 1, p. B-7.

Eichel, Larry. "'Values Voters Seek Their Reward in Policy." *Philadelphia Inquirer,* November 7.

Episcopal Church. 2003. "Genetics: Approve Research on Stem Cells." Seventy-fourth General Convention, Episcopal Church. (www.episcopalchurch.org/19021_40459_ENG_Print.html).

Espinosa, Gaston, Virgilio Elizondo, and Jesse Miranda. 2003. "Hispanic Churches in American Public Life: Summary of Findings." University of Notre Dame, Institute for Latino Studies.

Farhi, Paul, and Vanessa Williams. 2004. "Politics and Pulpits Combine to Sway Swing-State Voters." *Washington Post,* October 25, p. A7.

Fears, Darryl. 2004. "Kerry Urged to Do More to Get Black Votes; Lack of Diversity among Top Campaign Officials, Absence in Community Are Concerns." *Washington Post,* June 29, p. A4.

Feldman, Stanley. 1988. "Structure and Consistency in Public Opinion: The Role of Core Beliefs and Values." *American Journal of Political Science* 32, no. 2: 416–40.

Ferdinand, Pamela. 2003. "Pols Take Hats off to Kerry for Coming to Boston Roast; Jokes Rib Senator's Jewish Ancestry." *Washington Post,* March 17.

Ferguson, Thomas. 2005. "Holy Owned Subsidiary: Globalization, Religion, and Politics in the 2004 Election." In *Defining Moment,* edited by William Crotty, pp. 187–210. Armonk, N.Y.: M. E. Sharpe.

Findlay, James F. 1993. *Church People in the Struggle: The National Council of Churches and the Black Freedom Movement, 1950–1970.* Oxford University Press.

Fineman, Howard, and Tamara Lipper. 2005. "The Cellular Divide." *Newsweek,* June 6, pp. 22–25.

Fiorina, Morris P. 2004. " 'Holy War' over Moral Values or Contempt for Opinion?" *San Francisco Chronicle,* November 21, p. B-5.

Fiorina, Morris P., with Samuel J. Abrams, and Jeremy C. Pope. 2005. *Culture War? The Myth of a Polarized America.* New York: Longman.

Foer, Franklin. 2003–04. "Beyond Belief: Howard Dean's Religion Problem [series]." *New Republic,* December 29, January 5, January 12.

Fowler, Robert, Allen D. Hertzke, and Laura R. Olson. 1999. *Religion and Politics in America: Faith, Culture, and Strategic Choices,* 2nd ed. Boulder, Colo.: Westview Press.

Fowler, Robert, Allen Hertzke, Laura Olson, and Kevin Den Dulk. 2004. *Religion and Politics in America: Faith, Culture, and Strategic Choices,* 3rd ed. Boulder, Colo.: Westview Press.

Fox, Richard L., and Jennifer L. Lawless. 2004. "Entering the Arena? Gender and the Decision to Run for Office." *American Journal of Political Science* 48, no. 2: 264–80.

Frank, Thomas. 2004. *What's the Matter with Kansas? How Conservatives Won the Heart of America.* New York: Metropolitan Books.

Freedman, Paul. 2004. "The Gay Marriage Myth: Terrorism, Not Values, Drove Bush's Re-election." *Slate,* November 5. (www.slate.com/id/2109275/).

Freidrich, Robert J. 1982. "In Defense of Multiplicative Terms in Multiple Regression Equations." *American Journal of Political Science* 34, no. 4 (December): 797–833.

Fuchs, Lawrence H. 1967. *John F. Kennedy and American Catholicism.* New York: Meredith Press.

———. 1990. *The American Kaleidoscope: Race, Ethnicity, and the Civic Culture.* Wesleyan University Press.

Gertner, Jon. 2004. "The Very, Very Personal Is the Political." *New York Times Magazine,* February 15.

Gilens, Martin. 1999. *Why Americans Hate Welfare.* University of Chicago Press.

Gilgoff, Dan, and Bret Schulte. 2004. "The Morals and Values Crowd." *U.S. News and World Report,* November 15.

Gimpel, James G., and Karen Kaufmann. 2001. "Impossible Dream or Distant Reality? Republican Efforts to Attract Latino Voters." Center for Immigration Studies, August (www.cis.org/articles/2001/back901.html).

Goodstein, Laurie. 2004. "Politicians Face Censure from Bishops on Abortion Rights." *New York Times,* June 19.

Gorski, Eric. 2004. "Values Vote a Powerful New Force." *Denver Post,* November 5, p. A-1.

Greeley, Andrew M. 1977. "How Conservative Are American Catholics?" *Political Science Quarterly* 92, no. 2 (Summer): 199–218.

———. 1981. *The Religious Imagination.* New York: Sadlier.

———. 1989. "Protestant and Catholic: Is the Analogical Imagination Extinct?" *American Sociological Review* 54, no. 4 (August): 460–85.

———. 1990. *The Catholic Myth: The Behavior and Beliefs of American Catholics.* New York: Collier Books.

———. 1994. "The Demography of American Catholics: 1965–1990." In *The Sociology of Andrew Greeley,* edited by Andrew Greeley. Atlanta: Scholars Press.

———. 1997. "Defection among Hispanics (Updated)." *America* 177 (September 27): 12–3.

Green, Donald, Bradley Palmquist, and Eric Schickler. 2002. *Partisan Hearts and Minds: Political Parties and the Social Identities of Voters.* Yale University Press.

Green, John C. 2000a. "Antigay: Varieties of Opposition to Gay Rights." In *The Politics of Gay Rights,* edited by Craig A. Rimmerman, Kenneth D. Wald, and Clyde Wilcox. University of Chicago Press.

————. 2000b. "Religion and Politics in the 1990s: Confrontations and Coalitions." In *Religion and American Politics: The 2000 Election in Context,* edited by Mark Silk, pp. 19–40. Hartford, Conn.: Center for the Study of Religion in Public Life.

————. 2004a. "The American Religious Landscape and Political Attitudes: A Baseline for 2004." Pew Forum on Religion and Public Life (pewforum.org/docs/index.php?DocID=55).

————. 2004b. "The Jesus Factor: Bush and Evangelicals." Internet interview. *PBS Frontline,* April 29 (www.pbs.org/wgbh/shows/jesus/evangelicals/bushand.html [November 2005]).

————. 2004c. "Winning Numbers." *Christian Century,* November 30.

Green, John C., and Daniel Coffey. 2006. *The State of the Parties,* 5th ed. Lanham, Md.: Rowman and Littlefield.

Green, John C., James L. Guth, and Cleveland R. Fraser. 1991. "Apostles and Apostates? Religion and Politics among Political Activists." In *The Bible and the Ballot Box,* edited by James L. Guth and John C. Green, pp. 113–36. Boulder, Colo.: Westview Press.

Green, John C., James L. Guth, and Kevin Hill. 1993. "Faith and Election: The Christian Right in Congressional Campaigns, 1978–1988." *Journal of Politics* 55, no. 1 (February): 80–91.

Green, John C., James L. Guth, Corwin E. Smidt, and Lyman A. Kellstedt. 1996. *Religion and the Culture Wars: Dispatches from the Front.* Lanham, Md.: Rowman and Littlefield.

Green, John C., and Paul S. Herrnson. 2002. *Responsible Partisanship? The Evolution of American Political Parties since 1950.* University Press of Kansas.

Green, John C., and John S. Jackson. 2007. "Party Profiles: 2004 National Convention Delegates," in *Rewiring Politics: Presidential Nominating Conventions in the Media Age,* edited by Costas Panagopoulos. Louisiana State University Press.

Green, John C., John S. Jackson, and Nancy L. Clayton. 1999. "Issue Networks and Party Elites in 1996." In *The State of the Parties,* 3rd ed., edited by John C. Green and Daniel M. Shea, pp. 105–19. Lanham, Md.: Rowman and Littlefield.

Green, John C., Mark J. Rozell, and Clyde Wilcox. 2001. "Social Movements and Party Politics: The Case of the Christian Right." *Journal for the Scientific Study of Religion* 40, no. 3: 413–26.

————, eds. 2003. *The Christian Right in American Politics: Marching to the Millennium.* Georgetown University Press.

————, eds. 2006. *The Values Campaign? The Christian Right and the 2004 Elections.* Georgetown University Press.

Green, John C., and Mark Silk. 2004. "Gendering the Religion Gap." *Religion in the News* 7, no. 1: 11–13.

Green, John C., Corwin E. Smidt, James L. Guth, and Lyman A. Kellstedt. 2005. "The American Religious Landscape and the 2004 Presidential Vote: Increased Polarization." Pew Forum on Religion and Public Life (pewforum.org/docs/index.php?DocID=64).

Green, John, Corwin Smidt, Lyman Kellstedt, and James Guth. 1997. "Bringing in the Sheaves: The Christian Right and White Protestantism." In *Sojourners in the Wilderness: The Christian Right in Comparative Perspective*, edited by Corwin Smidt and James Penning, pp. 75–92. Lanham, Md.: Rowman and Littlefield.

Green, John C., and Steve Waldman. 2004. "The Twelve Tribes of American Politics." BeliefNet, September 30 (www.beliefnet.com/story/153/story_15355_1.html).

Greenberg, Stanley B. 2004. *The Two Americas: Our Current Political Deadlock and How to Break It*. New York: St. Martin's Press.

Greenberger, Scott S., and Frank Phillips. 2005. "Romney Draws Fire on Stem Cells: Opposes the Use of Cloned Embryos." *Boston Globe,* February 11.

Grizzly Adams Productions. 2004. "George W. Bush: Faith in the White House." New York: Good Times DVD.

Guth, James L., and John C. Green. 1988. "The Christian Right in the Republican Party: The Case of Pat Robertson's Supporters." *Journal of Politics* 50 (February): 150–65.

———. 1993. "Religious Salience: The Core Measure?" In *Rediscovering the Impact of Religion on Political Behavior*, edited by David C. Leege and Lyman A. Kellstedt, pp. 157–74. Armonk, N.Y.: M. E. Sharpe.

Guth, James L., John C. Green, Lyman Kellstedt, and Corwin Smidt. 1995. "Onward, Christian Soldiers: Religious Activist Groups in American Politics." In *Interest Group Politics*, 4th ed., edited by Allan Cigler and Burdett Loomis, pp. 55–76. Washington, D.C.: CQ Press.

Guth, James L., John C. Green, Corwin E. Smidt, Lyman A. Kellstedt, and Margaret M. Poloma. 1997. *The Bully Pulpit: The Politics of Protestant Clergy*. University Press of Kansas.

Guth, James L., and Lyman A. Kellstedt. 2001. "Religion and Congress." In *In God We Trust: Religion and American Political Life*, edited by Corwin E. Smidt, pp. 213–33. Grand Rapids, Mich.: Baker Academic.

Guth, James L., Lyman A. Kellstedt, John C. Green, and Corwin E. Smidt. 1998. "Thunder on the Right? Religious Interest Group Mobilization in the 1996 Election." In *Interest Group Politics*, 5th ed., edited by Allan J. Cigler and Burdett A. Loomis, pp. 169–92. Washington, D.C.: CQ Press.

———. 2001. "America Fifty/Fifty." *First Things* 116 (October): 19–26.

———. 2002. "A Distant Thunder? Religious Mobilization in the 2000 Elections." In *Interest Group Politics*, 6th ed., edited by Allan J. Cigler and Burdett A. Loomis, pp. 161–84. Washington, D.C.: CQ Press.

Guth, James L, Lyman A. Kellstedt, Corwin E. Smidt, and John C. Green. 2006. "Religious Influences in the 2004 Presidential Election," *Presidential Studies Quarterly* 36 (June): 223–42.

Hall, Carl T. 2005. "Foes Closing the Gap in Stem-Cell Measure." *San Francisco Chronicle,* October 15.

Hall, Charles F. 1997. "The Christian Left: Who Are They and How Are They Different from the Christian Right?" *Review of Religious Research* 39 (September): 27–45.

Han, Hahrie. 2005. "Who Is Represented? The Impact of Issue Publics on Roll-Call Voting in the Senate." Working Paper. Wellesley College, August.

Hansen, Brian. 2004. "Cloning Debate." *CQ Researcher* 14, no. 37 (October 22): 877–900.

Hansen, John Mark. 1991. *Gaining Access: Congress and the Farm Lobby, 1919–1981.* University of Chicago Press.

Harding, James. 2004. "Electorate Puts Moral Concerns ahead of Policy." *Financial Times* (London), November 5.

Harris, Hamil R. 2001. "Blacks Reach out to Bush." *Washington Post,* January 27.

Harris, John F. 2004. "Victory Bears out Emphasis on Values; GOP Tactics Aimed at Cultural Divide." *Washington Post,* November 4.

Hart, Stephen. 2001. *Cultural Dilemmas of Progressive Politics.* University of Chicago Press.

Havergal, Frances. 1974. "Like a River Glorious." In *Hymns for the Living Church,* edited by Donald P. Hustad. Carol Stream, Ill.: Hope Publishing.

Hennesey, James S. J. 1981. *American Catholics: A History of the Roman Catholic Community in the United States.* Oxford University Press.

Hernandez, Raymond. 2005. "As Clinton Shifts Themes, Debate Arises on Her Motives." *New York Times,* February 1.

Hertzke, Allen. 1988. *Representing God in Washington.* University of Tennessee Press.

Hetherington, Marc J. 2001. "Resurgent Mass Partisanship: The Role of Elite Polarization." *American Political Science Review* 95, no. 3: 619–31.

Hillygus, D. Sunshine, and Todd G. Shields. 2005. "Moral Issues and Voter Decision Making in the 2004 Presidential Election." *PS: Political Science and Politics* 38, no. 2: 201–09.

Hochschild, Jennifer. 1981. *What's Fair: American Beliefs about Distributive Justice.* Harvard University Press.

Hofrenning, Daniel J. B. 1995. *In Washington but Not of It: The Prophetic Politics of Religious Lobbyists.* Temple University Press.

Hoge, Dean R., Benton Johnson, and Donald A. Luidens. 1994. *Vanishing Boundaries.* Louisville, Ky.: Westminister/John Knox Press.

Homans, George C. 1950. *The Human Group.* New York: Harcourt Brace.

Howard, Philip. 2003. "Digitizing the Social Contract: Producing American Political Culture in the Age of New Media." *Communication Review* 6, no. 3: 213–45.

Huckfeldt, R. Robert, Paul Allen Beck, Russell J. Dalton, and Jeffrey Levine. 1995. "Political Environments, Cohesive Social Groups, and the Communication of Public Opinion." *American Journal of Political Science* 39, no. 4: 1025–54.

Hunt, Larry. 2000. "Religion and Secular Status among Hispanics in the United States: Catholicism and the Varieties of Hispanic Protestantism." *Social Science Quarterly* 81, no. 1: 344–62.

Hunter, James Davison. 1991. *Culture Wars: The Struggle to Define America.* New York: Basic Books.

———. 1994. *Before the Shooting Begins: Searching for Democracy in America's Culture War.* New York: Macmillan.

Ingelhart, Ronald. 1971. "The Silent Revolution in Europe: Intergenerational Change in Post-Industrial Societies." *American Political Science Review* 65, no. 4: 991–1017.

———. 1977. *The Silent Revolution: Changing Values and Political Styles among Western Publics.* Princeton University Press.

Jackson, John S. 1992. "The Party-as-Organization: Party Elites and Party Reforms in Presidential Nominations and Conventions." In *Challenges to Party Government,* edited by John Kenneth White and Jerome M. Mileur, pp. 63–83. Southern Illinois University.

Jackson, John S., Nate Bigelow, and John C. Green. 2003. "The State of Party Elites: National Convention Delegates, 1992–2000." In *The State of the Parties: The Changing Role of Contemporary Parties,* 4th ed., edited by John C. Green and Rick Farmer, pp. 54–78. Lanham, Md.: Rowman and Littlefield.

———. 2006. "The State of Party Elites: National Convention Delegates, 1992–2004." In *The State of the Parties: The Changing Role of Contemporary Parties,* 5th ed., edited by John C. Green and Daniel Coffey. Lanham, Md.: Rowman and Littlefield.

Jackson, John S., Barbara L. Brown, and David Bositis. 1982. "Herbert McClosky and Friends Revisited." *American Politics Quarterly* 10 (April): 158–80.

Jackson, John S., and Nancy Clayton. 1996. "Leaders and Followers: Major Party Elites, Identifiers, and Issues, 1980–1992." In *The State of the Parties: The Changing Role of Contemporary Parties,* 2nd ed., edited by John C. Green and Daniel M. Shea, pp. 328–51. Lanham, Md.: Rowman and Littlefield.

Jackson, John S., and Robert A. Hitlin. 1976. "A Comparison of Party Elites: The Sanford Commission and the Delegates to the Democratic Mid-Term Conferences." *American Politics Quarterly* 4 (October): 441–81.

Jacobs, Lawrence. 2004. "Moral Values Takes Back Seat to Partisanship and the Economy in the 2004 Presidential Election." University of Minnesota, Humphrey Institute of Public Affairs (www.hhh.umn.edu/centers/csp/elections/moral_values.html).

Jacobson, Gary C. 2000. "Party Polarization in National Politics: The Electoral Connection." *Polarized Politics: The President and the Congress in a Partisan Era,* edited by Jon Bond and Richard Fleischer, pp. 9–30. Washington, D.C.: CQ Press.

Jennings, James. 1988. "The Puerto Rican Community: Its Political Background." In *Latinos and the Political System,* edited by F. Chris García. University of Notre Dame Press.

Jensen, Richard J. 1971. *The Winning of the Midwest: Social and Political Conflict, 1888–96.* University of Chicago Press.

Jones-Correa, Michael, and David Leal. 1996. "Becoming 'Hispanic': Secondary Pan-Ethnic Identification among Latin American–Origin Populations in the United States." *Hispanic Journal of Behavioral Sciences* 18, no. 2: 214–54.

Kaid, Lynda Lee, and Daniela V. Dimitrova. 2005. "The Television Advertising Battleground in the 2004 Presidential Election." *Journalism Studies* 6, no. 2: 165–75.

Katz, Elihu, and Paul F. Lazarsfeld. 1964. *Personal Influence.* New York: Free Press.

Kaufmann, Karen M., and John R. Petrocik. 1999. "The Changing Politics of American Men: Understanding the Sources of the Gender Gap." *American Journal of Political Science* 43, no. 3: 864–87.

Keefe, Susan, and Amado Padilla. 1987. *Chicano Ethnicity.* University of New Mexico Press.

Kellstedt, Lyman A., and John C. Green. 1993. "Knowing God's Many People: Denominational Preference and Political Behavior." In *Rediscovering the Religious Factor in American Politics,* edited by David C. Leege and Lyman A. Kellstedt. Armonk, N.Y.: M. E. Sharpe.

Kellstedt, Lyman A., John C. Green, James L. Guth, and Corwin E. Smidt. 1995. "Has Godot Finally Arrived? Religion and Realignment in 1994." *Public Perspective* 6, no. 4: 18–22.

———. 1996. "Grasping the Essentials: The Social Embodiment of Religion and Political Behavior." In *Religion and the Culture Wars,* edited by John C. Green, James L. Guth, Corwin E. Smidt, and Lyman A. Kellstedt, pp. 174–92. Landam, Md.: Rowman and Littlefield.

Kengor, Paul. 2004. *God and George W. Bush: A Spiritual Life.* New York: Regan Books.

Kenski, Henry, and William Lockwood. 1991. "Catholic Voting Behavior in 1988: A Critical Swing Vote." In *The Bible and the Ballot Box: Religion and Politics in the 1988 Election,* edited by James Guth and John Green. Boulder, Colo.: Westview.

King, Gary, Michael Tomz, and Jason Wittenberg. 2000. "Making the Most of Statistical Analyses: Improving Interpretation and Presentation." *American Journal of Political Science* 44 (April): 347–61.

Kirkpatrick, David D. 2004a. "Black Pastors Backing Bush Are Rarities, but Not Alone." *New York Times,* October 5, p. A15.

———. 2004b. "Bush Allies Till Fertile Soil, among Baptists, for Votes." *New York Times,* June 18.

———. 2004c. "Bush Campaign Seeks Help from Thousands of Congregations." *New York Times,* June 3.

———. 2004d. "Republicans Admit Mailing Campaign Literature Saying Liberals Will Ban Bible." *New York Times,* September 24, p. A20.

Kirkpatrick, David D., and Laurie Goodstein. 2004. "Group of Bishops Using Influence to Oppose Kerry." *New York Times,* October 12, p. A1.

Kirkpatrick, Jeane J. 1976. *The New Presidential Elite: Men and Women in National Politics.* New York: Russell Sage Foundation.

Kleppner, Paul. 1970. *The Cross of Culture: A Social Analysis of Midwest Politics, 1850–1900,* 2nd ed. New York: Free Press.

———. 1979. *The Third Electoral System: Parties, Voters, and Political Cultures.* University of North Carolina Press.

Kohut, Andrew, John C. Green, Scott Keeter, and Robert Toth. 2000. *The Diminishing Divide: Religion's Changing Role in American Politics.* Brookings.

Kosmin, Barry, and Ariela Keysar. 1995. "Party Political Preferences of U.S. Hispanics: The Varying Impact of Religion, Social Class, and Demographic Factors." *Ethnic and Racial Studies* 18, no. 2: 336–47.

Kralis, Barbara. 2004. "Will the Silence of U.S. Catholic Bishops Help Elect John Kerry?" *Intellectual Conservative*, October 19. (www.intellectualconservative.com/article3865.html [November 2005).

Krosnick, Jon A., and Lin Chiat Chang. 2001. "A Comparison of the Random Digit Dialing Telephone Survey Methodology with Internet Survey Methodology as Implemented by Knowledge Networks and Harris Interactive." Stanford University.

Lambro, Donald. 2004. "In Search of New Faces." *Washington Times Special Report*, November 7 (washingtontimes.com/specialreport/20041107-123932-3944r.htm).

Langer, Gary. 2004. "A Question of Values." *New York Times*, November 6.

Layman, Geoffrey. 1999. "Culture Wars in the American Party System: Religious and Cultural Change among Partisan Activists since 1972." *American Politics Quarterly* 27, no. 1: 89–121.

———. 2001. *The Great Divide: Religious and Cultural Conflict in American Party Politics.* Columbia University Press.

Layman, Geoffrey, and Thomas M. Carsey. 1999. "A Dynamic Model of Political Change among Party Activists." *Political Behavior* 21, no. 1: 17–41.

———. 2002. "Party Polarization and 'Conflict Extension' in the American Electorate." *American Journal of Political Science* 46, no. 4: 786–802.

Layman, Geoffrey C., and John C. Green. 2006. "Wars and Rumors of Wars: The Contexts of Cultural Conflict in American Political Behavior." *British Journal of Political Science* 36, no. 1: 61–89.

Lazarsfeld, Paul F., Bernard Berelson, and Hazel Gaudet. 1948. *The People's Choice: How the Voter Makes up His Mind in a Presidential Campaign.* Columbia University Press.

Leal, David. 2006. "Mexican-American and Cuban-American Public Opinion: Differences at the State Level?" In *Public Opinion in State Politics*, edited by Jeffrey Cohen. Stanford University Press.

———. Forthcoming. "Latino Public Opinion: Does It Exist?" In *Latino Politics: Identity, Mobilization, and Representation*, edited by Rodolfo Espino, David L. Leal, and Kenneth J. Meier. University of Virginia Press.

Leal, David, Matt Barreto, Jongho Lee, and Rodolfo de la Garza. 2005. "The Latino Vote in the 2004 Election." *PS: Political Science and Politics* 38 (January): 41–49.

Lee, Jongho, and Harry Pachon. 2005. "Leading the Way: The Analysis of the Effect of Religion on the Latino Vote." Paper presented at the annual meeting of the American Political Science Association, Washington, D.C., September 1–4.

Lee, Jongho, Harry P. Pachon, and Matt Barreto. 2002. "Guiding the Flock: Church as Vehicle of Latino Political Participation." Paper presented at the annual meeting of the American Political Science Association, Boston, Mass., August 29–September 1.

Leege, David C., and Lyman A. Kellstedt, ed. 1993. *Rediscovering the Religious Factor in American Politics.* Armonk, N.Y.: M. E. Sharpe.

Leege, David C., Paul D. Mueller, and Kenneth D. Wald. 2001. "The Politics of Cultural Differences in the 2000 Presidential Election: The Return of the Prodigal (Reagan) Generation." Paper delivered to the annual meeting of the American Political Science Association, San Francisco, August 30–September 2.

Leege, David C., Kenneth D. Wald, Paul D. Mueller, and Brian S. Krueger. 2002. *The Politics of Cultural Differences: Social Change and Voter Mobilization Strategies in the Post–New Deal Period.* Princeton University Press.

Lenski, Gerhardt. 1961. *The Religious Factor.* New York: Doubleday.

Lewis, Gregory B. 2005. "Same-Sex Marriage and the 2004 Presidential Election." *PS: Political Science and Politics* 38 (April): 195–99.

Littwin, Mike. "On the Road to the 2004 Election: You Don't Need a Map to Find America's Political Divide." *Rocky Mountain News,* November 17.

Long, J. Scott, and Jeremy Freese. 2001. *Regression Models for Categorical Dependent Variables Using Stata.* College Station, Tex.: Stata Press.

Maggiotto, Michael A., and Gary D. Wekkin. 2000. *Partisan Linkages in Southern Politics: Elites, Voters, and Identifiers.* University of Tennessee Press.

Magleby, David B., J. Quin Monson, and Kelly D. Patterson, eds. 2007. *Dancing without Partners: How Candidates, Parties, and Interest Groups Interact in the Presidential Campaign.* Lanham, Md.: Rowman and Littlefield.

Mansfield, Stephen. 2003. *The Faith of George W. Bush.* New York: Tarcher/Penguin.

Marcus, George E., W. Russell Neuman, Michael B. MacKuen, and John L. Sullivan. 1996. "Dynamic Models of Emotional Response: The Multiple Roles of Affect in Politics." In *Research in Micropolitics,* edited by Robert Y. Shapiro, Michael Delli Carpini, and Leonie Huddy. Greenwich, Conn.: JAI Press.

Marlin, George J. 2004. *The American Catholic Voter: 200 Years of Political Impact.* South Bend, Ind.: Saint Augustine's Press.

Marsh, Charles. 1997. *God's Long Summer: Stories of Faith and Civil Rights.* Princeton University Press.

Masci, David. 2001. "Evangelical Christians." *CQ Researcher* 11, no. 31 (September 14): 715–26.

McCarty, Nolan, Keith T. Poole, and Howard Rosenthal. 2006. *Polarized America: The Dance of Ideology and Unequal Riches.* MIT Press.

McClosky, Herbert, Paul Hoffman, and Rosemary O'Hara. 1960. "Issue Conflict and Consensus among Party Leaders and Followers." *American Political Science Review* 54, no. 2 (June): 406–27.

———. 1964. "Consensus and Ideology in American Politics." *American Political Science Review* 58, no. 2 (June): 361–82.

McCormick, Richard L. 1974. "Ethno-Cultural Interpretations of American Voting Behavior." *Political Science Quarterly* 89 (June): 351–77.

McDaniel, Eric L. 2003. "Black Clergy in the 2000 Election." *Journal for the Scientific Study of Religion* 42, no. 4: 533–46.

McDonald, Michael P. 2004. "Up, Up, and Away! Voter Participation in the 2004 Presidential Election." *Forum* 4, no. 2: 1–4.

McMahon, Kevin J. 2005. "A 'Moral Values Election?' The Culture War, the Supreme Court, and a Divided America." In *Winning the White House 2004*, edited by Kevin J. McMahon, David M. Rankin, Donald W. Beachler, and John K. White. New York: Palgrave.

Mendel, Ed. 2004. "Poll Finds Increasing Support for Stem Cell Research." *San Diego Union-Tribune*, October 31.

Mendelberg, Tali. 2001. *The Race Card: Campaign Strategy, Implicit Messages, and the Norm of Equality*. Princeton University Press.

Meyer, Dick. 2004a. "Moral Values Malarky." *Against the Grain*, November 5, 2004 (www.cbsnews.com/stories/2004/11/05/opinion/meyer/main653931.shtml).

———. 2004b. "How Did One Exit Poll Become the Story of How Bush Won? Good Question." *Washington Post*, December 5.

Milbank, Dana. 1999. "Candidates' Consultants Create the Customized Campaign." *New Republic*, July 5, pp. 22–27.

Miller, Arthur H., and Martin P. Wattenberg. 1984. "Politics from the Pulpit: Religiosity and the 1980 Elections." *Public Opinion Quarterly* 48, no. 1: 301–17.

Miller, Steve. 2001. "NAACP Votes to Fight Bush on His Faith-Based Initiative." *Washington Times*, July 11, p. A-6.

Miller, Warren E., and M. Kent Jennings. 1986. *Parties in Transition: A Longitudinal Study of Party Elites and Party Supporters*. New York: Sage.

Miller, Warren E., and J. Merrill Shanks. 1996. *The New American Voter*. Harvard University Press.

Mockabee, Stephen T. 2007 (forthcoming). "The Political Behavior of American Catholics: Change and Continuity." In *From Pews to Polling Places: Faith and Politics in the American Religious Mosaic*, edited by J. Matthew Wilson. Georgetown University Press.

Monson, J. Quin. 2004. "Get on TeleVision vs. Get on the Van: GOTV and the Ground War in 2002." In *The Last Hurrah? Soft Money and Issue Advocacy in the 2002 Congressional Elections*, edited by David B. Magleby and J. Quin Monson. Brookings.

Mueller, John. 1970. "Presidential Popularity from Truman to Johnson." *American Political Science Review* 64, no. 1: 18–34.

Muirhead, Russell, Nancy L. Rosenblum, Daniel Schlozman, and Francis X. Shen. 2005. "Religion in the 2004 Presidential Election." In *Divided States of America: The Slash and Burn Politics of the 2004 Presidential Election*, edited by Larry Sabato. New York: Longman.

Nagourney, Adam. 2001. "The Post-Sharpton Sharpton." *New York Times,* March 18, p. 42.

National Election Pool, Edison Media Research, and Mitosky Internal. 2005. National Election Pool General Election Exit Polls, 2004 [Computer file]. ICPSR version. Somerville, N.J.: Edison Media Research/New York: Mitofsky International [producers]. Ann Arbor, Mich.: Inter-University Consortium for Political and Social Research [distributor], 2005.

Nicholson, Stephen P. 2003. "The Political Environment and Ballot Proposition Awareness." *American Journal of Political Science* 47 (July): 403–10.

———. 2005. *Voting the Agenda: Candidates, Elections, and Ballot Propositions.* Princeton University Press.

Nicholson-Crotty, Sean, and Kenneth J. Meier. 2002. "In Defense of Single-State Studies." *State Politics and Policy Quarterly* 2, no. 4: 411–22.

Nisbet, Matthew C. 2004. "Public Opinion about Stem Cell Research and Human Cloning." *Public Opinion Quarterly* 68, no. 1: 131–54.

———. 2005. "The Competition for Worldviews: Values, Information, and Public Support for Stem Cell Research." *International Journal of Public Opinion Research* 17, no. 1: 90–112.

Noll, Mark, ed. 1990. *Religion & American Politics: From the Colonial Period to the 1980s.* Oxford University Press.

Oldfield, Duane M. 1996. *The Right and the Righteous: The Christian Right Confronts the Republican Party.* Lanham, Md.: Rowman and Littlefield.

Olson, Laura. 2007 (forthcoming). "Whither the Religious Left? Religiopolitical Progressivism in Twenty-First Century America." In *From Pews to Polling Places: Faith and Politics in the American Religious Mosaic,* edited by J. Matthew Wilson. Georgetown University Press.

Olson, Laura R., and John C. Green. 2006. "Symposium: Voting Gaps in the 2004 Presidential Election." *PS: Political Science and Politics* 39 (July): 443–72.

Oppel, Richard A., and Gustav Niebuhr. 2000. "Bush Meeting Focuses on Role of Religion." *New York Times,* December 21, p. 37.

Pachon, Harry, and Louis DeSipio. 1988. *The Latino Vote in 1988.* NALEO Background Paper 7. Washington, D.C.: NALEO Educational Fund.

Page, Susan. 2004. "Churchgoing Closely Tied to Voting Patterns." *USA Today,* June (www.usatoday.com/news/nation/2004-06-02-religion-gap_x.htm).

Parsons, Talcott. 1959. " 'Voting' and the Equilibrium of the American Political System." In *American Voting Behavior,* edited by Eugene Burdick and Arthur J. Brodbeck. Glencoe, Ill.: Free Press.

Petrocik, John R. 1996. "Issue Ownership in Presidential Elections, with a 1980 Case Study." *American Journal of Political Science* 40, no. 3: 825–50.

———. 2006. "Party Coalitions in the American Public: Morality Politics, Issue Agendas, and the 2004 Election." In *The State of the Parties,* 5th ed., edited by John C. Green and Daniel Coffey. Lanham, Md.: Rowman and Littlefield.

Pew Research Center. 2004a. "GOP the Religion-Friendly Party: But Stem Cell Issue May Help Democrats." August 24 (people-press.org/reports/display.php3? ReportID=223).

———. 2004b. "Race Tightens Again, Kerry's Image Improves," released October 20, 2004 (people-press.org/reports/display.php3?ReportID=229).

———. 2004c. "Swing Voters Slow to Decide, Still Cross-Pressured." October 27, 2004 (people-press.org/reports/display.php3?ReportID=231).

———. 2004d. "Voters Liked Campaign 2004, But Too Much 'Mud-Slinging': Moral Values: How Important?" November 11. (people-press.org/reports/display. php3?ReportID=233).

———. 2005a. "Beyond Red vs. Blue: Republicans Divided about Role of Government; Democrats by Social and Personal Values." May 10, 2005 (people-press.org/ reports/display.php3?ReportID=242).

———. 2005b. "Politics and Values in a 51%-48% Nation: National Security More Linked with Partisan Affiliation." *Trends 2005,* January 24. (people-press.org/ reports/display.php3?ReportID=236).

Phillips, Frank, and Brian C. Mooney. 2003. "1986 Statement Counters Kerry's Stand on Heritage." *Boston Globe,* March 6 (3rd ed), p. A1.

Phillips, Kevin P. 1969. *The Emerging Republican Majority.* New Rochelle, N.Y.: Arlington House.

Pineau, Vicki, and Daniel Slotwiner. 2003. "Probability Samples vs. Volunteer Respondents in Internet Research: Defining Potential Effects on Data and Decision-Making in Marketing Applications." White Paper. Knowledge Networks (www. knowledgenetworks.com/insights/docs/Volunteer%20white%20paper%20 11-19-03.pdf).

Pollack, Andrew. 2004. "Measure Passed, California Weighs Its Future as a Stem Cell Epicenter." *New York Times,* November 4.

Pomper, Gerald M. 2005. "The Presidential Election: The Ills of American Politics after 9/11." In *The Elections of 2004,* edited by Michael Nelson. Washington, D.C.: CQ Press.

Pontifical Academy for Life. 2000. "Declaration on the Production and the Scientific and Therapeutic Use of Human Embryonic Stem Cells." Vatican City, Rome (www.vatican.va/roman_curia/pontifical_academies/acdlife/documents/rc_pa_ac dlife_doc_20000824_cellule-staminali_en.html).

Pool, Ithiel de Sola, Robert P. Abelson, and Stewart L. Popkin. 1965. *Candidates, Issues, and Strategies: A Computer Simulation of the 1960 and 1964 Presidential Elections.* MIT Press.

Prendergast, William B. 1999. *The Catholic Voter in American Politics: The Passing of the Democratic Monolith.* Georgetown University Press.

Putnam, Robert D. 2000. *Bowling Alone: The Collapse and Revival of American Community.* New York: Simon and Schuster.

Quinley, Harold. 1974. *The Prophetic Clergy.* New York: John Wiley.

Rahn, Wendy M., John Brehm, and Neil Carlson. 1999. "National Elections as Institutions for Building Social Capital." In *Civic Engagement in American Democracy,* edited by Morris Fiorina and Theda Skocpol, pp. 111–60. Brookings and Russell Sage.

Rauschenbusch, Walter. 1964. *Christianity and the Social Crisis.* New York: Harper and Row.

Reed, Ralph. 1996. *Active Faith: How Christians Are Changing the Soul of American Politics.* New York: Free Press.

Ritter, John. 2004. "Calif. Measures May Sway Nation." *USA Today,* October 28.

Robinson, William S. 1950. "Ecological Correlations and the Behavior of Individuals." *American Sociological Review* 15, no.3: 351–57.

Rosen, Hanna. 2005. "Beyond Belief." *Atlantic Monthly* 295, no. 1 (January/February): 117–20.

Rosenbaum, David E. 2004. "A Closer Look at the Stem Cell Record." *New York Times,* October 28.

Rosenstone, Steven J., John Mark Hansen, and Keith Reeves. 2003. *Mobilization, Participation, and Democracy in America.* New York: Longman.

Rothenberg, Stuart, and Frank Newport. 1984. *The Evangelical Voter: Religion and Politics in America.* Washington, D.C.: Free Congress Research and Education Foundation.

Sanderson, Jennifer. 2004. "New Charges Fuel Senate Race." *Argus Leader,* October 21, p. B1.

Shouse, Ben. 2004. "Advocate Promotes Religious Stance." *Argus Leader,* October 5, p. B1.

Slackman, Michael. 2003. "Jackson's Neutrality Hindering Sharpton Campaign." *New York Times,* October 29, p. 14.

Slackman, Michael, and Marjorie Connelly. 2004. "Sharpton Claims Success but Reassesses Campaign." *New York Times,* March 3, p. 18.

Slater, Wayne. 2004. "The Jesus Factor: The Evangelical Vote [Internet interview]." *PBS Frontline,* April 29 (www.pbs.org/wgbh/shows/jesus/evangelicals/vote.html [November 2005]).

Slevin, Peter. 2006. " 'St. Jack' and the Bullies in the Pulpit: John Danforth Says It's Time the GOP Center Took on the Christian Right." *Washington Post,* February 2, p. C1.

Smidt, Corwin E., Lyman A. Kellstedt, John C. Green, and James L. Guth. 1994. "The Characteristics of Christian Political Activists: An Interest Group Analysis." In *Christian Political Activism at the Crossroads,* edited by William Stevenson, pp. 133–71. Lanham, Md.: University Press of America.

———. 2003. "Religion and Politics in the United States." In *The Secular and the Sacred,* edited by William Safran, pp. 32–53. London: Frank Cass.

Smidt, Corwin E., and James Penning. 1997. *Sojourners in the Wilderness: The Christian Right in Comparative Perspective.* Lanham, Md.: Rowman and Littlefield.

Smith, Christian. 1998. *American Evangelicalism: Embattled and Thriving.* University of Chicago Press.

Smith, Daniel, Matt DeSantis, and Jason Kassel. 2005. "Was Rove Right? Evangelicals and the Impact of Gay Marriage in the 2004 Election." Paper presented at the fifth annual State Politics and Policy Conference, Michigan State University, East Lansing, Mich., May 12–14.

Smith, Daniel, and Caroline Tolbert. 2001. "The Initiative to Party: Partisanship and Ballot Initiatives in California." *Party Politics* 7, no. 6: 739–57.

Smith, Elizabeth Theiss, and Richard Braunstein. 2007. "The Nationalization of Local Politics: The South Dakota U.S. Senate Race." In *Electing Congress: New Rules for an Old Game,* edited by David B. Magleby, J. Quin Monson, and Kelly D. Patterson. Upper Saddle River, N.J.: Prentice-Hall.

Steensland, Brian, Jerry Z. Park, Mark D. Regnerus, Lynn D. Robinson, W. Bradford Wilcox, and Robert D. Woodberry. 2000. "The Measure of American Religion: Toward Improving the State of the Art." *Social Forces* 79, no. 1: 291–318.

Stevenson, Richard A. 2004. "Bush Urges Blacks to Reconsider Allegiance to Democratic Party." *New York Times,* July 24, p. 1.

Suro, Roberto, Richard Fry, and Jeffrey Passel. 2005. "Hispanics and the 2004 Election: Population, Electorate, and Votes." Washington, D.C.: Pew Hispanic Center.

Suskind, Ron. 2004. "Without a Doubt." *New York Times Magazine,* October 17.

Swidler, Ann. 1986. "Culture in Action: Symbols and Strategies." *American Sociological Review* 51, no. 2: 273–86.

Swierenga, Robert P. 1990. "Ethno-Religious Political Behavior in the Mid-Nineteenth Century: Voting, Values, Cultures." In *Religion and American Politics: From the Colonial Period to the 1980s,* edited by Mark A. Noll, pp. 146–71. Oxford University Press.

Tate, Katherine. 1993. *From Protest to Politics: The New Black Voters in American Elections.* Harvard University Press.

Teixeira, Ruy. 2004. "44 Percent of Hispanics Voted for Bush?" November 24 (www.alternet.org/election04/20606/).

Tomz, Michael, Jason Wittenberg, and Gary King. 2001. CLARIFY: Software for Interpreting and Presenting Statistical Results, version 2.0. Harvard University, June 1 (gking.harvard.edu).

Tomz, Michael, Jason Wittenberg, and Gary King. 2003. CLARIFY: Software for Interpreting and Presenting Statistical Results, version 2.1. Stanford University, University of Wisconsin, and Harvard University, January 5 (gking.harvard.edu).

Toner, Robin. 2004. "Democrats Join Fray on Marriage." *New York Times,* February 26.

Treier, Shawn, and Sunshine Hillygus. 2005. "The Structure and Meaning of Political Ideology." Presented at the 2005 annual meeting of the American Political Science Association, Washington, D.C., September 1–4.

Trueba, Enrique (Henry). 1999. *Latinos Unidos: From Cultural Diversity to the Politics of Solidarity.* Lanham, Md.: Rowman and Littlefield.

Van Allen, Rodger. 1974. *The Commonweal and American Catholicism: The Magazine, the Movement, the Meaning.* Philadelphia: Fortress Press.

Vedantam, Shankar. 2005. "Study Ties Political Leanings to Hidden Biases." *Washington Post,* January 30, p. A5.

Verba, Sidney, Kay Lehman Schlozman, and Henry E. Brady. 1995. *Voice and Equality: Civic Voluntarism in American Politics.* Harvard University Press.

Viscusi, W. Kip, Joel Huber, and Jason Bell. 2004. "The Value of Regional Water Quality Improvements." Harvard Law and Economics Discussion Paper 477. Harvard University, John M. Olin Center, June (www.law.harvard.edu/programs/olin_center/papers/pdf/477.pdf).

Wald, Kenneth D. 2003. *Religion and Politics in the United States,* 4th ed. Lanham, Md.: Rowman and Littlefield.

Wald, Kenneth D., Lyman A. Kellstedt, and David C. Leege. 1993. "Church Involvement and Political Behavior." In *Rediscovering the Religious Factor in American Politics,* edited by David C. Leege and Lyman A. Kellstedt. Armonk, N.Y.: M. E. Sharpe.

Wald, Kenneth D., Dennis E. Owen, and Samuel S. Hill Jr. 1988. "Churches as Political Communities." *American Political Science Review* 82, no. 2: 531–48.

———. 1990. "Political Cohesion in Churches." *Journal of Politics* 52, no. 1: 197–215.

Wald, Kenneth, and Lee Sigelman. 1997. "Romancing the Jews: The Christian Right in Search of Strange Bedfellows." In *Sojourners in the Wilderness: The Christian Right in Comparative Perspective,* edited by Corwin Smidt and James Penning, pp. 139–68. Lanham, Md.: Rowman and Littlefield.

Waldman, Amy. 1995. "Why We Need a Religious Left." *Washington Monthly* 27 (December): 37–43.

Walker, Jack. 1991. *Mobilizing Interest Groups in America.* University of Michigan Press.

Wallis, Jim. 2005. *God's Politics: Why the Right Gets It Wrong and the Left Doesn't Get It.* New York: HarperCollins.

Walton, Hanes, Jr., and Robert C. Smith. 2006. *American Politics and the African American Quest for Universal Freedom,* 3rd ed. New York: Pearson Longman.

Welch, Michael R., and David C. Leege. 1988. "Religious Predictors of Catholic Parishioners' Socio-Political Attitudes." *Journal for the Scientific Study of Religion* 27, no. 4: 536–52.

White, Gayle. 2004. "Let Abortion Guide Vote, Catholics Told." *Atlanta Journal Constitution,* September 17, p. A1.

White, John K. 2003. *The Values Divide.* New York: Chatham House.

———. 2005. "The Armageddon Election." In *Defining Moment,* edited by William Crotty, pp. 211–35. Armonk, N.Y.: M. E. Sharpe.

White House, Office of the Press Secretary. 2001. "President Discusses Stem Cell Research." August 9 (www.whitehouse.gov/news/releases/2001/08/20010809-2.html).

Wilcox, Clyde. 1992. *God's Warriors: The Christian Right in Twentieth-Century America.* Johns Hopkins University Press.

Wilcox, Clyde, and Carin Larson. 2006. *Onward Christian Soldiers? The Religious Right in American Politics,* 3d ed. Boulder, Colo.: Westview Press.

Wilcox, Clyde, Lee Sigelman, and Elizabeth Cook. 1989. "Some Like It Hot: Individual Differences in Responses to Group Feeling Thermometers." *Public Opinion Quarterly* 53, no. 2 (Summer): 246–57.

Wildavsky, Aaron. 1987. "Choosing Preferences by Constructing Institutions: A Cultural Theory of Preference Formation." *American Political Science Review* 81, no. 1: 3–21.

Williams, Rhys H., ed. 1997. *Culture Wars in American Politics: Critical Reviews of a Popular Myth.* New York: De Gruyter.

Wilson, Robert L. 1988. *Biases and Blind Spots: Methodism and Foreign Policy since World War II.* Wilmore, Ky.: Bristol Books.

Wolfe, Alan. 1998. *One Nation, After All.* New York: Viking.

Wothke, Werner, and James L. Arbuckle. 1996. "Full-Information Missing Data Analysis with Amos." SPSS White Paper. Chicago: SPSS.

Wuthnow, Robert. 1988. *The Restructuring of American Religion.* Princeton University Press.

———. 1989. *The Struggle for America's Soul: Evangelicals, Liberals, and Secularism.* Grand Rapids, Mich.: Eerdmans.

Contributors

David E. Campbell
University of Notre Dame

John C. Green
University of Akron
Pew Forum on Religion and
Public Life

James L. Guth
Furman University

D. Sunshine Hillygus
Harvard University

Laura S. Hussey
University of Baltimore

John S. Jackson
Southern Illinois University
(emeritus)

Scott Keeter
Pew Research Center for the People
and the Press

Lyman A. Kellstedt
Wheaton College (emeritus)

Geoffrey C. Layman
University of Maryland–College Park

David L. Leal
University of Texas–Austin

David C. Leege
University of Notre Dame (emeritus)

Eric L. McDaniel
University of Texas–Austin

J. Quin Monson
Brigham Young University

Barbara Norrander
University of Arizona

Jan Norrander
University of Minnesota

J. Baxter Oliphant
Brigham Young University

Corwin E. Smidt
Calvin College

J. Matthew Wilson
Southern Methodist University

Index

Religiosity: and African American voters, 225–27, 229; and traditionalist conservative voters, 255. *See* Worship attendance frequency

Religious activists: and centrist liberals, 240; and mainline Protestants, 56; and party elites, 55–60

Religious centrists. *See* Centrists, religious

Religious conservatives: and cultural policy attitudes, 101–02; and gay marriage, 101–02, 124–25; microtargeting of, 100–04; mobilization of, 95–119; and parental notification laws, 101–02; and party identification, 58–60; and religious right, 58; and Republican Party, 235; and terrorism issue, 102; theologies and practices of, 237–38

Religious left, 232–56; and activism, 56; and Catholics, 56–58, 177, 240–41, 244; and civil rights movement, 233–34; constituencies of, 239–42; and culture war, 255; and delegate representation, 50–51; and economic issues, 234, 251, 252; and environmental issues, 233–34, 243–45; and evangelical Protestants, 241; and foreign policy issues, 243, 246, 252; and gay marriage issue, 248–49; historical background of, 233–36; ideological fragmentation of, 265; and impact on *2004* election, 249–54; and Iraq war, 246–47; and Jews, 241; and Latino Catholics, 240–41; and mainline Protestants, 234, 240–41, 244; and modernist liberals, 254–55; and moral issues, 247–49, 251, 252; and partisan realignment, 235; and party elites, 39, 40; political definition of, 237; and political issues, 243–49; and religious centrists and traditionalists, 238–39; social-demographic characteristics of, 242–43; theological definition of, 237–38; and traditionalist liberals, 239–42, 244; and voter turnout, 251, 253–54

Religious liberals, 56–58, 237–38. *See* Religious left

Religious mobilization, 55–60

Religious modernists. *See* Modernists, religious

Religious profile of *2004* convention delegates, 42–44

Religious right: and activism, 56; and Catholics, 241–42; and culture war, 242; and delegate representation, 50–51; demographics of, 242–43; development of, 232–33; and evangelical Protestants, 90–91; and gay marriage issue, 129; and mainline Protestants, 241–42; mobilization of, 265; and mobilization of evangelicals, 98; and moral issues, 247–49; and party elites, 39, 40; and religious conservatives, 58; and theological issues, 240; and voter turnout, 254

Religious traditionalism, 16–17, 35–36

Republican National Committee (RNC): and direct mail campaigns, 108, 112, 113, 263; and mobilization of religious conservatives, 96, 97, 100–04

Republican Party: and abortion attitudes, 47–48, 53; and African American vote, 99, 218–19, 230; and black Protestants, 222–24, 230; constituencies, 23–24; and convention delegates, 43; and cultural policy positions, 73–75; and direct mail campaigns, 96, 106, 107; and evangelicals, 2, 7, 23, 25, 28, 87–88, 91, 99, 141, 181, 183–84, 188–89, 191–97, 266; and gay marriage issue, 73–75, 127; and ideology, 45–46, 53; and Latinos, 23–24, 27, 29, 199–200; and Latter-day Saints, 6–7, 23, 26, 28–29; and mainline Protestants, 23–24, 26, 30, 39, 269–70; and mobilization of religious conservatives, 115; and partisan realignment, 87–88, 99, 168, 187–89; party elites and partisan publics, 50–51; platform on abortion in *2004*, 72; and "religion